NEUROSCIENCE AND CRITIQUE

Recent years have seen a rapid growth in neuroscientific research, and an expansion beyond basic research to incorporate elements of the arts, humanities and social sciences. Some have suggested that the neurosciences will bring about major transformations in the understanding of our selves, our culture and our society. Ongoing debates within psychology, philosophy and literature about the implications of these developments within the neurosciences, and the emerging fields of educational neuroscience, neuroeconomics and neuro-aesthetics also bear witness to a "neurological turn" which is currently taking place.

Neuroscience and Critique is a groundbreaking edited collection that reflects on the impact of neuroscience in contemporary social science and the humanities. It is the first book to consider possibilities for a critique of the theories, practices and implications of contemporary neuroscience. Bringing together leading scholars from several disciplines, the contributors draw upon a range of perspectives, including cognitive neuroscience, critical philosophy, psychoanalysis and feminism, and also critically examine several key ideas in contemporary neuroscience, including:

- The idea of "neural personhood"
- Theories of emotion in affective neuroscience
- Empathy, intersubjectivity and the notion of "embodied simulation"
- The concept of an "emo-rational" actor within neuroeconomics

The volume will stimulate further debate in the emerging field of interdisciplinary studies in neuroscience and will appeal to researchers and advanced students in a number of disciplines, including psychology, philosophy and critical studies.

Jan De Vos is a post-doctoral FWO Research Fellow at the Centre for Critical Philosophy at Ghent University, Belgium. His main research area is that of the neurological turn and its implications for ideology critique.

Ed Pluth is Professor and Chair of the Philosophy Department at California State University, Chico, USA. He works on issues and figures in contemporary continental philosophy, with special attention to how language and the extra-linguistic are put into relation to each other, and what this relation implies generally about the status of thinking and conscious life.

NEUROSCIENCE AND CRITIQUE

Exploring the Limits of the Neurological Turn

Edited by Jan De Vos and Ed Pluth

Routledge
Taylor & Francis Group

LONDON AND NEW YORK

First published 2016
by Routledge
2 Park Square, Milton Park, Abingdon, Oxon, OX14 4RN

and by Routledge
711 Third Avenue, New York, NY 10017

Routledge is an imprint of the Taylor & Francis Group, an informa business

© 2016 Jan De Vos and Ed Pluth

British Library Cataloguing in Publication Data
A catalogue record for this book is available from the British Library

Library of Congress Cataloging-in-Publication Data
Neuroscience and critique: exploring the limits of the neurological turn /
edited by Jan De Vos, Ed Pluth.
    p.; cm.
Includes bibliographical references and index.
    I. Vos, Jan de, 1967- , editor. II. Pluth, Ed, editor.
[DNLM: 1. Neurosciences. 2. Culture. 3. Humanities. 4. Psychoanalytic Theory. WL 100]
QP360
612.8—dc23

2015021514

ISBN: 978-1-138-88733-6 (hbk)
ISBN: 978-1-138-88735-0 (pbk)
ISBN: 978-1-315-71418-9 (ebk)

Typeset in Bembo
by codeMantra
Printed in Great Britain by Ashford Colour Press Ltd

CONTENTS

LIST OF CONTRIBUTORS

Nima Bassiri, University of Chicago, USA

Ariane Bazan, Université Libre de Bruxelles, Belgium

Marc De Kesel, Saint-Paul University, Ottawa, Canada

Jan De Vos, Centre for Critical Philosophy, Ghent University, Belgium

Joseph Dumit, University of California Davis, USA

Vittorio Gallese, University of Parma, Italy

Philipp Haueis, Max Planck Institut for Human Cognitive and Brain Sciences Leipzig, Germany

Adrian Johnston, University of New Mexico at Albuquerque and Emory Psycho-analytic Institute in Atlanta, USA

Cynthia Kraus, University of Lausanne, Switzerland

Ed Pluth, California State University, Chico, USA

Jessica Pykett, University of Birmingham, UK

Peter Reynaert, University of Antwerp, Belgium

Jan Slaby, Free University Berlin, Germany

Mark Solms, University of Cape Town, South Africa

INTRODUCTION

Who Needs Critique?

Jan De Vos and Ed Pluth

> If I have a brain that understands for me, a cortical region who has a conscience for me, a neural network which decides upon a regimen for me, and so forth, I need not trouble myself at all. I need not think: (...) others will readily undertake the irksome business for me.

You might recognize in this passage a rather liberal rewriting of Kant's famous lines from "What is Enlightenment?".[1] For Kant, an immature humanity outsourced its thinking to other people, to external authorities. Today it seems that the brain has taken over this role. As Elizabeth Rottenberg succinctly remarks in relation to Kant's discussion of our immaturity: "it is so nice not to need to think" (Rottenberg, 2012, p. 138).

The concept of interpassivity is relevant here (see Pfaller, 2000; Žižek, 1997). When we speak, the Other speaks through us, our desire is the Other's desire ... so, given this situation, why heed any call to do any thinking or desiring for ourselves? It's impossible anyway! Rottenberg suggests that there could be a sort of ironic pleasure in this outsourcing of responsibility: it is so nice not to need to think. The pleasure itself, if it is too burdensome or awkward, could be outsourced too, and taken on by the neuro-discourses themselves!

So, maybe Bartleby expresses our current situation very well: we prefer not to be critical. The neurosciences may be even forcing the humanities to adopt this extreme passivity, thereby renouncing their historical vocation: for the neurosciences themselves seem to have taken over the role of critique quite well, shattering so many of our humanist illusions – agency, free will, love, empathy, altruism, none of these are what they seem to be.

But who is taking up the critical task today with respect to the neurosciences, and what kind of critique of them is possible? Recent years have seen a rapid growth in neuroscientific research and an expansion of its insights into the arts, humanities and social sciences. It has been suggested that the neurosciences will bring about major transformations in the understanding of ourselves, our culture and our society. In academia one finds debates within psychology, philosophy and literature about the implications of developments within the neurosciences, and the emerging fields of educational neuroscience, neuroeconomics and neuro-aesthetics also bear witness to the 'neurological turn' that is currently taking place. Is the expectation, even in academia – even in the humanities themselves – not widespread that the neurosciences will explain it all?

A reactionary humanist might consider the neuro-turn an absolute threat and reject it as much as possible. Three points about this:

1. What would de-neurologizing the humanities involve? Would it make any sense to cleanse the fields of education, work, the public space and politics of their neuro-mania? Why would this be done – to bring back things like true education, true work, a true public space, a true politics? To rid them of any influence from the neurosciences? The problem is that it is not obvious what any of that would be.[2]

2. Moreover, it does not make any sense to go back to a time before the neuro-turn because the neuro-turn has itself now deeply affected and shaped what it is to be a subject. That is, it is clear that the neurosciences have spawned in only a few decades a burgeoning neuro-culture, as well as a neural model of subjectivity (cf. Fernando Vidal's [2007] *Cerebral subject*, Nikolas Rose's [2006] *Neurochemical self* ...). How we experience ourselves and the world increasingly depends on, relies on, is informed by neurological notions, rather than on psychological or internalistic ones. Ortega hence, argues that it is "impossible to differentiate the brain as a scientific object and the brain as an object of extra-scientific culture" (Ortega, 2011, p. 28). To simply criticize or reject the idea that 'we are our brains' would overlook the crucial fact that we have already become brain-people, tremendously conscious that we are our brains: thinking things, deciding things, desiring things – things, in the end, that are us more than us, to paraphrase Lacan. If what being a subject is now fully formed by neurological ideas, what good would it do for the humanities to reject this model?[3]

3. We are used to the idea that the neurosciences might have something to tell us about culture and subjectivity. But it is hard to imagine how the humanities can tell us something about the neurosciences. Perhaps we just do not have the theoretical toolbox for thinking correctly the relation, or perhaps non-relation, if that's what it is, between the neurosciences and the humanities. Instead of rejecting the neuro-turn outright, such a toolbox is instead what should be developed.

What are the conditions for a critique of the neurosciences from the humanities, then? Here is one place to begin: is it not the case that, as some of the chapters in this book attempt to show, there are some difficulties involved in brain discourse itself? That is, some of the authors argue that there might be some basic and inevitable paradoxes, deadlocks and even aporias within the neurosciences that structurally prevent the field of the neurosciences from being fully unified and closed. If this is true, then the appropriate question might be: *how much critique do the neurosciences really need?* Because now, counter to some uses of the neurosciences for non-emancipatory and de-subjectivizing purposes (see its use in neoliberal politics), it may be the case that there is room within the neurosciences themselves for another version of brain-discourse. Neuroscience seems perfectly capable of self-critique. Just think about the allegation of neo-phrenology from Bao and Pöppel, who write:

> An uncritical use of new imaging technology may open the door to a new kind of old fashioned phrenology, i.e., looking at specific areas only and neglecting the interconnectivity of a neuronal network.
> *(Bao & Pöppel, 2012, p. 2144)*

But their network idea may be just a more sophisticated phrenology in which aspects of the human mind are still localized, only not just in one place, but many. That is, the network idea cannot but start from a localization of the components of the network. A neuroscientist could argue that neuroscience itself will reveal this: it could argue that there are fluid networks and multi-usable brain units, and we now have the capacity to show where they are and how they work. Consider how plasticity, epigenesis and mirror neurons offer a naturalistic foundation for a critique of neuroscience, a foundation that emerges from neuroscientific work itself, bypassing any influence from the humanities altogether.

But have the neurosciences really bypassed the humanities on this point? Plasticity, for example, was arguably a concept first developed within the humanities. What, then, about other concepts from the humanities that are not taken up by the hard sciences, ones that are perhaps not considered useful or relevant, and especially, not scanable? Is it a shortcoming on the part of the humanities that this is so, or could it not also be considered a shortcoming within the neurosciences that they have nothing to say about them? Consider here the so-called *skandalons* of psychoanalysis (e.g., the unconsciousness, the death drive, jouissance …). To take this line of thought one step further, perhaps it is not appropriate or legitimate anymore for the neurosciences to merely neglect or reject these negativities, especially since they can be seen to return in their own research and their theory formations. That is, the neurosciences themselves touch on the issues of our egolessness, our lack of free will, our illusions about love … and this is where they find themselves directly on the terrain of the human sciences, philosophy and good old psychoanalysis.

To be sure, this situation in which the neurosciences find themselves on the other side of the mirror, as it were, back in the domain of the humanities, is homologous to the situation of the human sciences themselves when they turn to the neurosciences, or when they critique them. Here, the humanities too cannot but find the same aporias, the same paradoxes, the same impossibilities that were always thwarting their very own praxes. At least the neuro-turn makes it possible for us to question the longstanding division of labour between the human and the natural sciences. In a way, it is this rather simple and straightforward issue that is at stake in each chapter in this volume. What is pursued in this volume is something other than a simple humanistic critique of the neurosciences. Rather more in line with the sense of critique that is operative in the Kantian project, this volume engages in questions about the conditions of possibility, impossibility and the domain, or range, of different sciences and disciplines.

The neurosciences, which are both situated within culture and in turn influence culture, inevitably give rise to questions about the borders and ranges of the sciences and other disciplines. How far does the legitimacy of the neurosciences extend? How is the relation of neuroscience to the humanities to be thought? The authors in this volume share a common interest in addressing this aspect of critique, which threatens to be overlooked or misunderstood not only in culture but in the everyday practice of the neurosciences themselves.

In order to approach this issue the book is divided into three parts. Part one, "Which Critique", explores the conditions for critique itself. It opens with an essay by Marc De Kesel. De Kesel discusses the links between the rise of science and the modern subject. Associating the concept of the subject with the negative, the void and ultimately with freedom, De Kesel analyzes recent attempts to find a sort of ontological ground for such things in the works of Verplaetse and Malabou. Whether nature is understood to be deterministic (in the case of Verplaetse) or free (in the case of Malabou), what these projects overlook, De Kesel argues, is the potential groundlessness of freedom itself. He suggests that there may be a correlate in nature for this freedom that is being overlooked, one found in the psychoanalytic notion of the death drive, in a nature that destroys itself. Jan De Vos opens the next essay with a discussion of the position from which critique tends to take place, which often seems like a third-party, neutral perspective. De Vos argues that the neurosciences have made it difficult for the humanities to assume such a neutral role, and that the neurosciences offer themselves now as the very point of view – like a view from nowhere – from which critique can take place. However, De Vos analyzes the notion of 'folk-psychology', relied on heavily in neuroscientific critiques and finds that the very notion of a naive, pre-scientific point of view that the neurosciences might critique is problematic: it, in fact, relies upon a particular psychological theory. Nima Bassiri's essay, "Who Are We, Then, If We Are Indeed Our Brains", begins with an enlightening discussion on the nature of critique, pointing out that it has never been something merely negative, but also always affirmative. But with respect to the neurosciences, what is the situation of critique? And is an external critique of any science legitimate? Bassiri discusses Feyerabend's critique of the sciences in this context and moves on to a consideration of the social, political and legal practices that surround or encourage scientific enquiry. Specifically, Bassiri looks at how railway accidents and traumas in the nineteenth century were connected to a simultaneous questioning of the concept of legal personhood: were victims of such accidents malingerers, faking their conditions? Bassiri explores how the neurosciences have been connected to anxieties about shifting notions of personhood, and indeed with a "crisis" in subjectivity itself. Peter Reynaert concludes part one with the argument that there is something like a category error being committed with certain uses of the neurosciences. Finding an original version of Ryle's notion of a category error in Husserl's *Logical Investigations*, Reynaert argues that Husserl's notion of material absurdity applies to some naturalistic approaches to consciousness. The error consists in mistaking the essence of consciousness with that of a physical thing. Reynaert delves into Husserl's differing analyses of the essences of physical bodies and living bodies in order to make his point, ultimately concluding that this naturalistic category mistake has baleful effects on human freedom.

Part two, "Some Critiques", begins with Jessica Pykett's essay "From Global Economic Change to Neuromolecular Capitalism". Pykett discusses the emergence of neuroeconomics and its links to behavioral economics, both of which are hugely influential for the development of contemporary public policies. From a perspective rooted in geography, Pykett critiques the models of human behavior and decision-making that are relied on in both fields. Cynthia Kraus, in her essay "What is the Feminist Critique of Neurosciences? A Call for Dissensus Studies", studies the way in which calls for dialogue between neuroscientists on the one hand and humanists and social scientists on the other make it sound as if each are part of a gendered couple, with the humanities and social sciences put in the role of the peacemaker. But Kraus argues that both fields are better served by the preservation and articulation of disagreement rather than consensus, and as an example, she looks at how 'dissensus' served to bring about changes to the theory and practice governing 'intersex' newborns. Next, Philipp Haueis and Jan Slaby discuss the Human Brain Project, a large-scale project funded by the European Union, which has drawn criticisms from some for its advocacy of 'in silico' experimentation over 'in vitro' brain research. Haueis and Slaby discuss the wide-ranging effects this project could have. Finally, concluding part two, Adrian Johnston responds to some criticisms of his work expressed in several essays by Ed Pluth. Johnston argues that his attempt to bring contemporary neuroscience and psychoanalysis together does not amount to a problematic verificationism, although he concedes that his position does entail a 'weak' reductionism. Far from leading to any marginalization of psychoanalysis, Johnston finds that dialogue with the neurosciences is crucial for its continued development, success and legitimacy.

Part three, "Critical Praxes", includes essays by three researchers in the neurosciences. Ariane Bazan, working on the intersection of psychoanalysis and the neurosciences, makes the claim that, contrary to most accounts of the relationship, it is in fact psychoanalytic theory and practice that should be doing more to inform neuroscientific research. Vittorio Gallese, well known for his pioneering research on mirror neurons, explores the topic of intersubjectivity, arguing that the theory of embodied simulation offers us an empirical basis for what is commonly referred to as "mind reading". Finally, Mark Solms discusses empathy. Leaning on Freudian theory, Solms finds neurological support for the idea that empathy is an "achievement", and that the theory of embodied simulation advanced by Gallese is not enough to account for it. Solms offers a case study of one of his patients, a stroke victim with damage to part of the brain involved in empathy, to illustrate his point. In a concluding afterward, Joseph Dumit offers an overview of the papers in this volume, and suggests that there may be a weakness to the neurosciences despite their evident strength. The weakness Dumit has in mind involves not only the neurosciences' dependence on shaky and competitive funding models, but also the legitimacy of their models for what it is to be human. Dumit calls on the neurosciences to challenge and transform the humanistic models they are already relying on in their research programs.

Notes

1. "If I have a book that understands for me, a spiritual advisor who has a conscience for me, a doctor who decides upon a regimen for me, and so forth, I need not trouble myself at all. I need not think, if only I can pay; others will readily undertake the irksome business for me" (Kant, 1999, p. 17).
2. Remember in this respect José Saramago's words: "we will know less and less what is a human being". Perhaps the neuro-turn above all reveals that we never knew much to begin with (Saramago, 2008).
3. In this respect are the humanities not always doomed to be one step behind the hard sciences? It is the hard sciences that seem to be doing all the work when it comes to shaping subjectivity and society – they are the deciders. The humanities would be in a position similar to that of journalists in the well-known story Ron Suskind told during the George W. Bush administration. One of Bush's senior aides told him that "guys like me were 'in what we call the reality-based community', which he defined as people who 'believe that solutions emerge from your judicious study of discernible reality'. I nodded and murmured something about enlightenment principles and empiricism. He cut me off. 'That's not the way the world really works anymore', he continued. 'We're an empire now, and when we act, we create our own reality. And while you're studying that reality – judiciously, as you will – we'll act again, creating other new realities, which you can study too, and that's how things will sort out. We're history's actors … and you, all of you, will be left to just study what we do'" (Suskind, 2004). In the empire of the sciences, the humanities would be left in the lame, clean-up role of meticulously recording and debating the effects the sciences are having on us …

References

Bao, Y., & Pöppel, E. (2012). Anthropological universals and cultural specifics: Conceptual and methodological challenges in cultural neuroscience. *Neuroscience & Biobehavioral Reviews, 36*(9), 2143–2146.

Kant, I. (1999). An answer to the question: What is enlightenment? In J. G. Mary & W. Allen (Eds.), *Practical Philosophy* (11–22). Cambridge: Cambridge University Press.

Ortega, F. (2011). Toward a genealogy of neuroascesis. *Neurocultures. Glimpses into an Expanding Universe* (27–44). Frankfurt and New York, NY: Peter Lang.

Ortega, F., & Vidal, F. (2007). Mapping the cerebral subject in contemporary culture. *Reciis, Electronic Journal of Communication Information & Innovation in Health, 1*(2), 255–259.

Pfaller, R. (2000). *Interpassivität: Studien über delegiertes Genießen*. Wien/New York, NY: Springer.

Rose, N. (2006). *The Politics of Life Itself: Biomedicine, Power & Subjectivity in the Twenty-First Century*. Princeton, NJ: Princeton University Press.

Rottenberg, E. (2012). Psychoanalytic critique and beyond. In K. de Boer & R. Sonderegger (Eds.), *Conceptions of Critique in Modern and Contemporary Philosophy* (137–155). New York, NY: Palgrave Macmillan.

Saramago, J. (2008). *Death with Interruptions*. London: Harvill Secker.

Suskind, R. (2004). Faith, certainty and the presidency of George W. Bush. *The New York Times Magazine,* (October 17). Retrieved from http://www.nytimes.com/2004/10/17/magazine/17BUSH.html?_r=2&.

Žižek, S. (1997). *The Plague of Fantasies*. New York, NY: Verso.

PART I

Which Critique?

1

THE BRAIN: A NOSTALGIC DREAM

Some Notes on Neuroscience and the Problem of Modern Knowledge

Marc De Kesel

> … I believe that everything is imagined …
>
> (Julien Offray de La Mettrie)

Since the origins of Western thinking in Ancient Greece, science and criticism have always gone hand in hand. Plato was the first to define scientific thinking as critique – 'κρίνειν' (*krinein*) in his language: making a distinction, the distinction between what *is* and what *is not*, between real and illusionary, true and false. Since Plato it is commonsensical to say that criticism leads to science and that science is impossible without criticism. No wonder then that the explosion of critical thought in the eighteenth century's Enlightenment was contemporaneous with the emergence of modern science.

Yet, it is in the age of the Enlightenment that the definition of science had to be adjusted because of modernity's paradigmatic shift. Science remained critical in essence, still distinguishing true and false, but no longer what *is* from what *is not*. Science and criticism were no longer considered to know being qua being, or to have access to *das Ding an sich*, as Kant said. Science was not giving voice to reality *as it is*. From now on, science was to be considered as a construction based upon empirical experience which, as such, is unable to comprehend the 'essence' of the experienced things.

Was this problematic? On the contrary. By omitting the ontological pretentions it had claimed since its origin, science was no longer 'limited from within'. 'De-ontologized', it gained an immense freedom and was now finally able to explore the universe limitlessly. It made modern man intervene in nature on the most minuscule level of atomic structure, as well as to visit the moon and gain knowledge about the center and origin of the universe, billions of light-years away.[1]

And yet, some specific knowledge did become problematic: the knowledge *of* that knowledge, and more precisely, the knowledge of the *subject* of that knowledge. For, indeed, since modernity and its de-ontologized science, we no longer really know what precisely knowing *is*. We lack an insight into its ontological nature, into its being *qua being*. And, similarly, we lack any ontological knowledge about the *being* of ourselves in our capacity of being the subject of scientific knowledge.

Immanuel Kant was clear about this issue: scientific knowledge is certainly possible, but about the one who knows as well as about knowing itself, science cannot be but hypothetical. The agent that thinks – the *Ich denke* – is a hypothetic idea of pure reason, 'hypothetic' if only because it claimed knowledge about that which cannot be traced back to empirical experience (Kant, 1998, p. 246 ff). The same goes for thinking *as such,* or, what amounts to the same thing, for reason *itself*. Reason cannot be observed empirically; it can only be experienced while being practiced. It is impossible to make reason the object of experience or empirical observation. Which is why, Kant concludes, reason definitely cannot be the object of scientific knowledge.

Is this a problem for Kant? It is first of all a strange thing, as he notices. For the Enlightenment, with its explosive critical thought and its new – Newtonian – physical science, is entirely the result of a thinking that has rediscovered its freedom, as it has emancipated itself from its medieval ontological predecessor. Yet, being the result of free thought, what it lays bare in nature is not freedom but laws, the so-called 'natural laws'. Free thinking does not discover nor recognize its own freedom in the nature it is examining. Nowhere does science empirically observe freedom, let alone the free nature of its own thinking.

The only situation in which freedom can be experienced, Kant says, is *moral* reasoning. Asking myself how to act ethically, I discover the ability to *freely* subject myself to the universal law of reason – which is what I do when I apply the *categorical imperative* to my moral behavior. In a world in which murder is commonplace, only by the force of my free reason can I see on the one hand that a world in which murder is allowed generates an unfree universe and that, on the other hand, in a world where murder is forbidden, freedom is rendered possible. Subjecting myself freely to the prohibition on murder, I discover my rational freedom and cannot but suppose that also reality itself has something to do with that freedom.

Science lays bare the laws of the nature it examines, but the freedom operating in scientific praxis escapes that grip. And yet, this is precisely the way in which science 'proves' freedom, according to Kant: freedom shows something which escapes the determinism of laws. So we do know that freedom exists, Kant states, just like we know that freedom is that which reason in moral reflections discovers to be its essence, but we have no real (i.e., scientific) knowledge of it. And precisely in this respect freedom is free, i.e., not reducible it to natural (i.e., scientific) laws. Freedom is the highest and only authority man has to listen to, and that authority can only be obeyed: 'obeyed' by applying natural laws (in science); 'obeyed' by freely submitting oneself to the principle hypothesis underlying the reason that discovered those laws – a submission which, as Kant explains, happens in rational morality.

But is all this really so? Has science, critical as it is, not gone a step further, and discovered the laws of free thinking and the laws of freedom in general? In what follows I discuss the central thesis in the work of the Belgian philosopher Jan Verplaetse, a thesis announced in his 2009 book, *Localising the Moral Sense*, but fully elaborated in his not yet translated Dutch book of 2011 entitled, *Zonder vrije wil* (*Without Free Will*) (Verplaetse 2009; 2011). Verplaetse states that the progress that science has made since Kant allows us to reduce freedom to natural laws. The implication of this is that freedom as such no longer exists, nor does the moral feeling of guilt – so often accompanying our moral concerns. Verplaetse's main argument is that the advanced modern sciences – and first of all the neurosciences – require such a conclusion. In the second part I discuss another book which focuses on neuroscience as well, but draws the opposite conclusion. Catherine Malabou's *What Should We Do with Our Brain?* states that the functioning of the brain shows us precisely how free human being and his thinking is (Malabou, 2008). In the last part, I will return to the de-ontologized condition modern thought is in. Facing the problem of the science of the human, and more precisely the way science deals with ideological critique, I will show the limits of neurology's attempt to comprehend freedom.

Without Free Will

Today's neurosciences allow insights into the causal processes underlying our mental activities, including the one that we, from time immemorial, call 'free will'. But if these processes are really causal, so Verplaetse asks, does this not imply that the will is not as free as we think it is and that, even, such a thing as free will simply does not exist? For Verplaetse, this is the only possible conclusion. If neuroscientists themselves rarely draw that conclusion, it is because conclusions like that are by definition beyond the scope of their science.[2] But not beyond the scope of "philosophers", Verplaetse writes. For philosophy's domain is that of logical reasoning.[3] If A and B and C lead to conclusion D, then the "philosopher" has to draw that conclusion, however mad, untenable or counter-intuitive it might seem. If the free will can be traced back to strictly causal processes, if every choice can be traced back to a chain of necessary reactions within the neurological system, then the will is causally determined and, hence, not free. Ergo: free will does not exist. Inside of me, there is no kind of separate thing that escapes logical causality and freely chooses what to do or not, what to think or not, what to wish or not. Such a free 'thing' is a mere illusion. Even if for centuries people have believed in its existence, this does not make it any less illusory.

But is this really so? Have past centuries thought this way about free will? Have they really believed that, within us, there is a kind of 'homunculus' escaping the laws, which our nature listens to? Certainly not Aristotle, for instance. A will existing apart from what he calls 'φύσις' (*phusis*) and escaping its causality, is according to him nonsense. According to Aristotle, there is only one thing that escapes causality, namely causality *as such,* or, what amounts to the same thing, *being* as such. And since everything and everyone that *is* shares being, everything and everyone participates in freedom, although each 'species' does this in a different way or degree. Thomas Aquinas, as well as medieval scholastic thinking in general, considered this problem in a similar way, except that for them, there is only one instance for whom Verplaetse's qualification of a free will is entirely valid: God. God is the only one who is not bound to causal reality, since he is creator of it, having freely made reality out of nothing – 'freely', i.e., for no reason except his unbound sovereignty and infinite goodness.

When this God 'died' during the sixteenth and seventeenth centuries something of his freedom was taken over by the new modern subject, the Cartesian *cogito*. Methodologically doubting all that there is, man discovered something that definitely escaped his doubt: his doubting *itself*, the 'self' undoubtedly present in his doubting, in his thinking. This is the way Descartes has put it, who considered the act of thinking as supported by a '*res*', a 'thing', a 'substance'.

Here – i.e., in the idea that next to my 'mechanically' functioning body ('*res extensa*'), there is an autonomous and free agency which is the soul ('*res cogitans*') – we meet the only historical reference to the 'free will' as defined by Verplaetse. But already in Descartes's own time, and certainly in the age after him, that idea was severely criticized. From Malebranche, through Spinoza and Leibniz, and up to the 'existential' analyses of Heidegger, Merleau-Ponty and Sartre, there have been numerous 'philosophical' attempts made to show the untenable character of that idea and to formulate more realistic alternatives, which do not deny human freedom, but acknowledge its inherently situational and finite condition.

In fact, Verplaetse's reference to neuroscience as well as the whole of his argument against the existence of a free will repeats a similar eighteenth century argumentation. The idea that all one can ascribe to the soul and free will can entirely be reduced to causal, bodily processes is a two and a half centuries old supposition. It was *L'homme machine* (*Man, a Machine*), a 'philosophical' manifesto by Julien Offray de La Mettrie from 1748, that 'solved' the problem of Cartesian dualism (man is two kinds of being, a free soul apart from a determined body) by declaring the soul to be non-existent (La Mettrie, 1996). The '*res extensa*', the material world determined by causal laws, was the only reality that exists.

La Mettrie's manifesto was decisive for the future of the modern 'science of the human', although his argument is in fact not very convincing, if only because it only says that it *will be* proved. The author again and again repeats that science *will* prove that everything we ascribe to the soul can be ascribed to bodily processes – which is to say that science has *not* delivered that proof *yet*. The future tense is still the main character of today's argumentations on this topic, including that of Verplaetse. Neuroscience is still in the position that it (only) *will* prove that the totality of our behaviors and our thoughts are merely causal and in no sense free processes.

And why is it so important for Verplaetse to prove that there is no free will, that everything a human being does can be traced back to strict causality? The crux of his answer can be put it in a seemingly paradoxical way: because that insight makes us really free. It more specifically makes us free from false ideas such as responsibility and guilt. And it delivers society from endless and useless moral and other 'reproaches', which people make to one another. If free will does not exist, people cannot be responsible for what they do and consequently cannot be accused of being guilty. After all the cause of one's behavior lays in the objective functioning of the brain – a cause that can scientifically be detected without accusing any person. We must free ourselves from those painful illusions that cause so much trouble and disturb so many juridical procedures. Responsibility and guilt must be evacuated from our courts. Juridical or moral questions should be treated in an enlightened, strictly rational way, seeking the answer to moral misbehavior by applying a strict deterministic causality excluding fantasies such as free will and responsibility. This, in a nutshell, is the mission of Verplaetse's crusade against the illusion of free will.

Even if all this is logically correct, Verplaetse's plea to leave behind imagination is naïve. As if we could simply get rid of such a thing as imagination. Would we be without guilty feeling once we know guilt is 'just imagination' and that the only real thing is merely a matter of neurological causality? Is consciousness that strong that it can annihilate feelings of guilt and responsibility once and for all?

Can a world in which nobody feels guilty be anything other than a world in which everyone acts *as if* s/he is without guilt, while in reality, s/he does feel guilty – at least guilty vis-à-vis a law saying one should not have feelings of guilt? Can a denial of a guilty conscience ever work other than as a law that forbids – and thus inadvertently feeds it?

It is strange that the 'philosopher' Verplaetse does not notice that the universe implied by his theory is in fact very similar to the Calvinistic universe of the seventeenth century. In its own way, Calvinism too declares guilty conscience senseless. Already before the beginning of time, God's predestination has determined someone's fate and arranged his entire life path in such a way that it could not escape universal causality.[4] Here, too, it was rather absurd to feel guilty about trespasses one has made, for one was unable to influence 'causal determinism'. Only, as quite soon became clear, the denial of that feeling made it all the more present, to such an extent that the consequences were nothing short of disastrous. Calvinist culture provoked a terrible and traumatic collective feeling of guilt. Can a life "without reproach", as Verplaetse defines it (2011, p. 24, 130), be anything other than a life in which I – just like everyone else – am on the verge of reproaching everyone that they are on the verge of reproaching me of something?

Guilt, reproaches, affects, feelings: even if Verplaetse is right that these are but products of our imagination, the question is whether the reduction of that imagination to facts (to neurological processes in the brain for instance) is legitimate at all. Is there not something in imagination which persists despite being reduced to something else? Does imagination not imply that there is, if not a free *ego*, at least something like 'freedom'? That, besides the causality of the brain and the neurological system, there is a space for freedom?

But what if the freedom present in imagination is nonetheless the product of the brain? What if the causality of the brain is not as strictly deterministic as Verplaetse claims it is? What if the brain is characterized by a plasticity that leaves room for a whimsicality comparable to that of the imagination?

Neuroscience as Ideology Critique

This is the thesis of Catherine Malabou's book, *What Should We Do with Our Brain?* (2008). The title itself indicates her distance from Verplaetse's thesis. It is not the brain which does something with us; it is us doing something with our brain. According to Malabou, the brain is not an inflexibly determined mechanism, but a process that is more flexible and changeable than we had for decades thought. The brain is in a way an active, and in that sense *free,* event. It is not a central computer directing the human machinery with a fixed, deterministic logic (Malabou 2008, p. 33), but an organism of great plasticity that actively interferes in coincidence and necessity.

> If neuronal function is an event or should bring about events, this is so precisely because it is itself able to create events, to eventualize *[evenementialiser]* the program and thus, in a certain sense, to deprogram it.
>
> *(2008, p. 8; Malabou's italics)*

Contrary to what we thought before, the brain is constantly in evolution. Again and again, it succeeds in adapting its 'program' to new situations and to 'deprogram' itself when necessary. In other words, the brain actively *makes* its own history, which is why it is able to recover and regenerate much more easily than we had presumed. And it does so in its own *particular* way. No brain is interchangeable with another one. "Plasticity thus adds the functions of artist and instructor in freedom and autonomy to its role as sculptor", Malabou writes (2008, p. 22).

We are far away from the kind of materialism that denies freedom and exchanges it with rigid determinism. But we definitely remain within the lines of materialism. A few pages before, we read:

> The difference between the brain and psychism is shrinking considerably, and we do not know it. 'We' end up coinciding completely with 'our brain' – because our brain is us, the intimate form of a 'proto-self', a sort of organic personality – and we do not know it. (2008, p. 8)

"… and we do not know it". This sentence is repeated throughout the book and betrays its main intention: scientific brain research is used to deny freedom, while in fact it gives freedom a solid foundation. Only the one who knows how the human brain works, really knows how free the human being is.

Freedom is a biological, neurological thing: this is what Malabou tries to explain. And, consequently, scientific brain research is in favor of human freedom and of free society. One of today's central questions is:

> How can we know how to respond in a plastic manner to the plasticity of the brain? If the brain is the biological organ determined to make supple its own biological determinations, if the brain is in some way a self-cultivating organ, which culture would correspond to it, which culture could no longer be a culture of biological determinism, could no longer be, in other words, a culture against nature? Which culture is the culture of neuronal liberation? Which world? Which society? (2008, p. 30)

Here, Malabou's analysis turns out to be an ideological critique. "Any vision of the brain is necessarily political", she writes (2008, p. 52). One can no longer consider the brain as a central power, a society built upon (biological) freedom must abandon any kind of centralism (2008, pp. 36–37). Referring to the plasticity of the brain, one must unmask the ideology of using the brain as support for its centralistic policy of power in which everything and everyone is supposed to be subjected to reigning 'determinism' (2008, p. 40).

But do society and politics not already function in accordance with the plastic model Malabou puts forward? Is this not exactly the way neoliberal capitalism is working? The latter does not ask for law-abiding servility, but self-control, innovation, flexibility, multitasking and networking – in short all kinds of capacities that fit perfectly with the plasticity of the brain. Malabou confirms that analogy. When she admits that depression and other mental deceases have social causes (exclusion from social networks, for instance), she immediately refers that observation to the malfunctioning of neuronal 'networking' and other brain functions.

But how, then, can brain theory be an exquisite tool with which to examine capitalism and its social debacle in an ideology in a critical way? Malabou writes: "It is not the identity of cerebral organization and socioeconomic organization that poses a problem, but rather the unconsciousness of this identity" (2008, p. 52). As we read earlier, the problem is "… that we do not know it".

If we had a correct idea of the way the brain functions (the opposite, for instance, of the way in which Verplaetse thinks it functions), then we should be able to see the limits of the flexibility capitalism is forcing us to accept (both as employee and employer). It would give a foundation to our protest against the dark sides of dominant economic culture. Yet, so Malabou adds, these dominant ideas "are precisely what induce us to keep the brain away from itself, to separate it from what it is" (2008, pp. 52–53). She concludes, it is time to abolish that distance or separation.

In other words, the brain has to finally discover 'itself'. And it *does* have a 'self', a 'proto-self', as Malabou calls it after Damasio (Malabou, 2008, p. 57), a "synthesis of all the plastic processes at work in the brain" (2008, p. 58). That neuronal (proto)-self is the basis for our conscious 'self', and so for consciousness in general, and for civilization, economy, politics and so on. But, therefore, we first have to gain knowledge about that neuronal 'self' and the 'continuity' between the neuronal and the mental.

Malabou argues that it is because we still fail to do this that ideology can slip in. She mentions "mental Darwinism", which reduces the plasticity of the brain and its 'self' too much to one-dimensional schemes of rigid determinism (2008, p. 65). In other words, it denies that our brain is dealing with reality (including ourselves) in a *creative* way. "The brain is our work and we do not know it", Malabou repeats here once again (2008, p. 66). This is why "it must be acknowledged that the neuronal liberation has not liberated us" (2008, p. 67). Despite the explosion of brain research, we still stick to the old deterministic ideologies of power.

> Once again, it seems that the neuronal revolution has revolutionized nothing *for us,* if it is true that our new brains serve only to displace ourselves better, work better, feel better, or obey better. The synthesis of the neuronal and the psychical thus fails to live up to its task: we are neither freer, nor smarter, nor happier. (2008, p. 68; the author's italics)

A revolutionary brain research should enable "resistance", argues Malabou:

> Resistance to flexibility, to this ideological norm advanced consciously or otherwise by a reductionist discourse that models and naturalizes the neuronal process in order to legitimate a certain social and political functioning. (2008, p. 68)

The brain is a dialectical process in which the neuronal and the mental go together by differing from one another. Their difference generates a freedom for which current brain research remains blind. Thus claims the author who not coincidentally wrote a doctoral thesis on Hegel, "the first philosopher to have made the word plasticity into a concept" (2008, p. 80). No unlimited flexibility, that other name for servile obedience, but dialectical plasticity, which contains a core of resistance to flexibility as an inherently "explosive" tendency (2008, pp. 73–74). A society based on freedom can only refer to that neuronal/mental model. It is the task of brain sciences to make us aware of this, so that we "know what to do with our brain".

New in Malabou's approach is the fact that natural science is analyzed as having both an ideological dimension and a mission of ideology critique. Most of the brain sciences, just like the one Verplaetse refers to, are still promoting a superseded deterministic 'world picture' that all too well fits with an authoritarian politics of power. And even where it is changed by a self-organizing plastic view on the brain, that science often supports subtle power mechanisms of self-control, flexibility, multi-tasking and so on. Only an advanced insight in the dialectical plasticity of the brain allows an adequate criticism of the hybrid mechanisms of power at work within our free, capitalist world.

The Brain: A Nostalgic Dream

Yet, why is it necessary to provide ideology critique a 'ground' in natural sciences? Why give cultural criticism a foundation in nature? There is an enormous amount of high-level twentieth century ideology critique – from Canguilhem to Foucault, from Adorno to Derrida, from Barthes to Lacan – that do *not* give their critical analyses a foundation in nature or natural sciences. They all stick to strict discourse analysis. They approach culture as a discursive reality, for a larger part treated as the result of mere imagination; and none of them feels the need to refer to any 'natural' base.

This is an observation which Malabou nowhere in her book thematizes explicitly. She supposes a foundation in nature to be a kind of 'must', providing a solid, ontological ground to modern criticism, including ideology critique, preparing the way "toward a biological alter-globalism" (the subtitle of the conclusion; 2008, p. 78). The way in which we (which is to say: our brain) are plastic and flexible, is the model and ground for the way civilization, culture, economy and politics are – and have to be – free.

Why this should be necessary is a question Malabou's book leaves untouched. Why does cultural criticism need an anchor point in nature? Or, more precisely, why does a critical distance from nature need a ground *within nature* (for this is what Malabou's thesis of the dialectical relation between the neuronal and the mental is about)? Should that distance from nature, in order to be what it is, not precisely acknowledge its *lack* of ground in nature? Should a theory of culture not depart from an unbridgeable gap between culture and nature – as for instance Claude Lévi-Strauss stated (referring to Jean-Jacques Rousseau who, according to him, was the founding father of the 'human sciences').[5]

Is this 'unnatural' distance with regard to nature not the reason why we are able, thanks to the power of natural sciences, to destroy nature? The catastrophic dimension of nuclear power is but one illustration. The knowledge of that power, which as we know has its origin in the human brain, enables us to bring us all back to the Stone Age in only a few seconds. Here we see how far-reaching brain power can be in its capacity of distancing itself from nature. Its limit coincides with nothing but the annihilation of nature, including the annihilation of the brain itself.

Is this 'death principle' underlying (and at the same time deconstructing) the working of the brain to be considered 'natural'? Or is it a matter of unnatural, 'mere' imagination? What about an imagination that does not exist, as Verplaetse would claim, but nonetheless is able to destroy all there is?

Here again, we meet the question raised at the beginning of this essay, the question about the 'nature' of thinking and, more specifically, the 'nature' of imagination. Has imagination – i.e., the faculty that allows us to distance ourselves from nature – a ground in nature (in our brain, in being qua being), or is it groundless, escaping natural determinacy, nature or being? And if this is the case, where then is the 'ground' of such groundless imagination?

To be clear, the question is not whether thinking and imagination has a natural *substratum*, for it surely has one. Without the brain, no thinking or imagination is possible. But the question is whether thinking and imagination can fully be understood as *proceeding from* that natural substratum, whether it can be exhaustibly understood as matter of nature.

And, a more important question that remains relevant when the latter is positively answered is: where and what is the motive of the will to understand thinking and imagination *from* – and *as* – its natural substratum? What motivates modernity's interest in grounding thought and imagination – and freedom in general – in nature? Is that motive purely scientific, or do we want to 'save' science, to save it more precisely from the consequences of its modern condition, i.e., of its disconnection from ontological being? Is our intention to found freedom in nature not affected by the nostalgia for a pre-modern ontological science that understood itself as firmly rooted in nature and being?

So, does scientific brain research, at least within the current public debate, not function first of all as the appeal to an 'authority' in order to defuse the modern groundlessness of thinking and imagination? Is the brain not a nostalgic dream, the name for that in which we hope to find a ground for the incurable groundlessness of our modern condition? Does brain research not function as an 'ideological' tool in order to hide or deny what is inherent to modern natural science – the *death drive,* the very concept that refers to its disconnection from nature and, consequently, to its genuine ability to destroy that nature?

Malabou tries to save brain studies from the dominant idea that they go hand in hand with a denial of freedom and the existence of a free will (as for instance in Verplaetse's theory). On the contrary, so she claims, the brain is an apotheosis of plasticity, which is the natural basis of the human freedom. But here, too, the question remains whether even that plasticity is not a way to deny the groundlessness of freedom and imagination, whether the 'anarchic' dimension of freedom can be traced back to the anarchic dimension of nature or of being.

Or, to put it in another way: where is the *death drive* in brain plasticity as conceived in Malabou's theory? Is the human brain's ability to destroy nature, including its own, found in its nature? This question – or, what amounts to the same thing, this malicious omnipotence of modern science – is left untouched in Malabou's book.

As it is left unthought in the entire current debate about the implications of brain research for the question of freedom.

Notes

1. See for instance Alexandre Koyré's classic study of the paradigm shift of modern science in the seventeenth century: *From the Closed World to the Open Universe* (Koyré, 1957).
2. Verplaetse, 2011: 16.
3. Repeatedly, Verplaetse emphasizes that his book is a "philosophical essay", even "philosophy in its purest form" (Verplaetse, 2011, p. 7; my translation, MDK). And what, according to the author, is "philosophy in its purest form"? *Logic*: this is the answer underlying Verplaetse's thesis. It is put forward on every page, but nowhere is it *argued* for *as such*. The supposition underlying the author's argument tells us that any claim that does not withstand logical scrutiny fails, is false, and speaks about things that do not exist. The idea that the free will exists is logically untenable, *ergo* free will does not exist, ergo freedom is an illusion. The first supposition behind this argument is that logic tells us what *is*. '*Logos*' is the way to *being*. The second supposition is that illusion, because it does not exist, has no reality at all. From the seventeenth century onwards, *modern* philosophy has put precisely these two suppositions into question. In the fifth century BC, the philosophical tradition started with the idea that logos/logic leads to being/truth. Since the seventeenth century, however, our modern condition has forced us to acknowledge that logos/logic can generate truth, even if it does not (and, even *cannot*) lead to being *as such*. This is the core of the Kantian critical project in philosophy. And – here we see modernity's impact on the second supposition – illusion, precisely *as* illusion, is not simply the opposite of reality: confronted with the impact of visual culture (to name only this phenomenon), twentieth century philosophy has learned to take this idea seriously. A reflection on both suppositions is apparently beyond the scope of Verplaetse's "philosophy". It is not a coincidence that his line of reasoning shows a deadlock similar to of the one found in seventeenth and eighteenth century philosophy, the centuries in which modernity was still struggling with its new 'scientific' paradigm (see further in this essay).
4. Verplaetse himself refers to predestination (Verplaetse, 2011: 47).
5. See the chapter "Jean-Jacques Rousseau, fondateur des sciences de l'homme", in Lévi-Strauss, 1976, pp. 33–43.

References

Kant, I. (1998). *Critique of Pure Reason*. Translated and edited by Paul Guyer & Allen W. Wood. Cambridge: Cambridge University Press.

Koryé, A. (1957). *From the Closed World to the Open Universe*. Baltimore, MD: The Johns Hopkins Press.

La Mettrie, Julien Offray de (1996). *Machine Man and Other Writings*. Cambridge: Cambridge University Press.

Malabou, C. (2008). *What Should We Do with Our Brain?* Foreword by Marc Jeanerod, Translated by Sebastian Rand. New York, NY: Fordham University Press.

Lévi-Strauss, C. (1976 [1973]). *Structural Anthropology, Vol 2*. New York, NY: Basic Books.

Verplaetse, Jan (2009). *Localising the Moral Sense: Neuroscience and the Search for the Cerebral Seat of Morality, 1800–1930*. Dordrecht: Springer.

Verplaetse, Jan (2011). *Zonder Vrije Wil. Een Filosofisch Essay Over Verantwoordelijkheid* [*Without Free Will. A Philosophical Essay on Responsibility*]. Amsterdam: Uitgeverij Nieuwezijds.

2

WHAT IS CRITIQUE IN THE ERA OF THE NEUROSCIENCES?

Jan De Vos

Introduction

At the end of a symposium critically assessing the use of neuroscience in parenting and family policy, one of the speakers summarized the day's results in the following terms: (1) nobody is against parental support and help; and (2) nobody is against neuroscience. Apart from the fact that this delineated two no-go zones, two zones where critique should not tread, it above all made the question of where, precisely, critique is to be launched, very pressing. Does critique not always posit itself at a remove from two other points? Just consider the typical phrase: "on the one hand … and on the other hand". In the symposium the two issues critically scrutinized were parental support and the neurosciences. Doing critique, hence, amounts to discerning the possible dichotomies, while assuming some kind of (Archimedean) point of view overlooking the binarized terrain.

This puts us in mind of the typical high school teacher who wants his pupils to be critical, to *think for themselves*, to *form their own opinions*. The problem is not that he actually wants you to think what he thinks, but rather, that, to a large extent, he does not really care what you think. His main goal is to have a proper debate: "there is nothing like a good discussion, right"? In this way he not only testifies to his Archimedean position – the point from which he steers and manages the sublunar, civilized warfare (the source of his little pleasures) – but also, and this is central, *he enjoins you to take part in it*. The pupils, too, have to become detached. They have to embrace all sorts of opinions, precisely by identifying themselves with his non-partisan, *uber*-critical point of view.

The same interpellation was brought about at the end of the critical symposium on the use and abuse of neuroscience in parenting: it addressed the participants as part of an aloof but critical people, overseeing both sides, assessing where matters truly stand or would need to stand. However, has this kind of critique, typical of the humanities, not precisely become outdated by the neuro-turn itself? It is clear that the neurosciences themselves offer a firm and ambitious critique, targeting our false consciousness, laying bare the illusions involved in love, altruism, rationality … showing us the bare facts, the materiality of all this. Hence, it could be argued that, as the neurosciences are able to (potentially) fully disclose the material base of rational and critical thinking, they actually deconstruct the illusory Archimedean position silently underpinning the humanities. Not only can neuroscience claim that there is no point outside the neurological from which to mount an Archimedean critique, it can also explain why traditional humanist critique is quite impotent when it comes to changes at the synaptic or the neuro-structural level.

However, perhaps the neuro-turn just lays bare a more fundamental impotence inherent to critique in the humanities. For, today more than ever, laying bare the "true state of affairs" proves to be a futile endeavor. This was nicely captured by Slavoj Žižek who reversed the well-known phrase from Marx's *Capital* – "they do not know it, but they are doing it" – turning it into: "they know very well what they are doing, but still, they are doing it". Žižek points out, leaning on Sloterdijk, that in these times of "cynical reason" the old models of ideology critique no longer work (Žižek, 1989, pp. 28–30). This is of course the longstanding issue of the impotence of critique, the impotence of reason, the impotence of knowledge. A classical attempt to counter, or at least to understand this, has precisely been the turn to a *psychological* explanation. Just consider a particular turn that happened in Marxist critiques as they were confronted in the 1930s with the fact that popular revolt did not automatically lead to socialism but rather to fascism, despite the Marxist critique revealing how capitalism works and what the role of the proletariat should be. It is to this that Freudo-Marxism tried to give an answer, turning to the domain of the psychological in order to counter the deadlock experienced by a pure, rational, knowledge-based critique. Today, however, we have shifted from a psychological back-up of critique to a neurological one. Think of W.E. Connolly, who in his book *Neuropolitics* addresses the inadequacy of rational choice theory and the intellectualist approach to deliberative democracy, arguing that "[t]he amygdala cannot be changed by argument alone" (Connolly, 2002, p. 206, n. 27). For Connolly, a new left and progressive movement should not shy away from addressing its voters on the affective level, reaching the appropriate brain areas even by subliminal pathways (Connolly, 2005, para 11).[1] The prefix neuro- has won its final battle, so it seems; it has conquered critique itself.

Neuro-Critique and Its Deadlock, Psychology

If critique has become neuro-critique, are we then still dealing with a triangle, with a point from which a critical gaze is launched at two "on the one hand … and on the other hand" points? Judging from the abstract of a paper on aesthetics by the neuroscientist Vittorio Gallese, it could be argued that the scheme of the critical triangle is still in place. Gallese writes:

> (…) cognitive neuroscience can surrender us from the forced choice between the totalizing relativism of social constructivism, which doesn't leave any room to the constitutive role of the brain-body in cognition, and the deterministic scientism of some quarters of evolutionary psychology, which aims at explaining art exclusively in terms of adaptation and modularity.
>
> *(Gallese, 2015)*

Or, if I am allowed to schematize this, cognitive neuroscience can mediate between the human sciences and psychology. In this way Gallese's move is interesting because it separates what often is considered a monolithic issue: the neuroscientific and the psychological. Gallese's neuroscientific "experimental aesthetics perspective" is a deconstructive critique of both the field of semiotic-hermeneutics *and* the psychological approach:

> We can now look at the aesthetic-symbolic dimension of human existence not only from a semiotic-hermeneutic perspective, but starting from the dimension of bodily presence. In so doing we can *deconstruct* some of the concepts we normally use when referring to intersubjectivity or to aesthetics and art, as well as when referring to the experience we make of them.
>
> *(Gallese, 2015, my emphasis)*

Experimental neuroscience here is pitted against, on the one hand, intersubjectivity and hermeneutics (the domain of the humanities), and on the other hand, to the experience we have of the world (the domain of psychology). Taking neuroscience to be setting up a critical triangle allows us to scrutinize the conditions of possibility of neuro-critique. As is well known, critique always solicits a meta-critique, evaluating the very possibility of evaluating something.

A question hence, could be: what are the limits of a deconstruction of neuroscience, and at what point does it produce, to use Bruno Latour's phrase, *fact-objects* that fill up the deconstructed and emptied-out space? For Latour, this is where critique, the drive to expose certain beliefs as mere fantasies, traditionally and necessarily ends up:

> Critical thought drained space, creating emptiness. Conversely, on the pretext that fact-objects appear to exist without us … critical thought lined up facts in tight ranks, forming a continuous, seamless "real world" without holes, without humans. Critical thought filled up space, creating fullness.
>
> *(Latour, 2010, p. 39)*

Neuroscience as critique denounces illusions of fullness, empties them out, but at the same time it engenders the fact-objects of the brain, the connectome, the synapse … and indeed, this forms a world without humans, the latter replaced by the brain that is living, thinking and loving in our place. The human has left the building, making way for the fact-specters of nature. But what is then the stuff of which these natural objects-apparitions are made? If the human is stripped of its old humanist and psychologistic attributions, do we end up with the real and concrete facts of human life as contained in the brain-object-icon – eating, drinking, having sex – topped off by some thinking and interacting in order to make the former possible in a cultural and somewhat sublimated way?

However, is it not precisely here, in the bare facts, that the old humanist and psychological assumptions come back to haunt what was meant to replace them? For one can argue that the deconstructive machine of the neurosciences necessarily has to start from humanist and psychological *theories*. To argue that X is understandable in terms of neurons, synaptic exchanges and brain areas requires certain humanist/psychological conceptions of X. Eventually, what is put under the scanner is not a body, it is even not the psychological features one wants to find the neural underpinning for: what is put under the scanner is, I argue, a psychological *theory*. Crucial for neuroscientific research on, for example, aggression, love or forgetting is the psychological theory that makes these issues operative, that is, to design the stimuli (images, videos or other forms of scenarios) offered to the subjects in, for example, the MRI tube. The choice between models from cognitive behavioral theoretical frameworks or from psychoanalysis, for example, is, obviously, decisive. Generally speaking, a clear-cut, black-and-white psychological theory will be more readily employed in a neuroscientific context than the more complex and less straight-forward models, as these are less amenable in experimental settings and laboratory environments. But not only do neuroscientific experiments start from psychology and its models, it is also with psychology that they can be said to end up. That is, eventually a typical neuroscientific experiment concludes, after having discussed brain areas, neurotransmitters and other neurological factors, with a theoretical-psychological speculation about the observed results. It is psychology that is mapped onto the brain, it is psychology that provides the pencils with which the brain is colored (De Vos, online first, October 17, 2014). This humanist/psychological filling-in of the fact-objects of neuroscience remains as a rule obscured.

Consequently, given that a neuroscientific approach is, necessarily, dependent on psychological models, it becomes doubtful whether the neurosciences can deliver an unproblematic, non-Archimedean perspective from which a neuro-critique can be launched. Critique always mobilizes some Olympic point from which the reflection sets out, a point external to the field in question so as to allow for an overview. Neuro-critique not only cannot escape this recourse to an external vantage point, it also has to scaffold its critical position with its silent partner, psychology: this is where the critical triangle threatens to collapse.

So perhaps we need to consider another, more classic, triangle, one that still puts philosophy or, for that matter, the human sciences in motion. This one would involve, on the one hand, the spontaneous, everyday folk-psychology of the human and, on the other, the objectified, scientific assessments of the human. Philosophy in this scheme can claim to offer a critical point of view to deal with both perspectives. In the two following sections I will engage with Ray Brassier's attempt to merge Wilfrid Sellars' critical realism with Thomas Metzinger's neuro-philosophical approach to the Self in order to re-mount a philosophical critique compatible with today's neurosciences. Then, I will mount a critique against this and engage with a specific psychoanalytic approach to subjectivity, reductionism and hence eventually, to critique.

Folk-Psychology, A Founding Myth

For Sellars, there are two images of man-in-the-the-world: "the manifest image of man" as a self-conscious rational agent and "the scientific image of man" as a complex physical system (Sellars, 1963). The manifest image, one could say, concerns our everyday, folk-psychological[2] way of dealing with ourselves, the others and the world; the scientific image is how science looks at the human and the world. Brassier describes the manifest image as the level of conceptual interpretation (giving and asking for reasons) and the scientific one as that of ontological description and explanation:

> In this regard, the genuine philosophical task, according to Sellars, would consist in achieving a properly stereoscopic integration of the manifest and scientific images, such that the language of rational intention would come to enrich scientific theory so as to allow the latter to be directly wedded to human purposes.
>
> *(Brassier, 2007, p. 6)*

Here we see the critical triangle. Again, as in the case with Gallese, I will question the possibility of an independent third point from which to mount a critique (in this case philosophy), and will scrutinize the role of psychology in this scheme (psychology is here given twice: on the one hand, as folk-psychology, and on the other, as its scientific pendant, [neuro]psychology).

Most interestingly, Sellars does not see folk-psychology as fully independent of science. As Brassier argues, "a proto-scientific theory lies at the heart of the normative structure of the manifest image": it is thus "not the domain of pre-theoretical immediacy" (Brassier, 2007, p. 3). Sellars himself writes that the manifest image is the framework in terms of which man comes to be aware of himself as man-in-the-world: "man couldn't be man until he encountered himself" (Sellars, 1963, p. 6). While the manifest image took shape "in the mists of pre-history", the scientific image is relatively young (Sellars, 1963, p. 5). The main difference is that the manifest image concerns concrete, experiential things ("persons, animals, lower forms of life and 'merely material' things") (Sellars, 1963, p. 9) while science involves the postulation of imperceptible entities to explain the behavior of perceptible things (Sellars, 1963, p. 7).

Philosophy, then, has the task of establishing a stereoscopic view, encompassing "in one view the two images of man-in-the-world" (Sellars, 1963, p. 6). Importantly, Sellars does not privilege the manifest image over the scientific one, nor the other way around. For Sellars the two images are not fully reducible to each other. He even argues that to the extent that the manifest image would not survive in the synoptic view, man himself would not survive. It would hence, be "folly to replace [the manifest image] piecemeal by fragments of the scientific image" (Sellars, 1963, p. 15). However, what makes it the case that the manifest image has a surplus which escapes the scientific grasp is not precisely clear. He does provide some hints: we do not get our folk-psychological outlook on life from a supposed direct and intimate contact with our own psychological states; rather, this is from the very start a matter of language and intersubjectivity (related to family, community and society). As this intersubjective manifest image is the basis for our self-understanding, it remains for Sellars out of the purview of science.[3]

But does this not still raise the question: why does the manifest image defy scientification? For, in the end, is Sellars' "giving and asking for reasons", determined by language and intersubjectivity, really a zone out of reach (or should we say, a no-go zone) for science? Are not precisely today's neurosciences, ranging from neuropsychology to neuro-aesthetics to neuropolitics, claiming jurisdiction here? However, whether this claim is legitimate or not might not be of central importance. The central issue, rather, is to understand why the irreducibility of the manifest image is crucial not only for the Sellarsian theoretical construction but also for what we here sweepingly might call the neuro-turn within the (human) sciences.

The point of entry here might be the predominance of the scopic element with Sellars (using terms as *images, stereoscopy, synoptic view* …), which he does not justify or elaborate on. To begin with, Sellars posits "man" as endowed with a naïve gaze; that is, a gaze embodied and embedded in history and intersubjectivity. This first gaze results in the manifest image. On the other hand, this perspective of "man-in-the-world" is redoubled in the scientific gaze, constituting thus a man, scientific man, not *in* but *outside* the world, looking from this Archimedean position at sublunar man. Here we could already ask if Sellars' all too easily advanced "man-*in*-the-world" gazing at itself, is indeed not above all an *image*, that is, a fiction, only seeing light through the scientific gaze itself? Or, put differently, the scientific gaze is only constituted by supposing a world out there and then within it a naïve, reflective "man-in-the world". But the main issue at stake here is that Sellars supplements these two gazes with a third one, the "synoptic view" of philosophy, turning the dual scheme thus into a triangle. Hence, Sellars needs the manifest image, the "man-in-the-world", and he needs it to be irreducible to science. Not only does this irreducibility constitute an object for the sciences: it creates the necessary outside for the sciences, and it also calls for the role of a third player, philosophy. For, it is only because science eventually "fails to provide a point of view outside the manifest image" (Sellars, 1963, p. 28) that philosophy can be called upon to deliver a stereoscopic view. The whole Sellarsian critical triangle thus stands or falls with the alleged irreducibility of the manifest image. The basis assumption of Sellars is thus that there is something like a folk-psychological man who testifies to some pre-scientific or extra-scientific realm that is only truly assessable from the philosophical, critical vantage point.

To make a bold statement, is the very idea of a folk-psychology not above all an invention closely related to the gesture of modernity and the birth of the modern sciences themselves? Consider, for example, David Hume, who in *A Treatise of Human Nature* could be said to have invented the very notion of a "folk-psychology":

> … whatever convincing arguments philosophers may fancy they can produce to establish the belief of objects independent of the mind, 'tis obvious these arguments are known but to very few, and that 'tis not by them, that children, peasants, and the greatest part of mankind are induc'd to attribute objects to some impressions, and deny them to others. Accordingly we find, that all the conclusions, which the vulgar form on this head, are directly contrary to those, which are confirm'd by philosophy.
>
> *(Hume, 2006[1739–1740], p. 129)*

Do we here not have one of the most puzzling philosophical conceptualizations of the Enlightenment, namely, the idea of a common sense, belonging to children, peasants and the greater part of mankind? Modern philosophy and psychology seem to be based on the invention of the extra-scientific naïve, common man with his folk-psychological ways of dealing with himself, others and the world. And this is precisely central to the neuro-turn in the human sciences: the myth of folk-psychology and the irreducible manifest image is the necessary counterpart, to be explained – but not to be explained away, as that would cut the ground out from under the neurosciences. However, certainly from a present-day perspective it is hard to maintain the idea of humanity's pre-scientific naïve presence in the world. A simple glance at the habitat and praxes of children and peasants invalidates the idea of a pre-scientific, naïve being immersed in reality. Do most parents not, for example, prepare a space for their newborn infant, a space which is designed to be safe, stimulating and structured according to the insights of pediatrics and psychology? Anyone a bit familiar with farming, on the other hand, knows that this profession is far removed from a straightforward, naïve or natural relation with the life-world (De Vos, 2013b). In modernity our being in the world, which one could argue collides with our reflection on it, passes fully over the scientific gaze.

But of course, one can object, Sellars does grant the manifest image its proto-scientific character. His notion of the manifest image is not an unmediated but is a proto-theoretical self-assessment. However, if central to Sellars' manifest image is that it is not fully reducible to the scientific image, it is precisely this irreducibility that could be contested. The advent of science, it can be argued, resulted in a fundamental shift of subjectivity in modernity. Science, as Edmund Husserl argued, "abstracts from everything subjective" (Husserl, 1970, p. 6). Hence, the modern sciences with their enormous capacity for objectification engendered not a so-called proto-scientific subject, but, rather, a full-blown 'subject of the sciences', looking at itself, others and the world, as a scientist. So contra Sellars' preservation of an irreducibility to the manifest image, and contra Husserl's refuge into the life-world, one could argue that both the folk-psychological man-in-the-world and the life-world are emptied out: we have all joined the ranks of the scientific community. We not only reflect upon our reasons for believing or thinking things from a scientific perspective: our 'giving and asking for reasons' and the very reasons themselves always already pass through scientific discourse, or, in psychoanalytic terms, through the scientific Other. This is in my opinion the basis of Slavoj Žižek's critique of the Husserlian concept of the life-world:

> Th[e] blending of Lebenswelt with science radically undermines the very notion of Lebenswelt as a field of everyday pre-scientific self-understanding and pre-theoretical life practice, from which science derives its meaning. (…) Lebenswelt has "lost its innocence" and become inherently defined by science. (…) Science as such, in the strict hermeneutic sense of the word, is unsignifying and as soon as it inherently begins to encroach on the Lebenswelt, the whole loses its meaning and we find ourselves in a void.
>
> *(Žižek, 1986)*

The modern subject is hence, not pre-scientific and even not proto-scientific: science does not merely color or influence our image of ourselves: science *is* our self-image. The modern subject is the subject of the sciences, and, with Žižek, we can call this the subject of the void. Hence, if Sellars writes that to the extent that the manifest image would not survive in the synoptic view, man himself would not survive, perhaps what he refrains from considering is the possibility that man indeed has not survived the advent of science: has the old 'man' not died, only without knowing it, only to live on like a zombie? At the least, here Sellars' critical triangle collapses.

Arguably, this is not the conclusion Ray Brassier makes when he engages with Sellars in his paper "The View from Nowhere" (2011). He instead attempts to reground the critical triangle and safeguard the vantage point of philosophy, precisely by claiming that, although the manifest image is not reducible to the scientific one, this irreducibility itself is not inaccessible to science. As we will see, Brassier, leaning on Thomas Metzinger, will claim that the neurosciences actually reveal a "point of view from nowhere", one that plays a role in the (illusionary) constitution of a Self.

There is No *No* Point of View from Nowhere

Brassier makes his point in a discussion with Habermas. Habermas clearly wants to preserve an irreducible, interpersonally constituted first-person perspective – Sellars' "manifest image" – fully disjoined from the scientific image and its third-person perspective. While, according to Brassier, Sellars is committed to the priority of the scientific image, Habermas is not. Brassier writes:

> Thus, according to Habermas, attempts to explain agency naturalistically fail because "the social constitution of the human mind which unfolds within interpersonal relationships can be made accessible only from the perspective of participants and cannot be captured from the perspective of an observer who objectivates everything into an event in the world".
>
> *(Brassier, 2011, p. 10)*

For Habermas self-objectification would irrevocably estrange us from ourselves: persons describing themselves in such a way "cannot recognize themselves as persons anymore" (Habermas quoted in: Brassier, 2011, p. 11). Here one could already remark that what Habermas misses is that this alienation perhaps is always already part, if not the core, of modern subjectivity as such. The question then is whether Brassier misses the same point, but I will return to this later. For the moment what is important is that Habermas evokes a 'point of view from nowhere', in order to immediately dismiss it. Brassier argues that this dismissal is a mistake. This is quotation of Habermas given by Brassier:

> The resistance to a naturalistic self-description stemming from our self-understanding as persons is explained by the fact that there is no getting round a dualism of epistemic perspectives that must interlock in order to make it possible for the mind, situated as it is within the world, to get an orienting overview of its own situation. Even the gaze of a purportedly absolute observer cannot sever the ties to one standpoint in particular, namely that of a counterfactually extended argumentation community.
>
> *(Habermas quoted in: Brassier, 2011, p. 12)*

Habermas, rejecting the priority of science's ontological descriptions and explanations, rebuffs the point of view from nowhere: "the gaze of a purportedly absolute observer" is always tied to the subject and its position in the community. It is precisely this point of view from nowhere that Brassier wants to re-establish. Brassier begins by arguing that the manifest image, although not reducible to the scientific image, ultimately is open to scientific inquiry, and it does not predetermine our understanding of what a person is. That is, the manifest image does not subordinate the ends of inquiry to human interests, since it can be studied scientifically. Hence, for Brassier the difference between Habermas and Sellars is that whereas both posit a linguistic embodiment of the normative order, Sellars' position, in contrast to Habermas', allows us to investigate how this linguistic embodiment and "this normative dimension might have arisen in the course of evolutionary and social history" (Brassier, 2011, p. 11). In other words, that there is "a constitutive link between subjectivity and rationality", Brassier writes, "is not to preclude the possibility of rationally investigating the biological roots of subjectivity" (Brassier, 2011, p. 9).

To pursue this path Brassier turns to Thomas Metzinger's "phenomenal self-model", since it would allow us to understand how normatively regulated social interactions actually supervene on neurobiological processes: the first-person subjective perspective arises out of sub-personal representational mechanisms at the neurobiological level (Brassier, 2011, p. 13). Metzinger's "phenomenal self-model" starts from a representational model to explain consciousness: "Conscious experience (…) consists in the activation of a coherent and transparent world model within a window of presence" (Metzinger cited in: Brassier, 2011, p. 13). Self-consciousness, then, is about the representing of the system's own states to itself. And here the notion of transparency is crucial, a notion which, as Brassier points out, is fundamentally a phenomenological rather than an epistemological one. That is, the Self is its own appearance only insofar as it does not perceive itself as a model. In other words, only insofar as it is transparent to itself, is the self phenomenologically constituted. Or, as Metzinger puts it, you can see through self-representations, they are cognitively impenetrable and not cognitively accessible for the system itself, and this unavailability of the representational character of the contents of conscious experience is the very base for our experience of having a self:

> Truly transparent phenomenal representations force a conscious system to functionally become a naïve realist with regard to their contents: whatever is transparently represented is experienced as real and as undoubtedly existing by this system.
>
> *(Metzinger cited in: Brassier, 2011, p. 14)*

We have a self as a result of the transparency (as 'a special kind of darkness') of the representations of ourselves. Brassier summarizes Metzinger's "phenomenal self model" (PSM) as follows:

> … it is precisely the system's lack of access to the process through which it generates its own self-model that engenders the condition of "autoepistemic closure" whereby the represented of the system's self-representation occludes the representing that gave rise to it.
>
> *(Brassier, 2011, p. 15)*

It is here, in a further twist of the phenomenal self model, that Brassier wants to ground the point of view from nowhere, precisely by anchoring it in the neuro-architecture itself. He proceeds to this by imagining, together with Metzinger, the possibility of a "selfless experience". That is, Metzinger contemplates the possibility of a system whose representational models would *not* be transparent but fully opaque. While in the case of transparency there is an introspective unavailability of all the earlier processing stages which have produced the Self, a system presented with opacity "would continuously recognize [the earlier processing stages] as a representational construct, as an internally generated internal structure" (Metzinger cited in: Brassier, 2011, p. 18). Such a system would not have a self, only a system-model: it would not instantiate selfhood. However, in that hypothetical case, the system would be burdened by a computational overload of representations: as Brassier argues, with Metzinger, it would have to find a way to deal with this in order to not get trapped into infinite loops of self-presentation.[4] Such a system would be, according to Metzinger, "nemocentric": it would be functionally egocentric, while remaining phenomenologically selfless.

Brassier argues that this nemocentric perspective is a strong argument for the neurocomputational processing underlying objectifying representation: it can serve to foreground the objective processes through which objectivity is partly produced. And this is where one might find *the view from nowhere* rejected by Habermas:

> The nemocentric subject of a hypothetically completed neuroscience in which all the possible neural correlates of representational states have been identified would provide an empirically situated and biologically embodied locus for the exhaustively objective "view from nowhere", which Habermas and others have denounced as a conceptual impossibility.
>
> *(Brassier, 2011, p. 18)*

So when Habermas claims that there is no escape from the subjective, first-person perspective – even the purportedly absolute observer is tainted by it – Brassier in contrast argues that precisely within that first-person perspective this objective 'point of view from nowhere' is potentially to be found. Rejecting on this ground Habermas' irreducibility of the subjective and the normative, Brassier thus validates and grounds Sellar's synoptic view as one that integrates the subjective and the objective, reasons and causes (Brassier, 2011, p. 19). Situating the point of view from nowhere primordially in the sub-personal dimension of the manifest image of man-in-the-world itself, Brassier aims at consolidating the critical triangle of Sellars.

Let me now formulate my critical point against this. To begin with, Brassier rightfully rejects the first-person perspective discourses à la Habermas and other phenomenological, hermeneutical approaches as he, leaning on Metzinger, attempts to, as it were, radically empty out the self. However, does Metzinger, and with him Brassier, in the end not refrain from completely emptying the self out? For it can be argued that Metzinger bases his phenomenal self model on the presupposition of a phenomenological everyday experience of oneself *as a self*. However, does this not amount to the construction of a straw man in order to then perform the decon-struction? Is not, in contrast, the basic primordial modern experience precisely one of the loss of the self, of selflessness or even un-selfness? This is where one could replace Metzinger's very starting point, the, albeit illusory, pre-reflexive experience of being someone, with the basic lesson of psychoanalysis: namely that the self, or better, the subject, only exists in relation to its non-being, its being split, its lack. This basic alienation is always already operative at the very phenomenological level: it is the inextricable shadow of any experience of being a self. It is this fundamental twist which is not taken into account by Metzinger. In this sense, Brassier's phrase "PSM is all we are" – speaking about a "full immersion" as he echoes Metzinger's terms "total simulation" (Brassier, 2011, p. 17) – is not unproblematic. I'd argue against this: to be immersed in the world requires a spot, a symptom, a doubt: is this real or is it a dream? This minimal doubt, that this self is not all (that it could be different, could be more …), that minimal alienation, and hence minimal distance is constitutive, as it opens a vantage point and a perspective for engaging with oneself, others and the world.

Hence, Metzinger, and with him Brassier, when trying to account for the allegedly folk-psychological notion of having a self – we are back here with the problem I found in Sellars, too – actually start from a psychological model of the unified self which they then attempt to explain.[5] Their account of the sub-personal neurobiological genesis of the self is, therefore, unwittingly swimming in psychologizing waters. Consider the concepts used by both Metzinger and Brassier in relation to PSM such as "exhibiting behavior", "self-regulation", "agency", "information processing" … These are by no means objective categories founded in biology: they refer to the specific psychological theories (which one could refute or deconstruct from other psychological theories) that inadvertently underlie the PSM model.

Against Metzinger's self and Sellars' manifest image of man, which apparently took shape "in the mists of pre-history", I oppose the modern subject as defined by Jacques Lacan as "the subject of the sciences" (Lacan, 1966). That is, since the advent of the modern sciences, modern man has come to look upon himself from an external scientific point of view. Hence, the manifest self-understanding of modern man is not only scientifically informed (or proto-theoretical as Sellars had it), it is as such structured as a scientific discourse. Does this in the end not mean that mod-ern subjectivity is centered around the scientific, objectifying point of view from nowhere? This would mean that the view from nowhere rejected by Habermas and sought for by Brassier in the realm of the sub-personal neurobiological genesis of the Self, is only understandable by the advent of scientific discourse itself.

From here it follows that the alleged outside of science – that is, the particular, the normative, the hermeneutic – by no means is an independent terrain that the 'human sciences' such as psychology, sociology – or for that matter, philosophy – could straightforwardly overlook and access. Giving weight and flesh to this outside of science requires the construction of a myth, the construction of a straw man, the resurrection of the humanistic subject. While Sellars' manifest image ultimately nods at this artificial *homo folk-psychologicus*, the question is if in the end Brassier too is not in its grip. To be clear, my point is not only that the manifest image of man-in-the-world is theory-laden, but, above all, that the manifest image, folk-psychology, or, for that matter, the alleged naïve-empirical notion of the everyday experience of being a self, only emerged with the gaze of the modern sciences.[6]

Could we then not radically think of the modern subject from *its zero level of subjectivity*, as that which structures, even at the basic phenomenological level, its being with itself, others and the world? The origin of this zero level of subjectivity is in the first instance to be situated within the objectivations of science: again, with Žižek, the sciences empty out the life-world, eventually leading to the void of sub-jectivity. The resulting non-sense subject (as opposed to Sellars' idea of man "giving and asking for reasons") is hence both the product of the modern sciences, and the very basis for the disinterested, emptied-out point of view from nowhere that makes modern science possible! Hence the "stain" in objectivity is not the subject as it is viewed in classical forms of critique (such as Habermas's) – a full humanistic sub-ject. It is instead the point of view from nowhere itself, it is the fact that objectivity cannot but be framed and formulated in terms of the zero-level of subjectivity. In short, the problem of objectivity is not the subject, it is the zero-level of subjectivity.

This is why we should subvert the classic understanding of the view from nowhere. Thomas Nagel's well-known book *The View from Nowhere* (Nagel, 1989) claims that there are two viewpoints to view the world from: the subjective and objective view-point. The subjective viewpoint is the allegedly obvious immediate and pre-reflective perspective, which, as Nagel points out, is precisely becoming visible by stepping fur-ther and further outside of oneself into an objective perspective. But for Nagel there are limits to this movement. One cannot fully transcend the initial starting point: even-tually the "view from nowhere" remains an impossibility. Now if in contrast Brassier, starting from a "hypothetically completed neuroscience" (which of course sounds a bit like, 'once, when we will have scanned the whole brain') does claim a "point of view from nowhere", I would give this a further twist and put forward: there is no no view from nowhere. That is, I argue that the 'manifest image of man' and so-called 'folk-psychology' are but myths of science: one cannot but look upon oneself, others and the world starting from a point of view from nowhere. And since modernity this point of view from nowhere has been connected to the objectifications of science. The modern subject looks at itself, others and the world from the point of view of the scientific Other. But to be more clear, this gaze is precisely launched from the impossibility nested within (and eventually grounding) objectivity, that is, from a zero-level of sub-jectivity which constitutes the modern subject as the subject of science. This means that in the end the true impossibility is not the impossibility of the objective view, as Nagel had it, but, rather, this impossibility is primordially situated at the level of the subjective view. There is no subjective view, there is no first-person perspective, there is no folk-psychology, there is no manifest image. The subjective view *is* the point from nowhere.

Conclusions

Is it not the *skandalon* of the emptied-out subject that was shunned in the move made at the end of the symposium I mentioned in the beginning of the chapter: the declaration of two no-go zones for critique, that (1) nobody is against parental support or help, and (2) nobody is against neuroscience? In this respect, it is above all the first indictment which is problematic, as it wants to safeguard a positivized, fleshed out, psychologized construct of parenting to serve as the correlate for the neurosciences. For, do we not all know what parenting is about and what can go wrong with it? This kind of (folk-)psychologisation, this kind of putting forward of unquestionable evidential facts, is what a critique of neuroscience must radically take as its primary target, only indirectly targeting neuroscience itself. Insofar as the latter poses as an explanation (or even as a deconstructive critique) of (folk-)psychology, it is but engaged in a Von Munchausen-like, auto-constructing move. But to be absolutely clear, no single neuroscientific approach will be able to steer clear of such a move. Things become even more problematic when neuroscience claims to fully transcend all traces of psychologisation!

And here the question of course is, what is the final ground of this critique of the neurosciences that I propose? Critique, of course, is defined by its own impossibility. As it has been argued in various ways by, for example, Koselleck (2000), Latour (2004), and Laclau (1997), critique has eventually no basis on which it can stand, it cannot but have a "darkness from which it works". The blind spot in the first critical triangle I've sketched – Gallese's positing of neuroscience as a critique vis-à-vis both the humanities and psychology – can, as I argued, be found in the neurosciences' structural, inevitable, but also occluded reliance on psychology. The blind spot of the second critical triangle, putting philosophy in gear vis-à-vis both the (neuro)sciences and folk-psychology, is eventually, as I argued, the denial of a zero-level of subjectivity, leading to the erroneous fleshing out of a (folk-)psychological subject believed to be in the end irreducible to the scientific image.

To explore the possibility of elevating this zero-level of subjectivity to the driving principle of a critique, let us use the so-called logic of representation as developed by Slavoj Žižek. Following Alain Badiou, Žižek differentiates between, on the one hand, "anti-philosophy" as the assertion of pure presence, irreducible and excessive with regard to the network of representations (Žižek, 2012, p. 841), and, on the other hand, the Hegelian position of positing nothing beyond phenomenality or beyond the field of representation (Žižek, 1989, p. 232). Hence, transposed to the field of science, the first, anti-philosophical option would be to understand subjectivity as that which remains or withstands the storms of the sciences and their objectifications. The second option considers representation itself as an excess to what it represents. I'll engage with both positions in more detail.

In the first, anti-philosophical option, 'what I am, what my true subjective core is', is conceived as that which remains after all the biological, neurological and psychological reductions. Here we have a 'too much', an excess at the site of subjectivity.

Bob Dylan's line "Dignity has never been photographed" could be rephrased as "subjectivity has never been fMR'ised': there is too much subject for the screen". This is where Habermas could been situated, and his argument that the social, interpersonal, first-person perspective is not reducible to the scientific image and its third-person perspective. From here a critique coming from the human sciences is launched reproaching the "hard sciences" for being tainted by this excess of subjectivity over objectivation. This is where, for example, the neurosciences are criticized for their being unwittingly embedded in cultural, political and economic contexts. But of course, the neurosciences could counter-argue that this field of the cultural, the political and the economical (from where the human sciences perform their critique) is by no means out of the reach of science itself: it can be criticized, deconstructed and incorporated by the neurosciences themselves. This is where Gallese and eventually also Brassier could be situated, who both put the neurosciences in the position of being able to fully grasp, potentially at least, the domain of (inter) subjectivity without anything left over. To be clear, even if one can object that these attempts to fully annex the human and the humanities rest upon an unrecognized and above all questionable reliance on psychologistic and humanistic notions (as I have shown earlier), one could still argue that there is some truth in their neuroscientific inspired deconstructive critique of the humanities. At the least it lays bare the fact that humanistic critique itself lacks the final ground for establishing a critical vantage point. Put differently, the neuro-turn as such did not effect a crisis in the humanities, it only brings into the open the already present or even longstanding crisis of the Humanities.

And here we can return to the second option in the logic of representation, which argues for too much on the side of objectivity. The garb of science, so to speak,[7] is too big for the world it wants to cover. This means not that there is too much subject for science, but, rather, that there is too much science for (or of) the subject. The modern subject is precisely nothing other than this too much; the subject *is* the excess, the surplus resulting from the sciences. This is the situation of the colourful brain scan engendering an oh-my-god-is-this-what-I-am subject: science creates a new subject, contemplating itself, others and the world from the scientific perspective. The Hegelian argument that philosophers cannot transcend their social and historical context (Hegel, 1991[1821]) should be hence, properly, that is, with an extra Hegelian twist, dialecticized: the modern subject as such is always already in its very kernel outside the social and the historical. Being the subject of science, I always already transcend the social and the historical, as I participate in the detached and objectifying scientific outlook on the human and the world. Hence, we might also need to give a twist to the classic scheme of Althusserian interpellation. For Althusser (Althusser, 1971) the subject arises only in an interpellation, that is, in a call to recognize itself in a certain image that is suggested to the individual. However, with the interpellation of modern science we actually do not identify with what we are said to be, but rather, and above all, we identify with the objectifying, scientific gaze, the perspective from which we are looked at. If science says, "look, that is what you are", we respond with an "oh really, let me look! It's amazing"!

It is with the latter option of the logic of representation that the zero-level of subjectivity could become the driving principle of critique. That is, the critique of the neurosciences should not be about the allegedly illusory objectivity the neurosciences possess (a critique wanting to lay bare its underlying cultural/political biases), but rather it should be a critique of subjectivity: addressing how modern subjectivity is linked to a vantage point (albeit a virtual and empty one) beyond culture, politics and history. A critique of the neurosciences should thus explore the conditions of (im)possibility of the modern academic subject and from there explore how in both the neurosciences and the human sciences it is more often than not missed that the human being has since long left the human zoo and joined the other side of the bars, that is, the ranks of the scholars. In this respect Ray Brassier most interestingly wrote:

> Nature is not our or anyone's 'home', nor a particularly beneficent progenitor. Philosophers would do well to desist from issuing any further injunctions about the need to re-establish the meaningfulness of existence, the purposefulness of life, or mend the shattered concord between man and nature. Philosophy should be more than a sop to the pathetic twinge of human self-esteem. Nihilism is not an existential quandary but a speculative opportunity. Thinking has interests that do not coincide with those of living; indeed, they can and have been pitted against the latter.
>
> *(Brassier, 2007, p. xi)*

But the question here would be if Brassier does not slide from nature to thinking without noticing it: is it nature or is it thinking which eventually is nobody's home? This can be solved by turning to Lacan, who wrote that the discourse of science leaves no place whatsoever for man (Lacan, 1991, p. 171). Or, as science objectifies, it inevitably empties out subjectivity. The subject is nowhere at home, neither in thinking, nor in nature – the latter being after all but the double of science. This homeless subject, this barred subject to use the Lacanian parlance, is what critique now more than ever should be about: it should be both its blind spot and its motor, its cause.

Epilogue

As is well known, what is most central in Karl Marx's appropriation of Hegel's dialectics was the fact that he distanced himself from Hegel's idealism of the Spirit by putting forward "real, corporeal man", occupying a world of "real natural objects" (Marx, 1988, p. 153). This is the basis for Marx's idea of an immanent critique, one that emphasizes the contradiction between ideologies and their real and objective effects. In the case of the neurosciences, a critique would be immanent if it would start from the promises of the neurosciences and would look for the impasses, that is, for where the neurosciences cannot live up to their promise to deliver a full materialist and objective approach of the human, and where they slip back into hermeneutic, psychologizing thinking frames. However here, I claim, the issue of the concrete real human being should be properly posited: the problem is not so much the difference between the false (ideal/ideological) neuro-psychologized human and an alleged real, concrete human, but rather, the problem – I repeat Hannah Arendt's (1989) contention on behaviorism here – is that the human being as he or she is conceived and fleshed out by the neurosciences would become all too true and concrete. That is, critique during the reign of the neurosciences should start from the actually, really existing neuro-turn and the concrete subject-positions it produces and enforces. Just consider processes of neurologisation and how these unfold in education, in professional life and in the public sphere in general. The rapidly growing area of neuro-education, for example, uses methods not unlike propaganda in order to convince everybody that we are our brain, that we should be our brain, that we have to become our brain. A brain education program in Flanders for fourteen- to eighteen-year-old pupils, for example, has a yearly closing festival, which is announced as "an entertaining mix of scientific presentations, live brain dissection, and workshops!" The party and the spectacle are the vehicle for the interpellative scheme: 'you are your brain' urges the pupils to look upon themselves from the perspective of the neurosciences.[8]

Perhaps one could argue that this ideologically steered neurologisation is above all about the misappropriations or all too swift popularizations of proper neuroscience itself. But what if these aberrations could be read as symptoms, signaling a return of the repressed, that is, revealing a particular truth about the neurosciences themselves, an *aporia* not dealt with? With this caveat maybe: this *aporia* eventually comes from elsewhere: that is, the symptom of the neurosciences is after all the inherited symptom of the humanities themselves. The reductionisms of the neurosciences, for example, are in the end to be traced down to the prior reductionisms in the human sciences themselves, as the latter reduce real concrete humans to cognitions, behaviors and other equally alienating concepts that are then put under the scanner.

If this critique could be thought to aim at saving a certain positive, humanistic subject beyond reductions, I firmly disagree: in the end, the only concrete and real human being my critique posits is the zero-level of subjectivity, the base level of concreteness, as this is what may become reified in the neuro-turn, precisely because the neurosciences are for structural reasons drawn to the siren song of the human sciences and to psychology in particular. If critique has to be a triangle, this is the one I propose: the (neuro)sciences – the psy-sciences – and (the gaze of) the zero-level subject. As this emptied-out subject, in Lacanian parlance, is not without its object – I'm referring of course to *object a* – this could be said to open up the very specific ontology and even materiality of psychoanalysis. At the very least one can argue that here the whole issue of reductionism evaporates: regarding the zero-level subject of psychoanalysis there is nothing to reduce.[9] Moreover, if reductionism is about one discipline explaining what for another discipline is but a given, psychoanalysis could even be given the role of the reductionist: albeit that this would be a negative reduction. Psychoanalysis reduces the all too fleshed-out neuropsychological subject to its bare, empty core.

Notes

1. For a critique, see (De Vos, 2013a).
2. Even though Sellars himself does not mention the concept of folk-psychology in his seminal text "Philosophy and the Scientific Image of Man" (1963), most of his interpreters connect the manifest image to it. See, for example, (de Vries, 2007).
3. It is here that Sellars differs from similar intentionalist and mentalist theories of folk-psychology. For example, also for Paul Churchland (1981) and Daniel C. Dennett (1987) folk-psychology is about the attribution of propositional attitudes and intentional states to others and ourselves in order to understand others and ourselves. But for Dennett folk-psychology is above all a biologically grounded issue, while for Churchland folk-psychology cannot but be flawed: so it needs to be replaced by scientific theories.
4. However, neither Brassier nor Metzinger explain how exactly such a system would be able to ward of this potentially infinite computational overload.
5. Hence I could echo the question of Jasper Feyaerts, who, while dealing with the same authors, entitled his lecture "Who needs to be disenchanted?" (Feyaerts, 2014). Metzinger is not deconstructing some folk-psychological, common sense notion of the self, rather what he is unwittingly targeting is classic academic self-psychology.
6. This is missed in the, in my opinion, misconstrued differentiation between "weak-phenomenological notions" of "what it is to be a self" and stronger theories of what a self is.
7. I am referring of course to Husserl's "garb of ideas" (Husserl, 1970).
8. In the manual given to the pupils we read, for example: "During puberty certain parts of the brain grow faster than others …" The youth, so it seems, have to be instructed on what it means to be young.
9. Elsewhere (De Vos, 2014) I have argued that with regard to the neurosciences, the theorems of psychoanalysis are eventually useless: you cannot put the unconscious, infantile sexuality, or the death-drive under a scanner. That is, these psychoanalytic *skandalons* in the end point to the zero-level of subjectivity with its specific materiality: that of *object a*. However, this uselessness of psychoanalysis, I've argued, can be said to be not without its effects either.

References

Althusser, L. (1971). Ideology and Ideological State Apparatuses (Notes Towards an Investigation). *Lenin and Philosophy and Other Essays*. London: New Left Books.

Arendt, H. (1989). *The Human Condition*. Chicago, IL: University of Chicago Press.

Brassier, R. (2007). *Nihil Unbound: Enlightenment and Extinction*. London: Palgrave Macmillan.

Brassier, R. (2011). The View from Nowhere. *Identities: Journal for Politics, Gender and Culture*, 17, 7–23.

Churchland, P. M. (1981). Eliminative materialism and the propositional attitudes. *The Journal of Philosophy, 78*, 67–90.

Connolly, W. E. (2002). *Neuropolitics: Thinking, Culture, Speed*. Minneapolis, MN: University of Minnesota Press.

Connolly, W. E. (2005). The media and think tank politics. *Theory & Event, 8*(4).

De Vos, J. (2013a). Interpassivity and the Political Invention of the Brain: Connolly's Neuropolitics versus Libet's Veto-right. *Theory & Event, 16*(2). doi: 10.1353/tae.2013.0034.

De Vos, J. (2013b). *Psychologization and the Subject of Late Modernity*. New York, NY: Palgrave Macmillan.

De Vos, J. (2014). Which materialism? Questioning the matrix of psychology, neurology, psychoanalysis and ideology critique. *Theory & Psychology, 24*(1), 76–93.

De Vos, J. (online first, October 17, 2014). The death and the resurrection of (psy)critique. The case of neuroeducation. *Foundations of Science*.

De Vries, W. (2007). Folk psychology, theories, and the Sellarsian roots. *Poznan Studies in the Philosophy of the Sciences and the Humanities, 92*(1), 53–84.

Dennett, D. C. (1987). *The Intentional Stance*. Cambridge, MA: MIT press.

Feyaerts, J. (2014). *Who needs to be disenchanted? The Destruction of the Manifest Image and its Residuum*. Paper presented at the Symposium Depsychologizing/Deneurologizing Modern Subjectivity?, Ghent University.

Gallese, V. (2015). The body, the brain, symbolic expression and its experience: an experimental aesthetics perspective. Retrieved March 25, 2015, from http://british-aesthetics. org/the-body-the-brain-symbolic-expression-and-its-experience-an-experimental-aesthetics-perspective/.

Hegel, G. W. F. (1991[1821]). *Elements of the Philosophy of Right* (A. W. Wood, Trans.). Cambridge: Cambridge University Press.

Hume, D. (2006[1739–1740]). *A Treatise of Human Nature* (D. Norton and M. Norton, Trans.). Oxford: Oxford University Press.

Husserl, E. (1970). *The Crisis of European Sciences and Transcendental Phenomenology: An Introduction to Phenomenological Philosophy* (D. Carr, Trans.). Evanston, IL: Northwestern University Press.

Koselleck, R. (2000). *Critique and crisis: Enlightenment and the Pathogenesis of Modern Society*. Cambridge, MA: MIT Press.

Lacan, J. (1966). La science et la vérité, *Ecrits* (855–877). Paris: Éditions du Seuil.

Lacan, J. (1991). *Le Séminaire, Livre XVII: L'envers de la Psychanalyse 1969–1970*. Paris: Seuil.

Laclau, E. (1997). The death and resurrection of the theory of ideology. *MLN, 112*(3), 297–321.

Latour, B. (2004). Why has critique run out of steam? From matters of fact to matters of concern. *Critical Inquiry, 30*(2), 225–248.

Latour, B. (2010). *On the Modern Cult of the Factish Gods*. Durham, NC: Duke University Press.

Marx, K. (1988). *The Economic and Philosophic Manuscripts of 1844 and The Communist Manifesto* (M. Milligan, Trans.). Buffalo, NY: Prometheus Books.

Nagel, T. (1989). *The View from Nowhere*. Oxford: Oxford University Press.

Sellars, W. (1963). Philosophy and the scientific image of man. In W. Sellars (Ed.), *Empiricism and the Philosophy of Mind* (1–40). London: Routlegde & Kegan Paul.

Žižek, S. (1986). "Pathological Narcissus" as a Socially Mandatory Form of Subjectivity. First published in the Croatian edition of *The Culture of Narcissism* by Christopher Lasch (*Narcisističa kultura*, Naprijed, Zagreb, 1986). Translation retrieved from http://www. manifesta.org/manifesta3/catalogue5.htm.

Žižek, S. (1989). *The Sublime Object of Ideology*. London: Verso.

Žižek, S. (2012). *Less Than Nothing: Hegel and the Shadow of Dialectical Materialism*. London: Verso Books.

3

WHO ARE WE, THEN, IF WE ARE INDEED OUR BRAINS?

Reconsidering a Critical Approach to Neuroscience[1]

Nima Bassiri

Cautious Critique

In a volume concerned with the relationship between (any) science and critique, it would be wise to tread lightly. After all, it has not been so long since the very question of critique was a topic of contestation within science studies and the history of science, precisely around what it means to, and whether or how one should, be critical or simply do critique vis-à-vis the sciences. It is not necessary to rehash these accounts; it is not altogether clear that they represent anything more than a caricatured disappointment with scholarly trends, disputes over disciplinary and methodological authority, and an unwarranted identification of 'critique' with negativity, undue skepticism, excessive suspicion and with an unmasking of what (so it is claimed) a critic has presumed to be either an epistemic ruse or ideological construct (Latour, 2004; Daston, 2009; Dear & Jasanoff, 2010).

Yet despite the vocalized objections against it, the critical enterprise has long been the object of broad and multi-disciplinary advocacy. The strongest recent advocates have understood critique in some relation to traditions of political philosophy, as an inquiry into the conditions of legitimacy of one or more systems of power and authority (or the conditions according to which the boundary between legitimacy and illegitimacy is demarcated and regulated) (Butler, 2002, 2009; Scott, 2007; Sonderegger & de Boer, 2012).[2] Critique from this standpoint yields an even more valuable set of possibilities, to the extent that it can refer to an interrogation of the suppositions that hold together implicit frameworks determining the acceptability of normative constraints that are not strictly political (in the narrow sense), but which pertain to the ways we come to know the world and ourselves – i.e., why we speak, behave, question and resist in certain ways and not in others, why some systems of knowledge exhibit more veridical authority in different times and places than others, how the difference between truth and falsehood is organized, stabilized and enacted within certain historical periods, knowledge systems, modes of scholarly practice, and so on (Macherey, 1998).

Such an understanding of critique, as broad as it is, does not readily translate into a singular practice, a formal set of rules or a disciplinary method. It can be confrontational in tone and substance (thereby appearing negative) or take the form of a more nuanced "stylization" of the regulatory norms it sets about to uncover (Butler, 1991). And while it is for this reason that critique appears destructive and even roguish, (Butler, 2009) it does not preclude some sort of fundamental affirmation.[3] Indeed, affirmation is one of the central functions of a critical operation. As Michel Foucault explained in his 1978 lecture, "What is Critique?", (2007) the delimitation of what is deemed illegitimate is done for the sake of uncovering a more fundamental basis of legitimacy. The early modern critical attitude towards governance did not ask how not to be governed *at all,* but rather "how not to be governed *like that*" (p. 44). It was an inquiry that was aimed at discovering the proper grounds of governance, and, to that extent, modern governance and political critique (that is, questioning the constraints and conditions of governance) went hand in hand, co-emergent as a new set of mechanisms by which structures of authority, effects of power and both the conduct *and counter-conduct* of subjects were interrelated and mutually developing (Davidson, 2011).

That critique may embed a rehabilitative ideal is particularly important when considering its role in relation to scientific knowledge. It leads to two questions. First, can and should the critic's intervention exceed the internal processes of criticism and self-correction that many believe already exist within the sciences (Feyerabend, 1998, pp. 260–62)? That is, should the only mode of critique in relation to science be *scientific* criticism? And second, is there a place in relation to scientific knowledge for something that even Foucault was not willing to dismiss – that rather than rehabilitation, critique could signify resistance, revolt, or a kind of "fundamental anarchism" (Foucault, 2007, p. 75)? Few scholars have engaged with this second question.

In an essay written shortly before Foucault's 1978 lecture, Paul Feyerabend warns of what he believes has become the tyrannical nature of scientific knowledge – an expression of truth so prevalent and powerful, that opposition to it is attainable only at the most dangerous costs. He writes,

> A truth that reigns without checks and balances is a tyrant who must be overthrown and any falsehood that can aid us in the overthrow of this tyrant is to be welcomed. It follows that 17th and 18th century science indeed *was* an instrument of liberation and enlightenment. It does not follow that science is bound to *remain* such an instrument. There is nothing inherent in science or in any other ideology that makes it *essentially* liberating. (1981, pp. 157–158)

Of particular concern for Feyerabend is the role science plays in education. In schools and the university, where 'scientific facts' are unquestionably presented to students with what sometimes amounts to religious zeal, scientific education reveals itself to be a veritable process of indoctrination. While criticism is championed, even in a student's earliest education, as a tool to be applied to the sphere of socio-politics, still "science is excepted from the criticism" (p. 157). Indeed, adopting a dissenting position vis-à-vis dominant scientific views, Feyerabend argues, is akin to heresy, an act that will become the subject of severe social castigation. "My criticism of modern science", he concludes, "is that it inhibits freedom of thought" (p. 158).

While radical, Feyerabend's position should not be confused with an expression of anti-science. Instead, it is an important and starkly presented reminder of an epistemological and certainly political imperative of the present: that pure and unadulterated opposition to or defiance of dominant scientific rationalities is tantamount in the West to absurdity and insolence; and that this represents an implicit and regulatory constraint according to which we are invariably required to think about ourselves and the world today. What Feyerabend enables us to see is that what is really at stake is not whether there is a place for critique vis-à-vis the sciences. At stake, instead, is the issue of who is permitted to perform it, what form it can take and how far it can extend.

This was the point *inadvertently* demonstrated by Lorraine Daston (2009), in her contentious and polemically received article, "Science Studies and the History of Science", where she effectively characterized the disciplinary difference between science studies and history of science as the difference between bad critique (or, suspicious unmasking and debunking) and good critique (i.e., historicizing, in a disciplinarily rigorous way) (pp. 805–808). In relation to the sciences, she implicitly reveals, a critical enterprise cannot forego some internal policing. After all, what Feyerabend tacitly suggests is that the very act of total, oppositional and anarchic resistance – the quasi-fiction of "originary freedom" that even Foucault (2007, p. 75) will not fully dismiss – somehow feels more possible in the context of politics (or at least appears to be a more warranted topic of philosophical consideration) than it does in relation to science, where it remains virtually unthinkable, a kind of modern unreason. The boundaries of a critical operation in relation to science appear to extend from passive acceptance of the myth that science performs its own critical self-correction to the perilous and threatening pursuit of total resistance to any scientific rationality. Within this spectrum, the critic must find her place. She is at the same time forced to tread lightly, to monitor her critical efforts and to ask judiciously of herself: How far should my critique extend? How far can it extend, given not only the restrictions set by others, but by those implicitly set by myself – that is, by my own inescapable policing of the limits, acceptability and even conceivability of a critical operation vis-à-vis the sciences? What I will propose in the remainder of the paper is that there is, perhaps, no satisfactory answer to this question, and that within this spectrum from compliance to resistance, the critic may never successfully identify a happy medium between inefficacy and rebuke. Perhaps, then, a different sense of the critique of science is in order, and the topic of neuroscience may very well facilitate just such a consideration.

Critique, Neuroscience (and Psychoanalysis)

It is perhaps most in relationship to the mind and brain sciences generally where the controversy of critique has become particularly apparent: is critique of science even warranted, or does it simply represent everything that is wrong with the anachronistic nature of the humanities and qualitative social sciences today (Pinker, 2013)? The brain sciences, especially, localize a set of scholarly anxieties, in part because at stake is the question – indeed, the future – of the human subject (Pelabrat & Hartouni, 2011; Pitts-Taylor, 2010). Few other scientific disciplines appear capable today of fully saturating the explanatory field of the subject, marking perhaps another historical moment when the humanities have felt disenfranchised from the very object of their disciplinary *raison d'être*; and few sciences do it with as much translational appeal as brain research does. Reactions across the humanities and social sciences have been mixed (Fitzgerald & Callard, 2015; Dumit, 2012). Some scholars have advocated for the value of thinking or working *with* (rather than against) the neurosciences, in the form of interactions, crosspollinations, "critical friendships" or other sorts of "entanglements" (Fuller, 2011, 2014; Fitzgerald & Callard, 2015; Rose & Abi-Rached, 2013, 2014).[4] These sorts of disciplinary solicitations or partnerships (the prescriptions for engagement can vary widely) are seen as more effective and reasoned variants to the enthusiastic adoption of neuroscientific approaches and methods in order to adjudicate questions internal to social science and humanities fields.

But, in truth, advocacy for interaction has been presented as an answer to the apparent problems and futility of another common approach – namely, the critique of neuroscientific claims and their disciplinary translatability (Cooter & Stein, 2013; Choudhury & Slaby, 2012).[5] Rose and Abi-Rached (2014) denounce the apparent 'hostility' of some social science to the various 'neuro-knowledges', concluding: "Critique is necessary, but is becoming unproductive" (p. 18). For Fitzgerald and Callard (2015) 'critique' has simply meant replacing neurobiological reductionism with "the ontological primacy of the sociocultural" (p. 7). For them, critics merely invert the ontological order of things and, to use the language of a somewhat analogous and longstanding debate in feminist theory, transform a biological essentialism into a biological constructivism.[6]

The value of the critical interventions mounted by those social scientists specifically reproached by the authors above is not at issue here; I do not plan to defend specific cases per se, though it might be worth acknowledging once again the extent to which 'critique', as a scholarly approach to scientific knowledge, remains constrained by devaluation and charges of retrograde unproductivity. And yet, to the extent that *some* critical work can and, perhaps, should be recuperated, it might be useful to begin by considering the underlying stakes of a sample of recent scholarly interventions that have explicitly adopted that designation.

A network of scholars, for instance, have loosely organized themselves around a project they have dubbed 'critical neuroscience' – publishing an edited volume of the same title.[7] The broad objectives of the project involve performing a reality check on what is seen as the troubling overreach of neuroscientific claims (Choudhury & Slaby, 2012, p. 6).[8] Through the explicit language of rehabilitation, the project exhibits the procedures of classical critique: scholars seek to restrain what is viewed as the unwarranted authority of neuroscience as an explanatory parameter for human, cultural or political developments and phenomena (p. 9); they attempt to introduce into the very rationality of the neurosciences (that is, the underlying epistemologies that organize the field but also the assumptions that orient methodologies and experimental protocols) an awareness or, rather, a self-awareness of the constructed nature of many of their core concepts as well as the unavoidably socio-political valency of many of their claims and generated facts (p. 30; Fitzgerald and Callard, 2015, p. 8). In the form of a direct encounter with practitioners, critical neuroscience amounts to a checking, intervening and refashioning of the neurosciences themselves.

Another variation of the self-avowed critique of neuroscience has taken the form of a marked disciplinary commitment to history-writing (Cooter, 2014; Cooter & Stein, 2013, pp. 214–228). Historians of science, particularly of neuroscience, these scholars argue, are in a prime position to demonstrate how the emergent authority of the neurosciences is a consequence of, among other things, complex political, economic and material contingencies rather than a consequence of quasi-metaphysical revelations of the brain's processes. Such an orientation, according to its advocates, would refashion the ahistorical presentism of neuroscience and reframe the prominence of brain research as an historical, and, therefore, conditional, *event*. Rigorous and critical historical reasoning can and must unseat the scholarly prominence of neurological and biomedical ideologies.

Putting aside their ontological commitments, and whether they have anything productive to offer the social studies of science and medicine, what appears to unite these two particular critical reactions – indeed perhaps most critiques of neuroscience – is that they attempt to *disengage* the category of the modern self, however slightly and however momentarily, from the veridical hold that brain research is increasing having over it – even if they do so by postulating novel conceptions of neural subjectivity, in marked contradistinction to what current brain science offers (Malabou, 2008; Wilson, 2011; Valk, 2012). The focus, then, of these critical labors has not been selfhood per se, but an implicit reclamation of the self, its extrication from the regime of neuroscientific reasoning. But it is precisely here where an alternative approach can be introduced, one whose difference is neither methodological nor disciplinary (my own approach is historical, after all). Such an approach involves adopting a different position with regards to what might be dubbed the neurological consolidations of selfhood – that is, the ways in which neurological discourses, very broadly construed, become predominant frameworks according to which we make sense of and tell the truth of who we are. It is to suggest that such consolidations are not a consequence simply of the increasing legitimacy of a pervasive neurological ideology. A motivating concern for critics today is how the neurosciences affect, impinge on and normatively stabilize and naturalize how we are constituted as subjects (and so how we fashion ourselves), not only according to novel cognitive and affective norms, but according to new biologies of gender and moral and political conduct; and so from this arises the impulse to reclaim the self to some degree, to think about how not to be neurological quite so much, or at least not quite like that.

But perhaps the question can be posed differently. Instead of asking how the neurosciences are encroaching on or unduly dictating the terms of subject-formation, we might instead ask: what would incite clinicians, researchers and even institutions for that matter to speak and think neurologically about people, when there may have been no essential reason to do so in principle? Why does it become medically necessary, epistemologically possible, even legally or politically acceptable, to reimagine the contours of the modern subject through recourse to neural accounts? Why does this reimagining occur in certain historical periods and not in others? And perhaps most centrally, what sorts of anxieties, impasses, or problems (not necessarily medical) does this way of thinking about ourselves resolve or address? With these sorts of questions as a point of commencement, the critique of neuroscience begins, not with the neurosciences, but instead with the self. How has selfhood as a category itself become a kind of problem – what sorts of indeterminacies or anxieties has it brought about – such that deployments of brain science (its explanatory frameworks and institutional force) function as a warranted, acceptable and in some cases necessary response – a seemingly crucial technology of the self, capable of stabilizing and rationalizing such anxieties.

Critique need not simply be concerned with extricating selfhood from the rationality of the neurosciences. It might instead function as an investigation into how and why the language of neuroscience would have been sutured into accounts of the self, and for reasons that were not inevitable, essential, or obvious. Instead of simply delimiting the so-called improprieties of brain science and its claims upon personhood or, similarly, stressing that the self does not essentially reside in neural matter, the critic might instead detail why the brain nevertheless needed to speak the truth of the self, even if for reasons whose contingencies can be entirely enumerated. The critic would expose these imperatives, though not for justificatory reasons.

I acknowledge that scholars have offered positions that are certainly in keeping with these views. I do not even oppose the project of the reclamation of the self; but should we not first understand who it is that the self has in fact already become? Should we not investigate the implicit demands that subtended that becoming and at some point pose the question: who are we, then, if we are indeed our brains? And should we not consider why we would have come to be 'made up' in this way, when there may have been no essential, inevitable, or natural reason for it (Hacking, 2002)? If the value of posing this sort of question lies in its historical demonstrability, it must do so in such a way as to enable a reconsideration of the present. One compelling point of entry into the discussion surrounding critique and neuroscience is the relationship (both past and present) between neuroscience and psychoanalysis. The convergence of neuroscience and psychoanalysis represents an interesting case study, as it is an affiliation long marked by assertions that the givenness of a rapprochement between the two fields is not entirely self-evident; that it was not for Freud and may not be so today. Whether neuroscience has a part to play in the continued development of psychoanalysis or, conversely, whether some general tenets of psychoanalysis or dynamic psychiatry should organize neuroscientific assumptions is an issue that has been justified, qualified and contested. For this reason, the two fields represent a point of convergence (of which there are no doubt many) through which we can examine the impulse to articulate the neurological truth of the self.

The additional value of considering this particular relationship is that, even today, it continues to exhibit an openness to historical consideration, simply to the extent that psychoanalysis as a practice and theoretical framework remains explicitly indebted to and embedded in a historically situated set of ideas in a way that brain research alone does not, at least not necessarily for its practitioners. And yet, what this has often meant is that an investigation into, for example, Freud's own transition from neurology to metapsychology has been completed with an eye to fulfilling a research program in the present; the utility of historical analysis has been determined according to its fitness, we might say, for the work of contemporary science.

Already, then, a critical labor would begin by sketching a different kind of history, one that moves away from a simple narrative of Freud's transition from neurology to metapsychology. Consequently, I will consider Freud's place more generally within a set of broader discussions in nineteenth-century neurology and behavioral medicine – a set of discussions that, as I will propose, were intervening in conceptions of what it means to be a person, both medically but also institutionally. While atypical, this historical approach to the relationship between psychoanalysis and neuroscience will provide an opportunity to consider the value of the critical approach I discuss.

Personhood, Pathology and Forensic Dilemmas

Turning now to the formative period of brain research beginning in the late nineteenth century, I will propose that this moment of the formalization and institutionalization of neurological knowledge beginning just after 1860 introduced a set of effects on medical conceptions of personhood, though not in ways we might immediately intuit. This period was not defined simply according to the predominance of localization debates and their effects in the fashioning a modern, biological "homo cerebralis" (Hagner, 1997). Or, rather, homo cerebralis did not as a category display any straightforward understandings of how a neurologically defined person or self might appear, or what new sorts of problems it might introduce. In fact, as I will suggest (and have done so elsewhere[9]), this period represented within brain and behavioral medicine a moment when the very categories of personhood and, particularly, personal identity were becoming problems, objects of medical and epistemological anxiety, in the face of new and unsettling pathologies. Given the apparent prevalence and clinical study of illnesses that could affect and induce radically altered states of consciousness – e.g., mental automatism, somnambulism, hypnotic states, double consciousness, multiple personality and so on – precisely at a time when entry into the political econo- mies of late nineteenth-century industrial capital seemed to demand a classical and stable sense of personhood, it is no wonder that this period would witness what the nineteenth-century psychiatrist James Crichton-Browne (1862–63) called the "morbid modifications" of personal identity itself. What transpired during this period, in other words, was the medical adjudication of illnesses that would not merely affect a person, but illnesses that constituted disaffections of personhood itself.

What made many of these disorders a particular source of anxiety, especially for the medical considerations of personhood, was that these clinical adjudications seemed in many cases, almost invariably, to be medico-legal in nature. Especially dis- rupted by these pathologies were the forensic demands that historically undergirded conceptions of the modern subject since the seventeenth century, demands loosely organized around the accountability, responsibility, transparency and authenticity of the self. This is not simply a consequence of psychiatry's long-standing professional and institutional relationship with the law (Goldstein, 2002). Medical questions aside, the relationship between personhood and forensic discourse is integral to what Mary Douglas (1992) understood to be the operative conception of selfhood at the heart of Western "enterprise" culture. She explains:

> The category of personhood has been filled by the need to meet the foren- sic requirements of a law-abiding society and an effective, rational judicial system (p. 43). [...] [A] unitary, responsible self-agent must be supposed to exist because it is intellectually, juridically and morally necessary. This is the prevailing forensic model of the person that best suits our culture. (p. 49)

Medical observations that would put into question certain forensic assump- tions of the self would be especially unsettling, not just legally but also culturally. Personhood – to the extent to which it could succumb to forensically troubling pathological transformations – would not simply be a categorical assumption on the part of clinicians, but in fact a problem, one that would need to be attended to as a medical but also forensic predicament. The medico-legal discussions that occasionally colored and sometimes fully saturated medical accounts (including Freud's, as I will show) were implicitly stipulating tacit parameters for what it means to be a person. In *Body and Will*, for example, Henry Maudsley (1884) describes a case of a patient suffering from major alternating fluctuations in affective states. He concedes, "An actual disruption of the *ego* this is not", while nevertheless acknowl- edging, "How changed the person now from what he was!" Maudsley's resolution to this conundrum is to grant, "To all intents and purposes he is a different person, another *ego*, at any rate so far as consciousness is concerned – subjectively though not objectively – since in all relations he feels, thinks and acts quite differently" (p. 311). In the strictest metaphysical sense, we would not say that the patient presents another mind; but the concern, as Maudlsey implies, is not philosophical, but is ultimately related to "actions and their merit", as Locke (1700, p. 346) once put it, and to questions of accountability and public concern that would ensue – that is, to a forensic, not philosophical, orientation to thinking about pathological transformations of personhood.

As I will discuss below, Freud is representative (though in ways we would not immediately intuit) of similar anxieties and preoccupations linked to new pathologies of personhood and, specifically, to certain institutional-forensic demands on the self. At the same time, he is also representative of the neurological and neuro-psychiatric efforts to rationalize and stabilize these novel pathological puzzles of the self with a new medical intelligibility.

Freud, Trauma and Simulation Crises

In an 1896 letter to Wilhelm Fliess, Freud (1950, pp. 185–192) directly linked his 1891 monograph *On Aphasia* to his emerging research on the retranscriptions of memory traces. He suggested in the letter that his monograph implicitly offered a neurophysiological analogue for an important aspect of his early theory of childhood sexual trauma – namely, how and why childhood sexual experiences are retroactively and pathogenically remembered as traumatic in adulthood. On the one hand, the link is useful for thinking about the transition between Freud's neurological writings and his early metapsychology (Bassiri, 2013, p. 100). Yet on the other hand, the link in itself was pivotal for Freud's earliest decipherment of the etiological underpinnings of hysteria. In "Aetiology of Hysteria" (1896), Freud (1962b) writes, "I therefore put forward the thesis that at the bottom of every case of hysteria there are *one or more occurrences of premature sexual experience. ... I* believe that this is an important finding, the discovery of a *caput Nili* in neuropathology".

Ian Hacking (1998, p. 32) has argued, "The two great but mysterious mental pathologies of the day were hysteria and epilepsy".[10] They were, at the very least, the two central so-called 'functional' neurological quandaries of the period between 1860 and 1905 – that is, disorders understood to be strictly somatic in nature, and yet unrelated to any localized histological damage or lesions (Killen, 2006; Bynum, 1985; Danziger, 1982). And the two clinicians most associated with these disorders were the seminal neurologists John Hughlings Jackson and Jean-Martin Charcot, both of whom began their respective careers in the early 1860s and who were formative in different ways for Freud. Much of what Freud drew from Charcot, however, was integral to how Freud developed a more expanded view of the relationship between trauma and hysteria. It was Charcot, Freud explained

(1962, p. 19), who promulgated an account of hysteria as a disorder that exhibited a lawful and wholly authentic symptomatology. Much of what substantiated the view that hysteria was both authentic and lawful was the recognition that hysteria was a disorder that could affect male patients in equal measure as female patients. Charcot had initially drawn upon hereditary and constitutional etiologies to describe the origins of female hysteria. But how a "vigorous artisan, well built, not enervated by high culture, the stoker of an engine for example, not previously emotional" (1889, p. 221) could present hysterical symptoms was, for Charcot, a question that could not be reduced to any constitutional explanations (Levin, 1974, p. 382).

The answer lay precisely in what Charcot thought was the instigating stimulus for the hysterical train-engine stoker: the hysteria would typically follow "an accident to the train, by a collision or running off the rails" (Charcot, 1889, p. 221). The hysterical symptoms were the consequence of a major traumatic shock, linked, in other words, to episodes and events that represented a generalized understanding of trauma as a frenetic violence upon the psyche – e.g., a concussive shock, a sensory overload, a penetrative disturbance – and thus a pathogenesis that could affect anyone (though some were more susceptible to it than others) (Micale, 2001; Caplan, 1995).

Freud eventually adopted this conception of a traumatically induced hysteria, or what more commonly went by the name of "traumatic neurosis"[11] – the pathogenic consequence of violences fundamentally tied to the precariously destructive features of late industrial modernity. As he writes, famously, in *Beyond the Pleasure Principle* (1961, p. 10), "A condition has long been known and described which occurs after severe mechanical concussions, railway disasters and other accidents involving a risk to life; it has been given the name of 'traumatic neurosis'".

Freud's various invocations, like Charcot's before him, of railway accidents as the source of the traumatic shock, and traumatically induced hysteria, are especially noteworthy. The idea that some psychoneuroses arise as a consequence of traumatic episodes has its origins, at least in part, in the convergence of neurology and discussions around industrial, typically railway, disasters beginning in the 1860s. It was in his 1866 *On Railway and Other Injuries of the Nervous System* that English surgeon John Eric Erichsen explicitly emphasized the direct injurious effect of railway travel and accidents on the neurological constitutions of passengers (Caplan, 1995, 2001; Schäffner, 2001; Schivelbusch, 1986). In the book's 1875 second edition, retitled *On Concussion of the Spine,* Erichsen described the extent to which railroad accidents produce varying degrees of what he called "nervous shock" at the psychological level alone, inducing an emotional state that he identified as hysteria (1875, pp. 194–95).

But Erichsen never entirely abandoned the notion that there was always some accompanying physical etiology in nervous shock. It was English railway surgeon Herbert Page who, in his 1883 *Injuries of the Spine and Spinal Cord Without Apparent Mechanical Lesion,* argued that shock could produce a purely psychogenic injury on a person's mental and even physical constitution (Caplan, 2001, p. 61). Charcot was attracted to Page's psychogenic theory of traumatic shock and concluded, as Page and Erichsen both did, that there were few stimuli that could produce a trauma strong enough to incite such a devastating pathogenesis (Levin, 1974, p. 382; Micale, 2001, p. 121). Only the railway accident – or, analogously, the industrial disaster – could give rise to these sorts of shocks.

With the continued elaboration of traumatic psychoneuroses in the ensuing decades, the clinicians most centrally involved in its theorization – particularly Hermann Oppenheim, but also Paul Möbius and Moritz Benedikt – drew from patients whose pathologies arose as a consequence of industrial, often labor-related, accidents either on railways or in factory settings (Lerner, 2001; Schmiedebach, 1999; Killen, 2006, pp. 91–98; Levin, 1974, p. 396). The period of the 1870s through 1890s witnessed the rise of disorders fundamentally coupled to the horrific failures of industrial technology and, correlatively, to the injurious effects of the labors and political economies of industrial modernity.[12]

But it was not simply the case that a subset of mental and neural pathologies were linked to industrial accidents. More specifically, the very relationship between pathology and accident was typically framed as a forensic and juridical affair. Herbert Page (1892, p. 139) put it quite simply: "Every case of railway injury is more or less the subject of medico-legal inquiry". Indeed the very question as to whether a pathological state and an industrial accident were related in the first place – causally or otherwise – became as much a forensic inquiry as a medical one, as a pattern of litigation by injured passengers against railroad companies became a norm throughout Europe by the middle of the century (Schmiedebach, 1999, p. 40; Caplan, 1995, p. 395). The monetary damages sought after industrial injuries did not subside even when liability legislation was substituted with nationalized social and accident insurance, as it was in Germany in 1884 (Killen, 2006, pp. 82–91).

Ultimately, the pathogeneses that potentially lay at the heart of technological development, industrial labor and, more generally, the political economies of the late nineteenth century meant that certain psychoneuroses (e.g., hysteria, traumatic neurosis) introduced a juridical problem quite different than the way in which the concept, say, of criminal responsibility framed the understanding of other nervous disorders of the nineteenth century, such as monomania and epilepsy (Goldstein, 2002, pp. 152–196). Indeed, the primary forensic inquiry that framed the examination of traumatically induced psychoneuroses was not responsibility or accountability, but rather authenticity.

Given the possibility of generous compensation, suspicion emerged around the motives of plaintiffs or injured parties, along with the belief that many were simply simulating illnesses, in an attempt to defraud railroad companies, employers or the state (Rabinbach, 1996, p. 67). Accident neurosis, then, was not just an object of legal adjudication, but indeed a medico-legal anxiety, precisely because of what Herbert Page and others were purporting, which is that injuries could take a purely psychological, not physical form. With these sorts of accident-induced psychoneuroses – these so-called 'functional' neurological disorders – there was no immediate way of differentiating authentic injury from its inauthentic simulation. This was an especially worrying prospect for Page. As an advocate for the viability of mental pathologies with no physical etiology, Page was especially preoccupied with the opportunities such a diagnostic category opened for the imposter and with the incredible lengths the malingerer would go to simulate pathological states (1885, p. 262–69).

But the essential problem concerning the potential simulation of disorders by imposters and malingerers was that it was extremely difficult to speak in terms of a strict dichotomy between authentic pathology and inauthentic simulation. This had primarily to do with the fact that simulation was itself understood to be a genre of pathological behavior, taking the occasional form of simulation or mimicry disorders – that is, imitative states that were specifically thought to be hypnotically induced or brought about when mental functioning was either traumatically or artificially diminished (Ellenberger, 1970, pp. 112–145, 750–62). Charcot, in particular, emphasized the extent to which hypnosis could induce certain kinds of pathological mimicry, where patients would involuntarily imitate not only the behaviors but also the pathologies of others (Levin, 1974, pp. 383–84; Killen, 2006, 71; Mayer, 2006).

This would imply that after a railway or industrial disaster, shock alone could throw an otherwise healthy person into a mildly hypnotic state – a state, furthermore, that was particularly conducive to suggestion. The highly impressionable patient would find herself, possibly from a doctor's prompting or from some inadvertent source, mimicking some other mental illness or physical ailment. The simulation would be wholly unintentional, though not devoid of pathology, since it was a legitimate part of the overall symptomatology of a hypnotic state generated by traumatic shock.

There was, however, no systematic definition of what exactly a simulation disorder entailed. Herbert Page, for instance, relied on the notion of "nervous mimicry" or "neuromimesis", introduced by English surgeon James Paget in 1873 (Paget, 1875). Paget conceded that neuromimetic conditions are often diagnostically described as cases of hysteria, but maintained that while it is common in hysteria, mimicry should be understood as a proper disorder in its own right, resulting from "sudden mental distresses" or even "exhaustion by overwork" (p. 192). Page drew fairly liberally from many aspects of Paget's account of nervous mimicry, save one: for Paget, pathological mimicries and simulations were essentially involuntary acts, since for him the authenticity of the neuromimetic disorder was necessarily analogous to its involuntary nature.

For Herbert Page, however, things were not so simple. He was certain, for instance, that many neuromimetic conditions were willfully induced by patients (Page, 1885, p. 221). And yet, even in such cases, the voluntary inducement of a simulated state was not necessarily equivalent to the intention to deceive or defraud. Something as ordinary as, what he calls, "simple exaggeration", where the suggestible sufferer of a recent traumatic shock feels compelled to amplify a set of symptoms, did not often indicate intent to deceive. For Page, certain neuromimetic states, particularly those that take the form of hyperbolic embellishments – what we might otherwise describe as mild fabrications, inventions and even falsifications – were themselves occasionally part of a pathological symptomatology (1885, p. 221). The clinician, Page maintained, must take great care to differentiate genuine fabrication (that is, malingering in the proper sense) from pathological fabrication (e.g., hysterical exaggeration).

When it came to pathological simulation the question of intent and authenticity could easily become especially obscure. This was particularly true in what were for some clinicians cases where the fully intentional, i.e., fraudulent, simulation of a pathological symptom actually induced the authentic emergence of the disorder itself. American physician Morton Prince discussed such a possibility in 1890 (Prince, 1975; Leys, 2000, ch. 2). He maintained that there could not always be a correspondence between malingering and the *inauthenticity* of a disease: "It is well known that many neuroses, although they may have originated in volitional attempts to deceive, nevertheless pass in time beyond the control of the will and persist as true pathologies" (p. 78). It was effectively possible for the malingerer to be both an imposter and a hysteric, or at least for the malingerer to *become* a hysteric, to submit to the authenticity of a disorder that she was initially only simulating. And that transition from malingering to hysteria would, from a diagnostic standpoint, be virtually imperceptible.

Simulation, then, was capable of fundamentally distorting the boundary between the authenticity and inauthenticity of a disorder, and thus the boundary between the patient and the imposter. It was, however, Freud who presented perhaps the most dramatic culmination of this view – not in his early discussions on hysterical imitation and identification in 1900 (Freud, 1953, pp. 149–150; Leys, 2000, pp. 35–40), but in a statement he made in the middle of October 1920, while acting as principle expert witness in the trial of Austrian physician Julius Wagner-Jauregg, who stood accused by the Commission for Military Violations of Duty of the medical mistreatment (through electrotherapy) of traumatized WWI soldiers (Freud, 2000, p. 35). Given that the soldiers in question alleged that they suffered from debilitating war neuroses, the discussion, perhaps inevitably, turned to the subject of the authenticity of the disease. It was Wagner-Jauregg's position that many of these soldiers were malingerers, deceptively intent on avoiding war duty.

Freud's thoughts on the matter are especially remarkable, given that they were part of an utterance made in a formal judicial context. He stated: "All neurotics are malingerers [*Simulanten*]; they simulate without knowing it, and this is their sickness" (Eissler, 1986, p. 62; Freud, 1972, p. 947). It is not so easy to ascertain exactly what Freud meant by this statement. There is more to this claim, I would propose, than the mere assertion that simulation is highly prevalent in cases of traumatic neuroses – or even potentially present in all of them.[13] There is also more to it than the contention that the authenticity of a neurotic disorder depends only upon an *unconscious* simulative performance, rather than a conscious one; or even that the intentional simulation of a disorder is itself sort of pathological. What Freud suggests is that *all* instances of psychoneurosis represent an undoing of the very difference between authenticity and mendacity. All neurotics are to some degree necessarily dissemblers and imposters, to the extent that some sort of imitation, replication, or fabrication is essential to psychopathology itself.

Now, the differentiation between the authenticity and the inauthenticity of a disorder was a predominantly forensic imperative. But what Freud's claim seems to exemplify, in the most general sense, is that there is something incommensurate between the medical versus the forensic epistemologies of the neuropsychiatric self of the late nineteenth and early twentieth century (which makes its utterance in a legal proceeding all the more noteworthy). Who we are, according to the neurological discourse and behavioral medicine of the period, presented challenges to who we should be, according to a set of legal and institutional constraints. Instead of either truly suffering from a neuro- or mental pathology or otherwise falsely lying about it, Freud claims that a person was in fact truly the former (the neurotic) by virtue of being the latter (the malingerer, the falsifier).

Although it represents a culmination of an extended set of anxieties around the problem of authenticity, simulation and medical fraud emerging during the decades of the 1860s and 1870s, Freud's utterance also functions as a re-embodiment of some of his earliest writings. To the extent that neurotic simulation is tantamount to the performance of replication, copying or redoubling, it is possible to link the 1920 formulation that all neurotics are simulators, to an earlier claim Freud had made about pathological doubling itself. He writes in 1893 that "in every hysteria we are dealing with a rudiment of what is called [in French] *'double conscience,'* dual consciousness, and that a tendency to such a dissociation and with it the emergence of abnormal states of consciousness … is the basic phenomenon of hysteria" (Freud, 1962a, p. 39). Here we see the simultaneous occurrence of diminished normal mentation, on the one hand, combined with the emergence of an altered abnormal state – one that could easily be imitative in nature (and for clinicians like Charcot and Page, it often was). Insofar as both statements share this dynamic feature of doubling or replication, it's possible to view the 1920 claim about the inherently simulative condition of psychopathology as an implicit elaboration of the sort of 'doubling' of mentation (and so of oneself) with which Freud framed the phenomenon of hysteria during the earliest period of his research.

But this internal link within Freud's writings embeds the anxieties and discussions about simulation – the so-called *duplicities* of the neurotic – within a larger preoccupation with the various *duplications* and multiplicities of personality, and other discussions about severely altered states of consciousness that were dramatically challenging standing accounts of personal identity, particularly as a consequence of the forensic and institutional dilemmas they introduced.[14] The significance of this brief historical narrative, then, is not about clarifying the relationship between Freud's neurology and metapsychology, but instead understanding how a trajectory in Freud's overall work was part of a broader style of thinking about personhood, and the institutional problems inherent to it, in nineteenth-century brain and behavioral medicine.

Specifically, when Herbert Page in *Injuries of the Spine* provided a technical explanation of the physiopathology of traumatic shock suffered in railway accidents, he relied on the writings of psychologist James Sully, who was in turn utilizing the concept of "nervous dissolution" from John Hughlings Jackson (Page, 1885, pp. 192–194; Sully, 1891, pp. 122–123). Traumatic shock for Page amounted to an immediate and usually only temporary "dissolution" in Jackson's specific, terminological sense. For Jackson, dissolution referred to a double event: a simultaneous diminishment of higher neurological (and thus mental) functioning along with the disinhibition of evolutionarily lower neural (thus mental) states; for Jackson the manifestation of lower states translated into the variety of 'insanities' of the late nineteenth century (Jackson, 1958).

This is what Freud implies when he defines hysteria as double consciousness in 1893 – a dissociation of higher mentation and a simultaneous rise of a lower, "abnormal consciousness". Indeed there is good reason to believe that Freud's account of this dynamic "doubling" of the mind is Jacksonian, at least to some degree; his views in *On Aphasia* from two years earlier were, according to Freud's own admission, almost entirely reliant on Jackson's neurophysiology (Bassiri, 2013, p. 96). On the other hand, for Herbert Page, who is indirectly invoking Jackson, these disinhibited abnormal states often translated into mimicries and simulative behaviors (Page, 1885, pp. 215–216); I suggest that Freud's account incorporates these simulative possibilities as well, though perhaps implicitly at first.

What's particularly noteworthy, with regards to Jackson himself, is that by the end of the 1880s, Jackson began describing this pathological phenomenon of "dissolution" as the disinhibition not only of an altered state of consciousness, but of a state of consciousness so different, that is should rightly be called an altogether "new person" (Jackson, 1958a). It was a conception that was for Jackson both medically and forensically valid, prompted as it was from implicit medico-legal questions concerning the accountability of patients during states of altered consciousness (Bassiri, 2015). With Jackson, Page and Freud, we can begin to see a certain conceptual continuity between simulating, doubling and becoming an altogether new person during neuropathic states. Freud's relationship to neurology goes well beyond standard narratives of an attenuated 'pre-psychoanalytic' period, one headed inevitably towards a metapsychology.

My point ultimately is that the historical discussions around simulation disorders, culminating with Freud, were quite shot through with the same difficulties introduced by the idea that in madness we are as much *not ourselves* as we in fact *become another,* an idea that was articulated quite explicitly by numerous nineteenth-century clinicians and researchers (in some ways, Jackson is the most conservative among them) – an idea, furthermore, that represented one of the most pointed ways in which late nineteenth-century neurological discourse and behavioral medicine subtended challenges to personal identity and its institutional imperatives. Nineteenth-century neurological discourse was not mobilized to salvage a stable conception of personhood but instead to provide a system of knowledge by which to ground and render intelligible these new deviations and abnormalities of the self, pathological possibilities that were intertwined with emerging forensic conundrums and novel political-economic concerns.

Who Are We, Then, If We Are Indeed Our Brains?

I argued in the first section of this paper that the spectrum of the critique of science ranged from compliance (no doubt unacceptable for the critic) to a virtually impossible mode of resistance; and that the critic needed to find her way somewhere within these set of possibilities. If the critique of neuroscience, in particular, is ultimately concerned with what might be called the neurological consolidations of the self, then many critics have tried to find their way, headlong against the neurosciences, by understanding such consolidations to mean the stabilization of the subject according to a set of regulatory norms imposed by a neuroscientific ideology. They have engaged in the critical labor of delimitation and reclamation, and it is a labor that, despite their cautiousness and mitigations, seems invariably at risk of being either inefficacious or the object of rebuke.

I suggested that another sense of critique might then be warranted, one where scientific knowledge and neuro- ideologies were not themselves the target. I've maintained throughout that critique of neuroscience should ultimately be concerned with the fashionings (and not the performative liberation) of the self, and that critique would be a way of coming to terms with the fact that the neural consolidation of self is representative of certain crises of the modern subject. This is what I sought to demonstrate in the historical analysis above: that a system of knowledge was mobilized to make sense of people, at a moment when the category of personhood found itself in a precarious moment of indeterminacy and preoccupation.

I propose such a view of critique, not because I agree with some scholars that critical labors are unproductive or harmful, but because critique may very well have meant something different all along. A critical labor should be concerned with the constitutions and transformations of the self, at least to the extent that – as Butler (2002), by way of Foucault, has argued – critique is itself a kind of virtue, a concern for oneself, a practice of self-fashioning, an inquiry into one's own self-constitutions. What better arena to engage in such combined investigations *and practices* than around the neurological consolidations of the self, the crises that induce them and the possibilities for self-stylizations that they engender?[15]

The relevance to our present moment derives precisely from this approach, and the inquiry into the relationship between neuroscience and psychoanalysis can be useful in this regard, as much today as it was with Freud. I do not maintain, of course, that the interface between psychoanalysis and neuroscience reinvent itself according to discussions of accident neuroses, simulation disorders and a preoccupation with medico-legal duplicity. These anxieties are linked to a prior historical moment. But perhaps we have our own anxieties today, ways in which our accounts of who we are or who we should be have become a problem, so to speak – medically and epistemologically, but also politically and economically. Perhaps personhood has once again become the object of some sort of anxiety, preoccupation or concern such that deployments of brain science have (once again) become acceptable and even necessary. And perhaps the inquiry into the continuing relationship between psychoanalysis and neuroscience might allow us – in ways we would not have necessarily intuited – to account for the incitement to tell the neurological truth of ourselves, while also offering a possible contemporary position from which we can step back from (rather than dismantle) the demands of knowledge production in order to see what provocations motivate that production in the first place.

Notes

1. Versions of this paper were presented at the Neuroscience and History workshop at Columbia University and at the Department of the Social Studies of Medicine at McGill University. I am grateful to organizers and participants at both events. I'm also grateful to the volume editors as well as to Andrew Gerber, Satyel Larson, Mark Robinson, and Simon Taylor for comments on earlier versions of this paper.
2. Indirectly relevant are the discussions and disputes distinguishing Frankfurt School critical theory from Karl Popper's "critical rationalism" (Adorno, 1976).
3. Cf. Derrida (2004, p. 162).
4. In fairness, Fitzgerald and Callard (2015) distinguish their conception of "entanglement" with other interactionist impulses, though I have schematically organized them together.
5. See also Martin (2000).
6. Judith Butler's resolution to this dichotomy might be a useful alternative for discussions around the neurosciences. See Butler (1993), especially the introduction and chapter 1.
7. http://www.critical-neuroscience.org/.
8. See also Ortega & Vidal (2007), Vidal (2009), and Slaby, Haueis, & Choudhury (2012).
9. See Bassiri (2015).
10. See also Drinka (1984, chapter 4).
11. For more on the transformations to Freud's theory of trauma, see Laplanche and Pontalis (1973, pp. 465–69) and Leys (2000, ch. 1).
12. American neurologist George Miller Beard explicitly discusses the neuropathogenic effects of industrial labor in his *American Nervousness* (1881, p. 102). See also Killen (2006, p. 51).
13. Cf. Killen (2006), p. 103.
14. See also Hacking (1991, 1991a, 1995).
15. I am drawing here on Butler (2002, p. 221). See also Malabou (2015).

References

Adorno, T. (1976). *The Positivistic Dispute in German Sociology*. London: Heinemann.
Bassiri, N. (2013). Freud and the Matter of the Brain: On the Rearrangements of Neuropsychoanalysis. *Critical Inquiry, 40*, 83–108.

Bassiri, N. (2015). Epileptic Insanity and Personal Identity: John Hughlings Jackson and the Formations of the Neuropathic Self. In D. Bates and N. Bassiri (Eds.), *Plasticity and Pathology: On the Formation of the Neural Subject*. New York, NY: Fordham University Press.

Beard, G.M. (1881). *American Nervousness, Its Causes and Consequences: A Supplement to Nervous Exhaustion (Neurasthenia)*. New York, NY: G. P. Putnam's Sons.

Butler, J. (1990). *Gender Trouble: Feminism and the Subversion of Identity*. New York, NY: Routledge.

Butler, J. (1993). *Bodies That Matter: On the Discursive Limits of 'Sex.'* London: Routledge.

Butler, J. (2002). What is Critique? An Essay on Foucault's Virtue. In D. Ingram (Ed.), *The Political*. Malden, MA: Wiley-Blackwell.

Butler, J. (2009). Critique, Dissent, Disciplinarity. *Critical Inquiry, 35*, 773–95.

Bynum, W.F. (1985). The Nervous Patient in Eighteenth- and Nineteenth-Century Britain: the Psychiatric Origins of British Neurology. In W.F. Bynum, R. Porter, & M. Shepard (Eds.), *The Anatomy of Madness: Essays in the History of Psychiatry, Volume 1: People and Ideas*. New York, NY: Tavistock.

Caplan, E.M. (1995). Trains, Brains, and Sprains: Railway Spine and the Origins of Psychoneuroses. *Bulletin of the History of Medicine, 69*, 387–419.

Caplan, E.M. (2001). Trains and Trauma in the American Gilded Age. In M. S. Micale & P. Lerner (Eds.), *Traumatic Pasts: History, Psychiatry, and Trauma in the Modern Age, 1870–1930*. Cambridge, UK: Cambridge University Press.

Charcot, J.M. (1889). *Clinical Lectures on Diseases of the Nervous System*, Vol. 3. London: New Sydenham.

Choudhury S., & Slaby, J. (Eds.). (2012). *Critical Neuroscience: A Handbook of the Social and Cultural Contexts of Neuroscience*. Malden, MA: Wiley-Blackwell.

Cooter R., & Stein, C. (2013). *Writing History in the Age of Biomedicine*. New Haven, CT: Yale University Press.

Cooter, R. (2014). Neural Veils and the Will to Historical Critique: Why Historians of Science Need to Take the Neuro-Turn Seriously. *Isis, 105*, 100–154.

Crichton-Browne, J. (1862–63). Personal Identity and its Morbid Modifications. *Journal of Mental Science, 8*, 385–95; 535–45.

Danziger, K. (1982). Mid-Nineteenth-Century British Psycho-Physiology: A Neglected Chapter in the History of Psychology. In W. R. Woodward & M. G. Ash (Eds.), *The Problematic Science: Psychology in Nineteenth-Century Thought*. New York, NY: Praeger.

Daston, L. (2009). Science Studies and the History of Science. *Critical Inquiry, 35*, 798–813.

Davidson, A. (2011). In Praise of Counter-Conduct. *History of the Human Sciences, 24*, 25–41.

Dear, P., & Jasanoff, S. (2010). Dismantling Boundaries in Science and Technology Studies. *Isis, 101*, 759–74.

Derrida, J. (2004). *Eyes of the University: Right to Philosophy 2*. Stanford, CA: Stanford University Press.

Douglas, M. (1992). The Person in an Enterprise Culture. In S. H. Heap & A. Ross (Eds.), *Understanding the Enterprise Culture: Themes in the Work of Mary Douglas*. Edinburgh: Edinburgh University Press.

Drinka, G.F. (1984). *The Birth of Neurosis: Myth, Malady, and the Victorians*. New York, NY: Simon and Schuster.

Dumit, J. (2012). Afterword: Twisting the Neurohelix. In M. Littlefield & J. Johnson (Eds.), *The Neuroscientific Turn: Transdisciplinarity in the Age of the Brain*. Ann Arbor, MI: University of Michigan Press.

Eissler, K.R. (1986). *Freud as an Expert Witness: The Discussion of War Neuroses between Freud and Wagner-Jauregg*. Madison, CT: International Universities Press.

Ellenberger, H. (1970). *The Discovery of the Unconscious: the History and Evolution of Dynamic Psychiatry*. New York, NY: Basic Books.

Erichsen, J.E. (1875). *On Concussion of the Spine: Nervous Shock and Other Obscure Injuries of the Nervous System in Their Clinical and Medico-Legal Aspects*. New York, NY: William Wood.

Feyerabend, P. (1981). How to Defend Society Against Science. In I. Hacking (Ed.), *Scientific Revolutions*. Oxford: Oxford University Press.

Feyerabend, P. (1998). Galileo and the Tyranny of Truth. In *Farewell to Reason*. New York, NY: Verso.

Fitzgerald, D., & Callard, F. (2015). Social Science and Neuroscience Beyond Interdisciplinarity: Experimental Entanglement. *Theory, Culture & Society, 32*, 3–32.

Foucault, M. (2007). What is Critique? In S. Lotringer (Ed.), *The Politics of Truth*. Los Angeles: Semiotext(e).

Freud, S. (1950). *Aus den Anfängen der Psychoanalyse*. London: Imago Publishing.

Freud, S. (1953). The Interpretation of Dreams. In J. Strachey (Ed.), *The Standard Edition of the Complete Psychological Works of Sigmund Freud*, Vol. 4. London: Hogarth.

Freud, S. (1961). *Beyond the Pleasure Principle*. New York, NY: Norton.

Freud, S. (1962). Charcot. In J. Strachey (Ed.), *The Standard Edition of the Complete Psychological Works of Sigmund Freud*, Vol. 3. London: Hogarth.

Freud, S. (1962a). On the Psychical Mechanism of Hysterical Phenomena. In J. Strachey (Ed.), *The Standard Edition of the Complete Psychological Works of Sigmund Freud*, Vol. 3. London: Hogarth.

Freud, S. (1962b). The Aetiology of Hysteria. In J. Strachey (Ed.), *The Standard Edition of the Complete Psychological Works of Sigmund Freud*, Vol. 3. London: Hogarth.

Freud, S. (1972). Über Kriegneurosen, Elektrotherapie, und Psychoanalyse: Ein Auszug aus dem Protokoll des Untersuchungverfahrens gegen Wagner-Jauregg im Oktober 1920. *Psyche: Zeitschrift für Psychoanalyse und ihre Anwendungen, 16*, 939–51.

Freud, S. (2000). Letter to Sándor Ferenczi 11 October 1920. In *The Correspondences of Sigmund Freud and Sándor Ferenczi, Vol. 3, 1920–1933*. Cambridge, MA: Harvard University Press.

Fuller, S. (2011). Putting the Brain at the Heart of General Education in the Twenty-First Century: A Proposal. *Interdisciplinary Science Reviews, 36*, 359–72.

Fuller, S. (2014). Neuroscience, Neurohistory, and the History of Science: A Tale of Two Brain Images. *Isis, 105*, 100–109.

Goldstein. J. (2002). *Console and Classify: The French Psychiatric Profession in the Nineteenth Century*. Chicago, IL: University of Chicago Press.

Hacking, I. (1991). Double Consciousness in Britain, 1815–1875. *Dissociation, 4*, 134–146.

Hacking, I. (1991a). Two Souls in One Body. *Critical Inquiry, 17*, 838–67.

Hacking, I. (1995). *Rewriting the Soul: Multiple Personality and the Sciences of Memory*. Princeton, NJ: Princeton University Press.

Hacking, I. (1998). *Mad Travelers: Reflections on the Reality of Transient Mental Illnesses*. Cambridge, MA: Harvard University Press.

Hacking, I. (2002). Making Up People. In *Historical Ontology*. Cambridge, MA: Harvard University Press.

Hagner, M. (1997). *Homo Cerebralis: Der Wandel vom Seelenorgan zum Gehirn*. Berlin: Verlag.

Harrington, R. (2001). The Railway Accident: Trains, Trauma, and Technological Crises in Nineteenth-Century Britain. In M. S. Micale & P. Lerner (Eds.), *Traumatic Pasts: History, Psychiatry, and Trauma in the Modern Age, 1870–1930*. Cambridge, UK: Cambridge University Press.

Jackson, J.H. (1958). Remarks on Evolution and Dissolution of the Nervous System. In J. Taylor (Ed.), *Selected Writings of John Hughlings Jackson*, Vol. 2. New York, NY: Basic Books.

Jackson, J.H. (1958a). The Factors of Insanities. In. J. Taylor (Ed.), *Selected Writings of John Hughlings Jackson*, Vol. 2. New York, NY: Basic Books.

Killen, A. (2006). *Berlin Electropolis: Shock, Nerves, and German Modernity.* Berkeley, CA: University of California Press.

Laplanche J., & Pontalis, J.B. (1973). *The Language of Psychoanalysis.* New York, NY: Norton.

Latour, B. (2004). Why Has Critique Run out of Steam? From Matters of Fact to Matters of Concern. *Critical Inquiry, 30,* 225–48.

Lerner, P. (2001). From Traumatic Neurosis to Male Hysteria: The Decline and Fall of Hermann Oppenheim, 1889–1919. In M. S. Micale & P. Lerner (Eds.), *Traumatic Pasts: History, Psychiatry, and Trauma in the Modern Age, 1870–1930.* Cambridge, UK: Cambridge University Press.

Levin, K. (1974). Freud's Paper 'On Male Hysteria' and the Conflict Between Anatomical and Physiological Models. *Bulletin of the History of Medicine, 48,* 377–97.

Leys, R. (2000). *Trauma: a Genealogy.* Chicago, IL: University of Chicago Press.

Locke, J. (1700). *An Essay Concerning Human Understanding.* Oxford: Oxford University Press.

Macherey, P. (1998). George Canguilhem's Philosophy of Science: Epistemology and History of Science. In W. Montag (Ed.), *In a Materialist Way: Selected Essays.* New York, NY: Verso.

Malabou, C. (2008). *What Should We Do With Our Brain?* New York, NY: Fordham University Press.

Malabou, C. (2015). "You Are (Not) Your Synapses": Towards a Critical Approach to Neuroscience. In D. Bates and N. Bassiri (Eds.), *Plasticity and Pathology: On the Formation of the Neural Subject.* New York, NY: Fordham University Press.

Martin, E. (2000). AES Presidential Address: Mind-Body Problems. *Ethnologist, 27,* 560–90.

Maudsley, H. (1884). *Body and Will, Being an Essay concerning Will in its Metaphysical, Physiological, and Pathological Aspects.* New York, NY: D. Appleton.

Mayer, A. (2006). Lost Objects: From the Laboratories of Hypnosis to the Psychoanalytic Setting. *Science in Context, 9,* 37–64.

Micale, M.S. (2001). Jean-Martin Charcot and *les névroses traumatiques:* from medicine to culture in French trauma theory of the late nineteenth century. In M. S. Micale & P. Lerner (Eds.), *Traumatic Pasts: History, Psychiatry, and Trauma in the Modern Age, 1870–1930.* Cambridge, UK: Cambridge University Press.

Ortega, F., & Vidal, F. (2007). Mapping the Cerebral Subject in Contemporary Culture. *Electronic Journal of Communication Information and Innovation in Health, 1,* 255–59.

Page, H. (1885). *Injuries of the Spine and Spinal Cord without Apparent Mechanical Lesion, and Nervous Shock in their Surgical and Medico-Legal Aspects,* Second edition. London: J. & A. Churchill.

Page, H. (1892). *Railway Injuries: With Special Reference to Those the Back and Nervous System in Their Medico-Legal and Clinical Aspects.* New York, NY: William Wood.

Paget, J. (1875). Nervous Mimicry. In *Clinical Lectures and Essays.* London: Longmans, Green, and Co.

Pelaprat, E., & Hartouni, V. (2011). The Neural Subject in Popular Culture and the End of Life. *Configurations, 19,* 385–406.

Pinker, S. (2013). Science is Not Your Enemy. *New Republic.* Retrieved from www.newrepublic.com/article/114127/science-not-enemy-humanities.

Pitts-Taylor, V. (2010). The Plastic Brain: Neoliberalism and the Neuronal Self. *Health, 14,* 635–52.

Prince, M. (1975). Association Neuroses: A Study of the Pathology of Hysterical Joint Affections, Neurasthenia and Allied Forms of Neuro-Mimesis (1890/91). In *Psychotherapy and Multiple Personality: Selected Essays.* Cambridge, MA: Harvard University Press.

Rabinbach, A. (1996). Social Knowledge, Social Risk, and the Politics of Industrial Accidents in Germany and France. In D. Rueschemeyer & T. Skocpol (Eds.), *States, Social Knowledge, and the Origins of Modern Social Policies*. Princeton, NJ: Princeton University Press.

Rose, N., & Abi-Rached, J.M. (2013). *Neuro: The New Brain Sciences and the Management of the Mind*. Princeton, NJ: Princeton University Press.

Rose. N., & Abi-Rached, J. (2014). Governing through the Brain: Neuropolitics, Neuroscience and Subjectivity. *Cambridge Anthropology, 32*, 3–23.

Schäffner, W. (2001). Events, Series, Trauma; The Probabilistic Revolution of the Mind in the Late Nineteenth and Early Twentieth Century. In M. S. Micale & P. Lerner (Eds.), *Traumatic Pasts: History, Psychiatry, and Trauma in the Modern Age, 1870–1930*. Cambridge, UK: Cambridge University Press.

Schivebusch, W. (1986). *The Railway Journey: The Industrialization of Time and Space in the 19th Century*. Berkeley, CA: University of California Press.

Schmiedebach, H.P. (1999). Post-Traumatic Neurosis in Nineteenth-Century Germany: A Disease in Political, Juridical and Professional Context. *History of Psychiatry, 10*, 27–57.

Scott, J.W. (2007). History-Writing as Critique. In S. Morgan, K. Jenkins, & A. Munslow (Eds.), *Manifestos for History*. London: Routledge.

Slaby, J., Haueis, P., & Choudhury, S. (2012). Neuroscience as Applied Hermeneutics: Towards a Critical Neuroscience of Political Theory. In Valk, F.V. (Ed.), *Essays on Neuroscience and Political Theory: Thinking the Body Politic*. New York, NY: Routledge.

Sonderegger, R., & de Boer, K. (Eds.). (2012). *Conceptions of Critique in Modern and Contemporary Philosophy*. New York, NY: Palgrave Macmillan.

Sully, J. (1891). *Illusions: A Psychological Study*. New York, NY: D. Appleton.

Valk, F.V. (2012). The Extension of Political Subjectivity. In Valk, F.V. (Ed.), *Essays on Neuroscience and Political Theory: Thinking the Body Politic*. New York, NY: Routledge.

Vidal, F. (2009). Brainhood, Anthropological Figure of Modernity. *History of the Human Sciences, 22*, 5–36.

Wilson, E. (2011). Another Neurological Scene. *History of the Present, 1*, 149–169.

4

NEUROSCIENTIFIC DYSTOPIA

Does Naturalism Commit a Category Mistake?

Peter Reynaert

Utopias have always promised a bright future for mankind, one in which science would play a distinctive role. Neuroscience would also play a prominent role in such utopias, since mental health and happiness are thought to be obtained by controlling the relevant brain processes behind them. Philosophically, the support for this point of view is naturalism: the conviction that man is basically a biological organism and that all problems can be solved by scientific means. Huxley's *Brave New World* and Orwell's *1984* are, however, famous novels about how these utopias can lead to horrific dystopias. In this essay, I want to argue that neuroscience runs the risk of becoming dystopic in a logical sense by committing a category-mistake. I explain how this notion, which was introduced by Ryle, actually goes back to Husserl's analysis of what he called a *metabasis eis allo genos* (a change to another genus). Husserl argued that the naturalistic understanding of human consciousness and mental processes as natural phenomena, that is, as brain-processes, is a fundamental theoretical mistake. And category mistakes have devastating consequences for the object under study. The miscategorization leads to a misunderstanding, which neglects fundamental properties of the object. In what follows, I will illustrate how this applies to naturalism's analysis of embodiment. In my conclusion I will briefly return to the potentially harmful effects of this category mistake for the problem of free will.

Nonsense Versus Absurdity

In the *4th Logical Investigation* Husserl distinguished absurdity from both sense and nonsense. He developed an a priori pure logical grammar, which aimed at identifying the laws that determine what sorts of expressions can be meaningfully combined (Thomasson, 2002, p. 123). This logical grammar was to be distinguished from the grammar of natural languages. The a priori laws of meaning not only serve to separate sense from nonsense, but also to distinguish nonsense (*Unsinn*) from absurdity or counter-sense (*Widersinn*). Nonsense involves a combination of expressions, and hence meanings, from different syntactic categories, and results in meaningless expressions such as: *a round or* or *a man and is* (Husserl, 1984, p. 334, 2001, vol. 2, p. 67). In the first example, three so-called syncategorematical expressions are combined. Syncategorematical expressions don't have an independent meaning of their own and can only be meaningfully used in combination with a categorematical expression. A noun is an example of such a categorematical expression. So an adjective like 'round' only makes sense when combined with a noun. Because it is meaningless, a nonsensical expression does not refer. No corresponding object exists for it. "Husserl's understanding of 'nonsense' is rather strict: he counts only those strings of words that are syntactically incorrect (so that they form a mere 'heap of words' and cannot be combined into any unified meaning) as strictly nonsensical, and thus as signs of differences in categories of meaning" (Thomasson, 2013).

Absurdity on the contrary is meaningful: an absurd expression does make sense, but it is nevertheless logically wrong. Because of this, absurd expressions are not thought to refer to any object either. Husserl identifies two kinds of absurdity: formal and material absurdity. Expressions are formally absurd when they violate purely formal, logical laws, like the law of contradiction, of double negation or the modus ponens law. "A round not-round thing" is formally or analytically absurd because it is contradictory. "Expressions are materially absurd if the impossibility of there being a corresponding object is based in the particular material concepts employed" (Thomasson, 2013). "A square is round" or "woody iron" are, by contrast, materially absurd expressions because of the particular meanings of 'round' and 'square' in geometry, and of 'woody' and 'iron' in physics (Husserl, 1984, pp. 334–335, 2001, vol. 2, p. 67). Yet, because they are still meaningful expressions, their absurdity is much more difficult to recognize. Doing so requires knowledge of the nature of the entities the expression is about – in this case geometrical and physical knowledge. Long before Carnap stated that there may exist meaningful expressions which are nonetheless devoid of cognitive significance, Husserl developed the same point. Yet where Carnap considers such expressions to be nonsensical, Husserl calls them instead absurd, and he insists that it is necessary to distinguish the two.[1]

Metabasis Eis Allo Genos

Correlated with the categories of meanings are ontological categories that are both formal and material. The formal 'categorial essences' include such things as the notion of an object in general, a state of affairs, a property, a relation and so on. Husserl distinguishes these formal ontological categories from material categories or essences, which he calls 'regions'. Material categories or essences classify entities according to their nature or essence. Hence regions are material a priori and distinct fields (*sachhaltig apriorische Sondergebiete*) (Husserl, 1974, p. 158, 1969, p. 150, 1985, p. 435). A material ontology would then outline the most general or generic properties of a regional being. Physical nature for instance has as its highest generic properties temporality, spatiality, causality and materiality, which together constitute the reality of this regional being (Husserl, 1952, pp. 41–45, 1989, pp. 44–49, 1971, pp. 25–37). The psyche lacks such materiality and spatiality and is thus, according to Husserl, a non-material causal reality, whose psychological processes are caused by and in turn cause bodily processes. A regional being is the object of a specific experience (Husserl, 1971, p. xviii, p. 38). For instance, the perception of a material thing differs descriptively from the experience of the psychological life of an animate being. Phenomenological description of this original experience is the basis of the material ontology Husserl develops, which identifies the essential (eidetic) ontological structures of any regional being. Any discovery of these highest essences is not only based on the description of the experienced object but also on the method of ideative abstraction (*ideierende Abstraktion*), which founds the specific material ontology of each of the regions.[2] There are as many ontologies as there are regional concepts (Husserl, 1971, p. 25). Every object with its material (i.e., non-formal) characteristics belongs to a region which can be identified with respect to its essential features.

The more fundamental material ontology of the world we experience, which Husserl later calls "the ontology of the life-world", leads to a distinction of the so-called fundamental regions or basic material ontological categories of this world.[3] In the second book of *Ideas*, Husserl claims that these three regions in the world of natural experience are physical nature, animate being and *Geist* or Spirit[4] (Husserl, 1971, p. xix). Animate being is the name for a living being with a psychological life. Spirit is the overarching term for all instances of human existence. The spiritual world (*geistige Welt*) contains human beings with their conscious, embodied existence, but in addition also the fundamental entities of the human world such as language, music, politics; but also all other instances of human culture. The use of the word *Geist* is to be understood in opposition to nature, as is clear from the debate about the specificity of the *Geisteswissenschaften* (human sciences) over and against the *Naturwissenschaften* (natural sciences). Husserl clearly argues against the idea of a unified science of the two regions and pleads for the methodological specificity of the *Geisteswissenschaften* for the study of humanity. This specificity is ultimately founded on the ontology of Spirit.

Scientific analysis and explanation must respect the ontology of their objects, which is something that must be taken into account in the conceptual framework used to study them.[5] With each different region comes a different set of concepts and thus a different type of explanation.[6] Husserl explicitly states that it is evident that we have to remove from our analysis every descriptive concept that is excluded by the regional concepts being used. "(…) the originary sense of the object cannot be annulled by any theory. It is the norm which must be presupposed and to which all possible theoretical cognition is rationally bound. Hereby is designated a universal rule for the fundamental clarification of all regional concepts – thus all concepts which delimit the domain of objects of a regional ontology (and therewith of all special and empirical disciplines of the regional sphere in question) (...)" (Husserl, 1952, p. 91, 1989, p. 97). When a scientific discipline explains a regional being by using or relying on concepts that should not be applied to it, a fundamental problem arises, a *metabasis eis allo genos* (a change to another genus) or, in Ryle's terms: a category mistake.

Husserl already identified this mistake in the *Prolegomena* to the *Logical Investigations* when he criticized logical psychologism:

> There is another, much more dangerous fault in the field-delimitation: the confusion of fields, the mixture of heterogeneous things in a putative field-unity, especially when this rests on a complete misreading of the objects whose investigation is to be the essential aim of the proposed science. Such an unnoticed *metabasis eis allo genos* can have the most damaging consequences: the setting up of invalid aims, the employment of methods wrong in principle, not commensurate with the discipline's true objects, (...).
>
> *(Husserl 2001, vol. 1, p. 13, 1975, p. 22)*

The theory which commits a metabasis results in what Husserl identified as material absurdity in his *4th Logical Investigation*. He repeats this in *Ideas II* when he says that not to take into account the essence of the object under study creates absurdity (*Widersinn*) (Husserl, 1952, p. 91, 1989, p. 96). The absurdity in question is the result of combining different ontological and conceptual categories that should be kept apart, because they refer to distinct ontological regions and entities. It is the task of philosophy as a theory of the a priori to help the sciences to avoid this absurdity, by gaining insight into the sense and essence of a scientific method in relation to its object (Husserl, 1975, p. 255, 2001, vol.1, p. 161, 1974, p. 10). So according to Husserl the classification and distinction of the sciences is dependent upon this notion of region (Husserl, 1971, p. 25). "Every science of facts (*Tatsachenwissenschaft*) has essential, theoretical foundations in eidetical ontologies", as Husserl explains in the first chapter of his *Ideas*, book I, entitled "Fact and Essence" (*Tatsache und Wesen*) (Husserl, 1976a, p. 23).

Naturalism and Material Absurdity

The naturalistic interpretation of human existence, and especially of consciousness, is an example of what Husserl calls material absurdity. Before explaining this point further, it should be remarked that naturalism has a complex meaning for Husserl. A first meaning concerns the falsification of ideal logical norms and laws in terms of inductively found psychological rules concerning the legitimate connection of mental states. This is what psychologism in logic does, as Husserl explains in his *Prolegomena*. Secondly, in the context of his transcendental phenomenology, he argues that "naturalism essentially misconstrues consciousness by treating it as a part of the world" (Moran, 2008, p. 1). Naturalism is understood here as the basic characteristic of the common natural attitude (*natürliche Einstellung*), which Husserl opposes to the more fundamental transcendental attitude. As he explains in the *Crisis*, it is a form of objectivism, which means that it starts from the common belief in the existence of the world, without clarifying its relation to transcendental consciousness. The naturalist does not perform the transcendental reduction. How non-transcendental, mundane or worldly consciousness is analyzed as a part of the world can further be specified, and this leads to a third notion of naturalism. Thirdly, and only this sense really matters in the present context, naturalism is characterized by what Husserl calls the naturalistic attitude. This attitude is, together with the personalistic attitude from which it substantially differs, based in the common natural attitude. It is foundational for what we now call physicalism, whereas the personalistic attitude founds the hermeneutical approach typical for the so-called human sciences (*Geisteswissenschaften*). So it makes sense to distinguish between a naturalism in a broad sense, characterized by the "natural attitude" *(natürliche Einstellung)*, as opposed to transcendentalism, and naturalism in a more narrow sense. The latter defines itself by the more specific "naturalistic attitude" (*natüralistische Einstellung)*, which is opposed to the personalistic attitude, and it gives rise to physicalism with regard to humanity (Husserl, 1952, pp. 139–142, 1989, pp. 147–150).[7] Given these distinctions, even the non-naturalistic *Geisteswissenschaftler* is a naturalist in the first broad sense.

Husserl makes the following remark about 'narrow' naturalism in *Philosophy as Rigorous Science*: "Hence the naturalist (…) sees nothing but nature and first and foremost physical nature. Everything that is is either itself physical, belonging to the unitary nexus of physical nature, or it is indeed something psychical, but then a variable that merely depends on the physical, at best a secondary, 'parallel accompanying fact'. All beings are of a psychophysical nature, that is, univocally determined in accordance with firm laws" (Husserl, 2002, pp. 253–254).

This naturalistic approach considers physical nature as the basis of everything there is and adopts the methods of the exact sciences to causally explain reality. In modern terms one could say that we are confronted here with both ontological and methodological naturalism.[8] Of course, Husserl is well aware of the fact that there exist what he calls psychophysical dependencies or conditionalities. In *Ideas II* and *III* he explains that our perceptual processes are causally related to our body. If you consider perception to be a psychological activity, then the psyche is a non-material reality, causally determined by bodily processes. Husserl speaks here of somatological causality, which concerns the relation between a subjective perceptual event and the body[9] (Husserl, 1952, p. 65, 1989, p. 70). In that sense, a naturalistic approach to human experience has obvious validity. But serious explanatory difficulties are already to be found at this basic level of human existence.

One can illustrate this point by considering Husserl's analysis of the lived body (*Leib*), which is primarily characterized by its sensitivity (*Empfindsamkeit*) (Husserl, 1952, p. 155, 1989, p. 163). The naturalist would approach the object to be studied (*Leib*) via notions that belong to physical nature (*Körper*). The result is a misidentification of the *Leib's* basic properties. Sensitivity is, for the naturalist, a psychological property of the organism that has to be explained by the organic, biochemical and neurological mechanisms underlying it. She wants a physio-psychological causal explanation. Husserl only partly agrees with a physio-psychological explanation since he accuses naturalism of material absurdity, but what this disagreement is precisely about needs clarification. Sensitivity certainly is a non-physical, psychological property of the *Leib*. Tactile sensitivity, for instance, does not constitute another physical property of the hand like its roughness or smoothness (Husserl, 1952, pp. 145–146, 1989, p. 152). No other material object besides a living organism is sensitive. It is also true that our sensitivity is conditioned by bodily processes. The body is stimulatable (*reizbar*), which means that physiological changes in its perceptual organs occur as the result of causal contact with external objects. Since sensations are consequences of these stimuli (*Reizerfolge*), changing sensitivity is the result of this dependency or conditionality and hence a psychophysical property. "The *Leib*, we can say, always has states of sensation, and which particular ones it has depends on the concomitant system of real circumstances under which it senses" (Husserl, 1952, p. 155, 1989, p. 162). So far, Husserl has no objections to a naturalistic search for and study of causal mechanisms underlying psychological/perceptual phenomena.

But sensations are more than mere physical stimuli; they are experiences. Husserl distinguishes stimulatability (*Reizbarkeit*) from sensitivity (*Empfindsamkeit*). The first concerns the body as a physical organism, whereas the second concerns the lived body or *Leib*, more precisely the subjective experience of being embodied. The body is not only covered by the skin which contains receptors that can be stimulated by physical contact, the skin is also a field of sensations (of touch and so on) (*Empfindungsfeld*) (Husserl, 1952, p. 154, 1989, p. 161). When we enter a hot room, it is not only the case that our heat sensors are activated. We also undergo a change in our sensation field that we call heat sensation and we consequently feel warm. Stimuli and sensations co-vary. When the stimuli change, this causes a change in the sensations.

Establishing causal covariance should be distinguished from reductively explaining consciousness in terms of neurophysiology. This means that although physiological changes of stimuli cause changes in the sensations, we still don't understand why this causal relation holds. The occurrence of physical stimuli does not explain why the sensations are experienced. The *Leib's* sensitivity is not a non-physical *consequence* of physical processes for Husserl (Husserl, 1952, p. 155, 1989, p. 163). This refers to the problem of why and how conscious experience arises from biological-physiological processes, i.e., the classical hard problem of consciousness.

"Making up a running list of observed psychoneural correlations does not amount to having an explanatory insight into why these particular correlations hold (…)" (Kim, 2006, p. 221). How physiology and experience are linked does not seem answerable within neurophysiology because experience as a subjective, conscious event does not even occur in it. Yet from a naturalistic point of view consciousness should be reduced to physiology. This first demands a definition of it in naturalistic terms, in order to causally reduce it to physiology. But because of its subjectivity, it cannot be described in neurophysiological terms, which refer to objective processes. So doing this is a category mistake and constitutes material absurdity, because by conceptualizing consciousness in a naturalist way, one denies its essence. Since this kind of conceptualizing is absurd, it becomes clear that a causal reductive explanation is highly problematical.

In a sense, one could say that Husserl addresses here what was later termed the problem of the explanatory gap, namely how physiological processes can give rise to conscious experiences. Husserl doesn't venture a closing of this gap, the very possibility of which he actually seems to reject. He merely records a plain fact when he writes: "(…) If my hand is touched or struck, then I sense it. We do not here have the hand as physical body and, connected with it, an extra-physical consequence. From the very outset it is (…) a hand *with* its field of sensation. (…) i.e., a physical-aesthesiological *unity*" (Husserl, 1952, p. 155, 1989, p. 163). The lived body must be this physical and aesthesiological *unity*, and hence a *Leib*, for physical stimuli to be experienced *as* sensations of warmth, sting, taste, touch, pain or whatever (Husserl, 1952, p. 155, 1989, p. 163). The physio-psychical conditionality or the co-variance thus only works when the body is already subjectively lived as *Leib*. Only then is the state of sensation of the body causally related to physiological processes, with which it co-varies. Sensitivity itself *as* an experience is not an effect of these processes since the causal mechanism between the natural and the experiential only works when consciousness, and more precisely subjective experience, is already in play.

The *Leib* is a very specific entity then, a subjective objectivity (*Subjektive Gegenständlichkeit*), with both material and subjective, non-material properties, between which there is a special causal link that correlates changes in the last properties with changes in the first (Husserl, 1952, p. 153, 1989, p. 160). The link is special because it does not imply that one of the two parties is constitutive for the other, since it only regulates their interdependence. It is not possible to reductively explain the causal link between the two properties (physiology and sensitivity) of the same object (*Leib-Körper*), but only to observe a relation of causal covariance. We have no explanatory insight into why sensed stimuli *are* sensations. That is why Husserl speaks of a physical-aesthesiological *unity*. Consequently, we can only separate these two aspects (physical and aesthesiological) in the abstract, and only in the abstract, Husserl emphasizes (Husserl, 1952, pp. 155–156, 1989, p. 163). We need here a complex approach that is at the same time naturalistic, i.e., psychophysical, *and* subjective, without reducing these analyses to one unique paradigm as the naturalist does. Accepting the necessity of an original unity of bodily and conscious processes, which cannot be reductively explained although the processes themselves are causally linked, doesn't lead to a dualistic interpretation of sensitivity. The *Leib* is a causal reality and can also be considered as a material object, but it differs from other material things since it has specific relations of dependency which concern its sensitivity. So it makes sense for Husserl to say that "sensations are not properties of the *Leib* as a physical thing" – sensations are not material but rather subjective properties – "but on the other hand, they are properties of the thing *Leib*" – which is more than just a physical object – since they are causal "effect properties" – they are affected by physiological changes, which result from the causal interaction of the body with other objects (Husserl, 1952, p. 146, 1989, pp. 153–154). The external cause of physiological stimuli also causes the sensations, but doesn't explain why the stimuli are sensed.

Although stimulus and sensation are both properties of the *Leib-Körper* and are causally linked, Husserl refuses to identify them because a sensation is not a physical but a subjective property. That is why he calls the *Leib* a subjective object. Consequently, reducing the *Leib* to a *Körper* (physical body) with purely physical and physiological properties, on which a psychical, mental, conscious layer is functionally dependent, as naturalism does according to Husserl, is an example of a category mistake. This miscomprehension of the body generates further (material) absurdity when one tries to understand the body's sensitivity by attempting to causally explain this non-material, subjective property by material, objective processes. The body simply is not originally experienced this way, but is subjectively lived (*erlebt*) or experienced. Even the naturalist must agree that the body is a *corps vécu (lived body)* as Merleau-Ponty says. The sensitivity of the body means that there is a pre-reflective self-givenness of bodily sensations, which we may term bodily self-awareness. These experienced sensations display all of the properties that define consciousness: subjectivity or first person givenness, immediacy and so on. The interpretation of the body as a physical reality (*Körper*) and the ensuing quest for a naturalistic explanation of consciousness presupposes this experience of the lived body, and rests on an approach which makes abstraction of this self-awareness.

As I remarked earlier, Husserl claims that in order to explain a phenomenon, you first have to take its nature into account. You find out what this nature is by carefully describing how the phenomenon is experienced and by applying the method of ideative abstraction to it. The naturalist is incapable of correctly describing the phenomenon of the lived body because of his theoretical bias. This bias entails, as cited above, that everything is either itself physical, or a (psychical) variable that functionally depends on the physical. As a result, the naturalist comes up with strange explanations of the properties of the lived body. When you start describing the body as a *Körper*, you then have to explain how those non-physical, psychical properties are linked to it. The naturalist conjures up the question of how non-conscious biological processes can give rise to the subjective experience of embodiment. This question can only arise because of an implicit dualism, which accepts a distinction between non-conscious physical processes and conscious experiences. This problem is of course unsolvable, as we know since we have been instructed about the explanatory gap. Following Husserl, this question is simply absurd. It is wrong because the analysis of the body's sensitivity is wrong. The body is not a non-conscious organism on which conscious processes supervene and whose causes have to be identified. Conscious embodiment will always stay a crux for any naturalistic analysis because it rests on a category mistake. The Mind-Body problem – how to reduce the mind to the body - is the result of the category mistake which consists in understanding the body (qua Leib) as a physical organism (qua Körper). A correct phenomenological description and ontological understanding elucidates that this reduction of *Leib* to *Körper* is unjustified and that there is no Mind-Body problem such as naturalism conceives of it.

Because the body is subjectively lived, because of the presence of this pre-reflective bodily self-awareness, it makes sense to say that the body itself experiences. As a sensing organism, the lived body is clearly more than just a physical cause of conscious experience, it is rather a constitutive element of it; therefore, the embodiment of a conscious person cannot be fully captured by a functional, psychophysical approach, which distinguishes between non-conscious bodily processes and conscious mental processes like sensations and then asks for their relation. Contrary to what naturalism claims, the body is not a physical cause of conscious perception. One should even say that certain bodily processes do not cause consciousness, but are themselves invested with it. This is clearly the case for the body's sensitivity. Lived embodiment is the essential mode of being of perceptual consciousness. Husserl calls the lived body a voluntarily movable organ of perception (*frei bewegliches Wahrnehmungsorgan*: Husserl, 1952, p. 56, 1989, p. 61). Embodiment is lived as a "*je peux*" (I can), i.e., a capacity to act.[10] Movement generates kinaesthetic sensations, which are sensed together with tactile and other sensations. Perception is only possible for a person who disposes of (*Walten*) her body as a voluntarily movable and sensitive organ of perception (Husserl, 1973, p. 128, 1976b, pp. 220–221). But the role of embodiment is not confined to perception. Lived embodiment is also the mode of existence of a person. It is the expression of personal life, which consists of the character, intentions, actions, decisions and so on of a person.

The absurdity of naturalism entails that the physicalist cannot succeed in explaining these other essential features of human existence such as subjectivity and intersubjectivity, intentionality and ethics, to name only the more important topics and core problems for any naturalistic approach. These features are either reduced or eliminated, and the naturalist claims that this is necessary in order to avoid what she calls unsolvable riddles and pseudo problems created by a non-naturalistic approach: the explanatory gap problem concerning consciousness, the problem of other minds, the problem of content and of the causality of intentional acts (free will) and the problem of the status of ethical and other values and norms. Yet a non-naturalistic phenomenological analysis shows these phenomena to be very well explicable, and the so-called *Scheinprobleme* identified by naturalism to be problems conjured up by naturalism itself. I referred to the absence of a Mind-Body problem for the phenomenological approach of lived embodiment, but one could also develop the theory of empathy to show how the so-called problem of inter-subjectivity is not at all a conundrum for phenomenology as naturalism pretends it should be.[11]

Naturalism is an abstract approach to humanity in the context of the natural attitude. Naturalism is an explanatory strategy, which is based on a more original experience. As Husserl remarks, we never encounter other humans as physical bodies on which a psychical layer is causally dependent. We naturally encounter other *persons*, and this means something completely different. Our most natural attitude is actually personalistic. If we try to reduce human behaviour to its physical causes, we not only import scientific categories into the human realm and hence commit a category-mistake, but we also eliminate what is typical for man. Husserl speaks of a "surplus" which is not thematized in the naturalistic approach (Husserl, 1952, p. 140, 1989, p. 147). To explain depression by a malfunction in the brain due to a reduction of serotonin and melatonin is a valid scientific insight, but it is an oversimplified abstraction and in that sense it doesn't really help to understand the behaviour of the depressed person and the other multiple personal, psychological, existential, social, relational and so on reasons of her pathology. Physiopsychical dependencies do not suffice to understand the subject and her properties, what Husserl also calls the personal or spiritual (*geistige*) individuality of man (Husserl, 1952, p. 139, 1989, p. 147). We also have to take into account how personality is motivated by social and cultural environment. In order to understand how man relates to his environment, categories such as causality and explanation can play no role. Motivation and understanding (*Motivation* and *Verstehen*) belong to another region. Physicalism, which reduces all phenomena to psychophysical processes, thus leads to a loss of man. "*Vom ganzen Menschen ist nichts mehr übrig*" (There is nothing left from man as such), says Husserl quite firmly (Husserl, 1992, p. 158). Human beings are more than psychophysical beings, and consequently understanding and explaining their existence requires another approach. For Husserl a correct explanation depends on a correct description, and it is here that naturalism fails. So both (description and explanation) are linked. Hence Husserl's argument is that once you correctly describe the phenomenon, you understand why naturalism's explanations are wrong. You then also understand why you need other, i.e., non-naturalistic explanations (hermeneutical ones, or social, cultural and so on).

Although physicalism can contribute to the study of human beings in so far as they are animated beings, it is nevertheless absurd *(widersinnig)* when it pretends to be the correct understanding and explanation of humanity. The naturalist doesn't talk nonsense (*Unsinn*) then, nor is what she is saying contradictory – she doesn't necessarily commit any logical mistakes as in the case of formal or analytical absurdity. But her approach to humanity is materially absurd by confusing regions. It is only in so far as human beings can be considered a part of physical and biological nature that naturalism concerning the organism is valid. But any claim to a complete understanding and explanation of human behaviour and culture is absurd, simply because man can't be reduced to an organism.

With Husserl I conclude that naturalism about human existence in general and about the body in particular results in a meaningful, non-contradictory but nevertheless absurd theory, which has to be exposed as the result of a category mistake. When it comes to understanding the body's sensitivity, it is clear that a causal explanation can only explain the functional dependency of sensations on stimuli, but can never elucidate the subjective experience of these sensations. Today, one could hear Husserl say that the explanatory gap is unbridgeable. But his claim is actually stronger. There is no explanatory gap, once one abandons the naturalistic approach and starts from the experience of the body as a freely moveable organ of perception and as the expression of personal life. This "subjective object" is subjectively experienced as the sensitive organ of perception, invested with consciousness. As remarked earlier, it is the mode of being of perceptual consciousness and of personal life, which from the outset is embodied. Any attempt to translate this into a naturalistic problematic, which searches to causally explain the presence of sensations and other mental processes in terms of non-conscious physiological processes, or to deny their existence on this basis (cf. the free-will discussion), commits a category mistake. One then applies to the body the notion of a physical organism, to which it is not reducible. Or to phrase it differently, sensitivity is a property of the lived body, but not in so far as it is a physical thing.[12]

Possibility of Apriori Knowledge

Ryle considered absurdities to be the key to detecting category differences. Thus, e.g., the statement "She came home in a flood of tears and a sedan-chair" (Ryle, 1949, p. 22) "is (…) absurd, because it conjoins terms of different categories" (Thomasson, 2013). For Husserl, this strategy is not available. Since materially absurd expressions are syntactically well formed and also meaningful, since they are neither non-sensical nor contradictory, the absurdity of the expression cannot be detected as easily as in Ryle's example. As indicated above, one needs ontological knowledge of the regions in question in order to identify that a category mistake is being made. Material absurdity is for Husserl a logical notion, based on ontology, and is not necessarily found in linguistic absurdity.

The ontological knowledge referred to here is an a priori, eidetical knowledge. It is arrived at by a process of abstraction that comes from phenomenological description. The exact nature of this description is a major subject for phenomenology, since the criticism of naturalism rests on the claim that a description in the so-called naturalistic attitude (*natüralistische Einstellung*) misreads the data. As Husserl said, back to the things themselves also means to describe them as they present themselves, without a bias induced by empiricism or naturalism. He firmly argued for the need for a more original approach to human existence in his *Ideas II*, where he showed that an unbiased description of what he termed "the world of natural experience" (*natürliche Erfahrung*) calls for the so-called personalistic attitude (*personalistische Einstellung*) which only guarantees a correct description of the region of *Geist* or human existence. Only the phenomenological description and analysis in this attitude can found the ontology of *Geist*, which is the tool to identify naturalism as committing a category mistake when it interprets and understands human existence as an element of physical nature. The phenomenological description and analysis of the lived body and the critique of its naturalistic interpretation as a *Körper* given above illustrates what this means.

Others have explained the method Husserl uses to obtain this a priori knowledge, which he calls ideative abstraction (*ideierende Abstraktion*).[13] So I can summarize here this threefold method. We start from the unbiased, original experience of an object and then try to identify its constitutive elements. We do that by varying freely, eventually with the help of fantasy, its form, properties and so on in order to determine the basic, structural elements which constitute the object. These features appear to us as invariant on the basis of overlapping syntheses (*Deckungssynthesen*) between the different fantasised variants of the object. Thirdly, these essential properties become the object of a proper act of thought, the so-called *Wesensschau* (eidetical intuition). Let us consider shortly each of these three aspects.

Original experience means that one tries to describe how the object is given, what kind of experience is necessary in order to experience this particular object. As I remarked before, Husserl insists for instance that we cannot experience our proper body as a physical object, because of its sensitivity. If I cut my finger, I immediately have a pain-experience. This is where to start from, namely how the body is given. Sensitivity is a basic property of this 'object', and one can describe what this means for the experience of the body: it is not a material object, but a so-called subjective object because it is subjectively lived. It is thus given in a specific experience, the experience of lived embodiment.

We identify the constitutive elements of the object with the help of fantasy, which enables us to freely alter the object. Through this process of free variation, it appears that even this fantasy has to comply with certain rules. If we try to determine for instance what is essential for a material object, we can arbitrarily alter its form, movement, properties and even venture to neglect common physical rules. But it is unalterable and necessary that the object will have to appear in a spatio-temporal continuum, and that this has implications for the way its properties appear. It follows for instance that every colour is spatially extended, that every tone has a duration, and so on. In this way we discover an a priori rule for the perception of a material object, more precisely that it has to appear as a spatio-temporal thing.

These rules also determine the essential, structural properties of the object itself, which are the object of the so-called overlapping syntheses. This synthesis picks out the element that is necessarily the same in all the different representations of the object, which is freely changed in fantasy.

Finally, this leads to the identification of a common core element, which is grasped as the *eidos*. This grasping is a form of thinking, more precisely categorical thought (*kategorisches Denken*). The 'idea of the object' designates a categorical or regional a priori norm which necessarily determines every further specification of an object that belongs to this category. Ideative abstraction results in the givenness of the eidos as the essence or the invariant core of the object. This essence is the object of a proper intuition, the so-called *Wesensschau*. So, although it is arrived at through a process of careful description of the experience of the object, which is then subjected to variation in order to identify its common constitutive elements with the help of overlapping syntheses, the essence itself is not an abstract concept which is the result of a process of generalization. The latter procedure leads to empirical generalization but not to the intuition of the essence. The eidetical method and its specific intuition are of a proper kind. Since Husserl developed this method in his struggle against psychologism, he clearly emphasizes its difference from empirical generalization. When one starts with a particular object and concentrates on one of its characteristics and then subjects it to imaginative variation, this aspect of the object, which appears as constant throughout the different variations, becomes the object of a new intuition, whereby it is grasped as an idea. One should avoid interpreting this in a platonic or metaphyscial sense, although the terminology is clearly platonic.[14] The eidetical structures are the essential structures of reality and do not exist in themselves. Husserl developed in *Ideas III* the example of the eidos of a material thing.[15] The analysis of the human, spiritual world and its essential structures can be found in *Ideas II*, which is a masterpiece of Husserlian constitutive analyses, where the experience and the correlative ontology of nature, animated nature and "spirit" are described. This leads to eidetical insight into what is typical of these three regions, and in what sense they need to be distinguished. Blurring these categorical distinctions by interpreting one of the regions with concepts that essentially belong to another region amounts to material absurdity. Naturalism with regard to human existence commits this absurdity when it naturalizes the mind.

Conclusion

My claim that naturalism commits a category-mistake has consequences for assessing neuroscience. Neuroscience is a variant of naturalism which reduces aspects of consciousness and human existence to brain processes. The identification of this mistake has both ontological and methodological consequences. The absurdity of naturalism implies that human consciousness and existence are conceptualized with notions and theories that cannot be applied to them, because they do not belong to the ontological region called nature. Second, and because of this, the scientific methods and theories developed for nature cannot be used to elucidate and understand human existence. Contemporary debates about the (un)reality of the free will for instance, whereby arguments against its existence are allegedly borrowed from neuroscientific research, are simply futile, because they illustrate par excellence the absurdity of the naturalist approach.

For the neuroscientist, we have a free will when our actions are caused by conscious intentions. Experiments by Libet and others prove that the conscious intention to act, as reported by the subjects, is preceded by a non-conscious readiness-potential that signals the beginning of the movement (Libet, 2002). Libet concludes that our brain has already decided to initiate the movement before we become aware of our intention to move. Hence the claim made by others that the conscious will is an illusion (Wegner, 2002). This claim rests on a set of highly problematical presuppositions. It accepts, as the basis for its refutation, the ideo-motor theory developed by W. James, who understands the free will of the self in terms of conscious intentions which cause an action. The free self is identified with consciousness and it is assigned a causal role. In order to escape the looming dualism of this theory, it is further assumed that consciousness is a (non-conscious) brain process (Place, 1956, Swaab, 2010). The neuroscientist claims that the readiness-potential in Libet's experiment has to be understood as the non-conscious neural correlate of the (unconscious) intention or decision to act, which is unconsciously taken by our brain. This identification of readiness-potential and intention or decision to act is problematic, as Mele showed (Mele, 2009). Furthermore, one might legitimately ask if it makes sense at all to ascribe typically personal activities like having intentions and making decisions to non-conscious neurological processes. Finally, no researcher has succeeded as yet in identifying the non-conscious neural correlates of a conscious intention (Desmurget, 2013). And it is not likely that this will ever be possible, since there is a theoretical problem here, a material absurdity, which consists in identifying an (un) conscious intention with a non-conscious brain activity. Awareness or consciousness cannot be attributed to neurological processes. These processes can be described in terms of biochemical and other biological terms. But it is logically impossible to discover a property that indexes consciousness or unconsciousness, because these are not material properties. A non-conscious neural correlate cannot have an extra neurological property that means conscious or unconscious intention. To assume it can is to commit a category mistake. So to conclude that we have no free will because unconscious intentions in the guise of non-conscious readiness-potentials already initiated the action, of which we only afterwards form a conscious intention, is a non-sequitur. The identification of the readiness-potential with the unconscious intention is the logical problem. If this criticism is correct, one must conclude that this research results in a rather trivial finding, namely that brain processes cause brain processes and that these cause in turn further bodily movements: the non-conscious readiness-potential, the presumed neural correlate of the unconscious intention, initiates the motor brain processes, which cause the action. It is hardly imaginable how this finding can teach us something about the problem of free will, yet some claim that these results have important consequences for our idea of responsibility, and that this might even require substantial revisions to our penal law in the future. So refuting with the help of neuroscientific research the notion of free will, on the basis of its identification with the causal role of conscious intentions in action, may not be an innocent scientific claim: making it all the more necessary to point out the material absurdity of this approach.

Notes

1. "(…) Metaphysics (…) is compelled (…) to combine meaningful words in such a way that neither an analytic (or contradictory) statement nor an empirical statement is produced". Carnap, 1959, p. 76.
2. Landgrebe, 1963, pp. 143–162.
3. About this ontology of the lifeworld and the problem of different regions, see Husserl, 1992, pp. 140–160.
4. For the definition of the regions, see Husserl, 1974, § 55; also Husserl, 1985, pp. 432 ff.; Husserl 1971, § 7, § 19; Husserl, 1995, § 62 and Beilage XVII.
5. Husserl, 1952, p. 91. Husserl, 1971, §§ 3, 5,6 and 7. Husserl writes that "the idea of each science", and more precisely "the idea of its method (is) founded on the proper essence of the idea of its object". Husserl, 1971, p. 13.
6. "(…) das Wesen der Gegenstände und das zugehörige Wesen möglicher Erfahrung von Gegenständen der betreffenden Kategorie (…) schreibt alles Prinzipielle der Methode vor". (The essence of the objects and the concomitant essence of the possible experience of objects of this particular category determine the method in principle.) Husserl, 1971, p. 22.
7. See the title of § 34 of Husserl, 1952: Necessity of the Distinction between the Naturalistic and the Personalistic Attitudes.
8. Papineau, D. (2009).
9. Husserl mentions the experience of eating Santonin, which makes us see things as yellow. (Husserl, 1952, pp. 62 ff., Husserl, 1989, pp. 67 ff.).
10. Merleau-Ponty, 1945, p. 160.
11. Gallagher, S., Zahavi, D. (2008) and the bibliography in this work.
12. For Husserl, the existence of non-material properties of physical objects is not limited to the body and does not constitute any mystery. The beauty of a landscape, the meaning of words, the religious significance of a church, are further examples of what he calls non-material, ideal properties of material objects. These objects have to exist materially in order for these properties to be present, but they cannot be identified with or reduced to any of their material properties.
13. See Lohmar, 2003.
14. See Fonfara, 2008.
15. See Husserl, 1971, pp. 25–37.

References

Carnap, R. (1959). The Elimination of Metaphysics Through Logical Analysis of Language. In A. Ayer (Ed.). *Logical Positivism* (60–81). New York, NY: Free Press.
Desmurget, M. (2013). Searching for the neural correlates of conscious intention. *Journal of Cognitive Neuroscience, 25(6)*, 830–3.

Fonfara, Dirk. (2008). *Husserls Überlegungen zum Eidos Welt in Forschungsmanuskripten der zwanziger und dreißiger Jahre mit einer Bezugnahme auf die, Ontologie der Lebenswelt" der Krisis-Schrift.* [Husserl's Reflections on the Essence World in Research Manuscripts of the 20s and 30s in Relation to the "Ontology of the Lifeworld" in the Crisisbook]. Retrieved from http://www.dgphil2008.de/fileadmin/download/Sektionsbeitraege/13-3_Fonfara.pdf.

Gallagher, S., & Zahavi, D. (2008). *The Phenomenological Mind.* New York, NY: Routledge.

Husserl, E. (1952). *Ideen zur einer Reinen Phänomenologie und Phänomenologischen Philosophie. Zweites Buch: Phänomenologische Untersuchungen zur Konstitution.* [Ideas Pertaining to a Pure Phenomenology and Phenomenological Philosophy. Second Book: Phenomenological Investigations of Constitution]. Husserliana 4. M. Biemel (Ed.). The Hague, Netherlands: Martinus Nijhoff.

Husserl, E. (1962). *Ideas: General Introduction to Pure Phenomenology.* Translated by W. R. Boyce Gibson. New York, NY: Collier Books.

Husserl, E. (1969). *Formal and Transcendental Logic.* Translated by D. Cairns. The Hague, Netherlands: Martinus Nijhoff.

Husserl, E. (1971). *Ideen zur einer reinen Phänomenologie und phänomenologischen Philosophie. Drittes Buch: Die Phänomenologie und die Fundamente der Wissenschaften.* [Ideas Pertaining to a Pure Phenomenology and Phenomenological Philosophy. Third book: Phenomenology and the Foundation of the Sciences]. Husserliana 5. M. Biemel (Ed.). The Hague, Netherlands: Martinus Nijhoff.

Husserl, E. (1973). *Cartesianische Meditationen und Pariser Vorträge.* [Cartesian Meditations and Parisian Lectures]. Husserliana 1. S. Strasser (Ed.). The Hague, Netherlands: Martinus Nijhoff.

Husserl, E. (1974). *Formale and transzendentale Logik. Versuch einer Kritik der logischen Vernunft.* [Formal and Transcendental Logic. Essay of a Critique of Logical Reason]. Husserliana 17. P. Janssen (Ed.). The Hague, Netherlands: Martinus Nijhoff.

Husserl, E. (1975) *Logische Untersuchungen. Erster Teil. Prolegomena zur reinen Logik. Text der 1. und der 2. Auflage. Halle: 1900, rev. ed. 1913.* [Logical Investigations. First Part. Prolegomena to a Pure Logic. Text of the 1. and 2. Edition. Halle 1900, rev. ed. 1913]. Husserliana 18. E. Holenstein (Ed.). The Hague, Netherlands: Martinus Nijhoff.

Husserl, E. (1976a) *Ideen zu einer reinen Phänomenologie und phänomenologischen Philosophie. Erstes Buch: Allgemeine Einführung in die reine Phänomenologie. 1. Halbband: Text der 1.–3. Auflage - Nachdruck.* [Ideas Pertaining to a Pure Phenomenology and Phenomenological Philosophy. First book: General Introduction into Pure Phenomenology]. Husserliana 3/1. K.Schuhmann (Ed.). The Hague, Netherlands: Martinus Nijhoff.

Husserl, E. (1976b*) Die Krisis der europäischen Wissenschaften und die transzendentale Phänomenologie. Eine Einleitung in die phänomenologische Philosophie.* [The Crisis of the European Sciences and Transcendental Phenomenology. An Introduction to Phenomenological Philosophy]. Husserliana 6. W. Biemel (Ed.). The Hague, Netherlands: Martinus Nijhoff.

Husserl, E. (1984). *Logische Untersuchungen. Zweiter Band: Untersuchungen zur Phänomenologie und Theorie der Erkenntnis.* [Logical Investigations. Second Volume: Research on Phenomenology and Theory of Knowledge]. Husserliana 19/1. U. Panzer (Ed.). The Hague: M. Nijhoff.

Husserl, E. (1985). *Erfahrung und Urteil.* [Experience and Judgment]. L. Landgrebe (Ed). Hamburg: Felix Meiner.

Husserl, E. (1989). *Ideas Pertaining to a Pure Phenomenology and to a Phenomenological Philosophy, Second Book. Studies in the Phenomenology of Constitution.* Coll. Works vol. 3. Translated by R. Rojcewicz and A. Schuwer. Dordrecht: Kluwer.

Husserl, E. (1992). *Die Krisis der europaischen Wissenschaften und die transzendentale Phänomenologie. Ergänzungsband. Texte aus dem Nachlass 1934–1937.* [The Crisis of the European

Sciences and Transcendental Phenomenology. Completing Volume. Texts from the Estate 1934–1937]. Husserliana 29. R. N. Smid (Ed.). The Hague, Netherlands: Kluwer Academic Publishers.

Husserl, E. (1995). *Logik und allgemeine Wissenschaftstheorie. Vorlesungen 1917/18. Mit ergänzenden Texten aus der ersten Fassung 1910/11.* [Logic and General Theory of Science. Lectures 1917/1918. With completing texts from the first draft 1910/1911]. Husserliana 30. U. Panzer (Ed). The Hague, Netherlands: Kluwer Academic Publishers.

Husserl, E. (2001). *Logical Investigations.* Translated by J. N. Findlay. London: Routledge.

Husserl, E. (2002). Philosophy as Rigorous Science. Translated by Marcus Brainard. *The New Yearbook for Phenomenology and Phenomenological Philosophy II,* 249–95.

Kim, J. (2006). *Philosophy of Mind.* Cambridge, MA: Westview Press.

Landgrebe, L. (1963). Seinsregionen und regionale Ontologien in Husserls Phänomenologie. [Ontological Regions and Regional Ontologies in Husserl's Phenomenology]. In L. Landgrebe, *Der Weg der Phänomenologie* (143–162). Gütersloh: Gerd Mohn.

Libet, B. (2002). Do We Have Free Will? In E. Kane (Ed.), *Oxford Handbook on Free Will* (551–564). New York, NY: Oxford University Press.

Lohmar, D. (2003). Die phänomenologische Methode der Wesensschau und ihre methodische Prezision als eidetische Variation in der 'Phänomenologischen Psychologie'. [The Phenomenological Method of Eidetic Intuition and its Methodical Precision as Eidetical Variation in 'Phenomenological Psychology']. In D. Lohmar (Ed.), *E. Husserl. Phänomenologische Psychologie* (XVII – XLI). Hamburg: Meiner.

Mele, A. (2009). *Effective Intentions: The Power of Conscious Will.* Oxford: Oxford University Press.

Merleau-Ponty, M. (1945). *Phénoménologie de la perception.* [Phenomenology of Perception]. Paris: Gallimard.

Moran, D. (2008*).* Husserl's transcendental philosophy and the critique of naturalism. *Continental Philosophy Review, 41(4),* 401–425.

Papineau, D. (2009). Naturalism. *The Stanford Encyclopedia of Philosophy.* Retrieved from http://plato.stanford.edu/archives/spr2009/entries/naturalism/.

Place, U.T. (1956). Is Consciousness a Brain Process? *British Journal of Psychology, 47,* 44–50.

Ryle, G. (1990). *The Concept of Mind.* London UK: Penguin.

Smart, J.J.C. (1953). A Note on Categories. *British Journal for the Philosophy of Science, 4(15),* 227–8.

Swaab, D. (2010). *Wij zijn ons Brein.* [We are our Brain]. Amsterdam: Atlas-Contact.

Thomasson, A.L. (2002). Phenomenology and the Development of Analytic Philosophy. *Southern Journal of Philosophy, Vol. XL,* Supplement, 115–142.

Thomasson, A.L. (2013). Categories. *The Stanford Encyclopedia of Philosophy.* Retrieved from http://plato.stanford.edu/archives/fall2013/entries/categories/.

Wegner, D. (2002). *The Illusion of Conscious Will.* Cambridge, MA: The MIT Press.

PART II

Some Critiques

5

FROM GLOBAL ECONOMIC CHANGE TO NEUROMOLECULAR CAPITALISM[1]

Jessica Pykett

Introduction

Both psychological and neuroscientific insights have risen to prominence in a number of academic, policy and cultural fields since at least the 1990s. These fields increasingly provide both the truth claims on which diverse forms of policy and practice are based, and – crucially – the basis for critiquing these claims. One area in which they have had a significant impact is on economic theory and methodology. Research on economic decision making has a long history spanning the development of game theory in the 1940s, to theories of judgment which came to prominence in the 1970s. At its most basic, game theory refers to a mathematical approach for understanding the logic of strategic decision making in social situations of interdependence and conflict, whereas theories of judgment have a more psychological emphasis on the perception and handling of information in circumstances of uncertainty and incomplete knowledge (Goldstein & Hogarth, 1997, p. 9). For the purposes of this chapter, a key point to grasp from these complex literatures is that these theories of decision-making have provided economists with an account of individual rational choices which can be statistically modelled and from which probabilistic courses of action can be inferred. What we now regard as the sub-discipline of behavioural economics, however, emerged from at least two major developments. Firstly, a recognition of the limitations of utility-based theories of rational choice, and secondly, it stemmed from extensive experimental evidence which shed light on how real human actors often failed to conform to these logical models. By 2002, when Daniel Kahneman and Vernon Smith had received the prestigious Nobel Prize for their research on judgment and decision-making, behavioural economics had had at least thirty years to mature, and the field's increasingly prominent public profile had ensured that it became a significant explanatory framework for human decision-making with a clear impact beyond the academy. Since this time, several popular behavioural economics inspired texts such as *Nudge* (Thaler & Sunstein, 2008), *Predictably Irrational* (Ariely, 2008) and *Thinking Fast and Slow* (Kahneman, 2012) have become international best sellers.

But what might be the political significance of the influence of psychological and neuroscientific approaches in economic theory? The popularisation of these ideas by publishers and the media, the intellectual groundwork of specific political think tanks and the personality-focused processes of international policy transfer have meant that behavioural economics has won favour with several national governments including for instance, the UK (see John et al. 2011; Jones et al. 2013; Oliver, 2013), the USA (Sunstein, 2013), Singapore (Low, 2011) and Australia (Australian Public Service Commission, 2007). Recent public policy initiatives informed by behavioural economics have included pension policies, personal tax compliance, anti-obesity and anti-smoking programmes, organ-donation, recycling initiatives and sustainable travel planning, amongst others. The core focus of such policies and initiatives is to establish a new set of guiding principles behind policy design and delivery, which starts from the premise that humans are not rational economic actors but subject to various heuristics and biases which make us vulnerable to all manner of pre-existing subtle influences on our behaviour. It is the role of governments within this scenario to understand what drives behaviour and to promote effective ways of guiding citizens towards making decisions which are in their own long-term best interests. In order to achieve this, there is an increasing emphasis on the medical methodology of Randomised Control Trials within social science, behavioural science and decision-making research. This method promises to provide evidence to show whether these policies and initiatives will *work*, thus saving potential wastage of scarce public funds (Haynes et al. 2012).

Such policy initiatives share an epistemological commitment to experimental methods with the economic decision-making research already discussed here. Extending this empiricism even further is a new emphasis on understanding the neurochemical and neurobiological correlates of economic decision-making. This baton has been taken up by a more recent disciplinary development within economics, that of neuroeconomics. Neuroeconomics refers to the use of neuroscientific techniques for understanding economic decision-making, and is a term said to have been coined in 2001 at a conference held by the Gruter Foundation of Law at Princeton University, when the Society for Neuroeconomics was established (Glimcher et al. 2009, p. 8). Its roots are again found both within the judgement and decision-making theories of Tversky and Kahneman (1974) and the experimental methodologies of cognitive neuroscience. Neuroeconomics has also developed a distinctly popular appeal, with popular science writers heralding a new dawn of understanding the decision-making moment (Lehrer, 2009), not least how our brains are susceptible to the increasingly sophisticated techniques of so-called neuromarketers (e.g., Zweig, 2007). What the neuroeconomists can promise, in distinction to those favouring behavioural explanations, is some foundational scientific principles rooted in biology, chemistry and psychophysics, to explain the driving forces and causal structures determining our observable behaviours, ingrained in our evolutionary development, and yet applicable to all manner of contemporary everyday economic situations.

This chapter does not provide a comprehensive genealogy of research on economic decision making nor on the intersections and historical dialogues between economics and psychology (for such an account, see Sent, 2004). Rather, it examines the role that the fields of neuroeconomics and behavioural economics have played in providing brain-based and behaviourist explanations of economic decision-making within contemporary policy-making cultures. By developing a geographical critique of these disciplinary phenomena as they have emerged and evolved, the chapter interrogates how such economic knowledges actively produce the subjects, practices and spaces of 'neuromolecular capitalism'. The discipline of geography has long spanned the natural and social sciences as well as the humanities, providing biosocial insight into the constructedness of 'human nature' at a range of scales. Geography has the mutually constitutive relationship between humans and their environment at its core, and for the purposes of this chapter is used to develop a critique of the intersections between the political economic context of capitalism and the invocation by policy makers of neuroscientific explanation at the molecular scale. In particular the chapter identifies the popularization of the figure of an irrational or 'emorational' actor at the centre of economic theory and public policy making, drawing attention to the behavioural assumptions, biological determinism and geographical blind-spots of these new ways of envisaging human nature. Mobilising conceptual resources within the discipline of human geography, the chapter provides a critical account of the interrelations between a neurologically 'flawed' (post-rational) economic actor and her global economic context.

The chapter aims to identify a set of philosophical and political concerns that are raised pertaining to neuromolecular capitalism as a political economic formation, the truth-status of which is understood to be confirmed by its biological materiality. These concerns are threefold. The first is to question the existence and characteristics of something called neuromolecular capitalism as an object of enquiry and to examine its broader popularisation in public policy making. The second draws attention to the behavioural assumptions of a turn to neuroscientific explanations of human action – challenging the certainty with which appeals to brain functioning and behaviour are made by policy strategists. The third considers questions of reductionism and biological determinism in these self-appointed 'new' ways of knowing (economic) worlds – highlighting some of the dangers associated with these standpoints when it comes to designing policies focused on 'irrational' economic behaviours. By connecting these concerns, it is my intention to show how neuroeconomics and behavioural economics have begun to provide us with popular understandings of the post-rational human subject. Where these understandings are utilised in public policy making, there is a positive feedback effect; neuromolecular capitalism is positioned here as part of a 'brain culture' which suffuses our social worlds (see Pykett, 2015). The chapter begins by interrogating the novelty of neuro-economics and behavioural economics, investigating their coherence and unpacking the relationship they imply between biology and economics. It outlines the central problematization of human rationality offered in both approaches to economics. The chapter then goes on to outline the implications of their opposing models of cognition for policy making in the contemporary era. In the final section, attention is drawn to research from human geography which sheds new light on what is politically at stake when public policy makers use neuroscientific and behavioural knowledges in order to tackle 'irrational' economic behaviours in a range of social spheres.

Economy Meets Neurobiology

Neuroeconomics uses neuroscientific methods such as electroencephalography (EEG), which measures electrical impulses in the brain, functional Magnetic Resonance Imaging (fMRI) scanning technologies which visualise blood flows as they differ from the 'resting state' brain, hormonal measurements in the blood, and skin conductance measurements which measure states of psychological arousal. In addition, experimental methods such as pre- and post-test measurements, questionnaires, visual stimuli, game theory scenarios or dilemmas are often used. The hormone and neurotransmitter, dopamine, appears to have been a particularly significant explanatory factor within neuroeconomic studies. It is the chemical which has been used to explain many of the habitual, non-reflexive or automatic behaviours which make us amenable to forms of nudging more associated with behavioural economics. Dopamine is used in theories of loss aversion (avoiding immediate losses rather than taking longer term gains), short-term thinking (future discounting) and coupled with mirror neurons (said to prove empathy and social imitation). For brand marketer Martin Lindstrom, dopamine is also the reason we just can't stop shopping. In his popular business book, *Buy-ology* (Lindstrom, 2009), he describes how neuromarketing can help us to understand how our unconscious minds drive our consumer behaviours. A special status is preserved for dopamine as the key to the science of successful advertising. It provides the pivotal explanation behind the sense of reward, euphoria and impulsiveness that we often attach to the experience of shopping, and our ultimate addiction to it. Dopamine has attained such a celebrity status in the emerging world of neuromarketing and the neuroscience of the popular imagination, that it was recently dubbed 'the Kim Kardashian of neurotransmitters' (Bell, 2013)[2]; the ubiquitous source of our impulsive, addictive and reward-seeking behaviours. As Bell points out, however, there is relatively little attention paid in the media to dopamine's more mundane (but no less fundamental) functions, such as the role it plays in regulating movement, stimulating lactation, causing paranoia, signalling when you have had a near-miss or in the avoidance of unpleasant feelings and memories.

No doubt neuroeconomists will want to distance themselves from the neuro-marketers who are paid to secure brand futures, despite sharing some fundamental principles and methods. Leaving that aside, neuroeconomics has been variously defined as "the study of how the brain makes economic decisions" (Houser & McCabe, 2008, p. xv); "the use of cognitive and brain sciences to uncover the dynamics underlying economic decision making" (Basso et al. 2010, p. 217); the bringing together of economic theory with the empirical methods of neurobiology (Politser, 2008, p. 3); or even as a challenge to common constructs of economics (Camerer et al. 2005, p. 31). Paul Glimcher, often credited with coining the term neuroeconomics, sees its main role in terms of using "the insights of economic theory in the study of behaviour, brain and mind" (2004).

Already we stumble upon a crucial question for neuroeconomics: is it the application of neurobiological insights to economic theory, or is it in fact the application of economic models to neurobiological empirics? Which is the direction of disciplinary travel here? And is there really anything new about the bringing together of biological science and economics to challenge our assumptions about human decision-making? One of the central claims of neuroeconomics is that *Homo Economicus* is no more than an outmoded and parsimonious fantasy of economic modelling; but in other respects, neuroeconomics does not challenge important modes of economistic thinking. As Glimcher (2004, p. 336), an expert in the choice behaviours of monkeys notes, "economics is a biological science. It is the study of how humans choose". In this sense, neuroeconomists may not simply be using new neuroscientific insights and methods to improve and refine economic theory; instead, they begin with an economic model of individual behaviour that fails to challenge classical utility-maximizing accounts of human decision-making after all. Let us turn then to the specifics of the relationship engendered between biological and economic thinking within neuroeconomics and behavioural economics. To this end, the following sections highlight the continuities and distinctions between the sub-disciplines of neuro- and behavioural economics, arguing that contrary to popular perceptions of these fields, they both actually fail to fully deconstruct the neoclassical figure of *Homo Economicus*. Both of these disciplinary perspectives turn out to rely on a notion of the irrational economic actor who is largely understood as separate from their wider environmental or geographical context. This has specific implications for how public policy makers conceive of (and in turn, construct) irrational economic behaviours.

Emorationality

As has been suggested above, the apparent demise of *Homo Economicus* is a subject given extensive treatment in nearly all of the existing literature on neuroeconomics, and provides an important continuity between neuroeconomics and behavioural economics (although there are some important distinctions as I shall go on to explain). Pointing out the naïve simplification of rational economic man is also the principal focal point of much of the literature which has popularised applications of neuroeconomics and behavioural economics. This problematisation of human rationality has a long precedent, with Herbert Simon's (1955) work on the bounded nature of rationality often cited as the precursor to the later establishment of behavioural economics. Simon showed that people make best-fit or 'satisficing' decisions in contexts in which access to information is necessarily limited. This observation was extended in the work of Tversky and Kahneman (1974), who identified the importance of subjective heuristic rules or biases applied to decision-making in situations of uncertainty, as opposed to a probabilistic or computational model assumed by neoclassical economists. These heuristics, relating to misrepresentations of probabilities and chance – relying on the most available or plausible clues as to the likelihood of something happening, or mistakenly 'anchoring' one's judgments to questionable starting points – lead predominantly to making *systematic* errors of judgment which fundamentally challenge the notion of the "idealized person" (Tversky and Kahneman, 1974, p. 19). Elsewhere, it has been argued that such heuristics are actually an efficient, accurate and sensible means by which people make decisions in the absence of full information and under conditions of uncertainty, leading Girgerenzer and Brighton (2009, p. 107) to find value in the personage of *Homo Heuristics*. The neurologically flawed individual is at the heart of these brain-based explanations of the economic actor (or economic-based explanations of the brain). But whilst the figure of the 'emorational man' (notably still a gendered figure) emerges as a challenge to the neoclassical characterisation of *homo economicus*, there are important methodological and conceptual distinctions in the way in which these fields model the brain. It is these distinctions which have consequences for those seeking to apply the insights of neuroeconomics and behavioural economics to problems in public policy, as the following section outlines.

Dualistic or Monistic Decision-Making in Policy

Despite apparent agreement between neuroeconomic and behavioural economic approaches on the post-rational human subject, important differences are too often brushed over in the imperative to seek new applications and policy implications derived from these research insights. Indeed some economists have argued that behavioural economics exists entirely *within* the neoclassical framework, finding the central dismissal of rational economic man problematic: "claims by behavioural economists that observed systematic 'irrationality' in human behaviour 'refutes' standard neoclassical theory should be rejected" (Ross et al. 2008, p. ix). Instead, the work of Ross et al. on neuroeconomics shows how economic models, including that of "true economic agents" can account for the deviation of real human behaviour from expected, generalizable and abstracted patterns.

In outlining "the politics of models", Schüll and Zaloom (2011, p. 528) provide one of the most comprehensive accounts of the distinctions between neuroeconomics and behavioural economics, based on interviews with many prominent proponents of neuroeconomics and behavioural economics. They identify a pivotal schism between "one- and two-brain models" of human cognition. For neuroeconomists and neuroscientists trained in biological methods, the decision-making subject has a holistic brain, albeit one characterised by internal conflict. This conflict is not reducible to a dualistic model or any notion of discrete functional brain regions; the brain must always work as a whole system, and theories of the brain must always be justified by real, physical and observable phenomena (Schüll & Zaloom, 2011, p. 522). In contrast, behavioural economists favour a two-brain model based on internal competition. This model opposes the rational, reasoning, abstract and long-term to the irrational, limbic, emotional, affective and impulsive parts of the brain. This is often used to account for what behavioural economists term 'hyperbolic discounting' or myopic decision-making, which appears to go against traditional models of rationality. It is a model which points towards the systematic *irrationality* of our heuristic biases and apparent inconsistencies (Schüll and Zaloom, 2011, p. 523). The key point here is that while there seems to be an apparent consensus within neuroeconomics and behavioural economics on the necessary demise of *Homo Economicus*, there are some crucial differences in the way in which they model the human brain. Thus, the relative status of biological explanation (in neuroeconomics) or economic explanation (in behavioural economics) is clearly distinguished. In the neuroeconomic account the monistic brain is viewed as a biophysical and observable reality, whilst the behavioural economic account posits a theoretical competition between economic choices made by the rational versus the irrational mind. This distinction is underplayed in the rush to popularise and utilise behavioural insights in public policy. Drawing attention back to these discontinuities therefore has the potential to provide fresh grounds on which to investigate the politics of contemporary attempts to govern that very irrationality, and explains why it is behavioural economics rather than neuroeconomics which has been most widely adopted in policy.

The notion of systematic irrationality features prominently in Thaler and Sunstein's (2008, p. 19) narrative of a battle between the 'automatic' and 'reflective' minds. They suggest policy interventions which address the need to cultivate the reflective mind, and demand decision-making environments which take advantage of the automatic mind to favour more 'desirable' choices. This approach has been taken up in recommendations for a more emotionally literate public policy from the UK's Cabinet Office/Institute for Government (Dolan et al. 2010). Here, Dan Ariely's (2008) work on the human propensity to be 'predictably irrational' is cited as a context for government to replace the traditional tools of taxation, information and hard regulation with smarter policy levers which fully recognise that "our behaviour is guided not by the perfect logic of a super-computer that can analyse the cost-benefits of every action" (Dolan et al. 2010, p. 13).

As Schüll and Zaloom (2011) note, policy makers can be rather selective when it comes to which conception of human (ir)rationality they choose; the 'one-brained' model from neuroeconomics or the 'two-brained' model posed by behavioural economics. The neuroeconomic approach necessitates policies which start from the position that people can be placed along a spectrum of competency in relation to their tendency toward short-termist and potentially self-defeating behaviours, and that these are pre-determined within their neural systems (Schüll & Zaloom 2011, p. 530). Policies based on neuroeconomic thinking therefore include education, pharmaceutical treatment, training in self-management and attempts to change a person's conscious values. Such policies would by their very nature be highly interventionist for those citizens marked out as more irrational or impulsive. By contrast, the account offered by behavioural economists (including both Camerer 'asymmetric paternalism' and Thaler and Suntein's 'libertarian paternalism') appears to be more popular in policy making precisely because of its conception of the human subject as two-brained and thus open to blanket forms of correction aimed at whole populations:

> Although dual-systems [behavioural economic] advocates recast this subject as neurological rather than moral, and as an incipient, rather than a consistent, rational actor, they preserve intact its essential capacity for rationality – and thus for governability within a liberal framework.
>
> *(Schüll and Zaloom, 2011, p. 532)*

Here we learn that for behavioural economists, people are ultimately rational but somehow led astray (by their conflicted minds, emotional drivers, internal biases and immediate decision-making environments). The libertarian paternalist approach sparked by behavioural economics therefore favours designing 'choice architectures' which nudge people's more rational and reasonable brains towards decisions which are not self-defeating, but welfare enhancing – without apparently compromising subjective freedoms. It is by brushing over the neurobiological complexity of (ir)rationality that behavioural economists can offer policy solutions that appeal to policy makers who seek liberal, individualised solutions to often intractable social and structural problems. At the very least, favouring this dualistic and economistic model of the brain and behaviour raises questions about the politics of governing practices based on selective conceptions of consciousness and the social. Arguably, however, both of the very specific constructions of the economic agent and human nature found among neuroeconomics and behavioural economics remain to be fully challenged. Because of the way in which they decouple the human subject from her environmental context. Is it really the case, as argued by the French government's Centre d'analyse stratégique, that *Homo Economicus* has been superseded by a more emotionally sensitive, psychologically complex and neurobiologically knowable *"homo consumerus"* (Oullier & Sauneron, 2010, p. 13)? Or is it more that the human brain itself is not well suited to capitalist economies? In essence, it is by discerning the precise models of the human subject selected by policy makers, and unpacking their basis in biological and economic thinking that we can generate an alternative analysis of a more geographically situated subject. Economic geography is well placed to take this analysis forward by forwarding understandings of the economic actor as both shaped by and an author of their environmental (cultural, social and economic) contexts. However, as the next section also argues, those economic geographers already explicitly interested in behavioural economics could go further in attending to the political implications of a world in which the economic actor is reconfigured as an irrational subject.

Cerebral Subjects in a Global Economic Context: A Human Geography Perspective

Neuroeconomics and behavioural economics within economic theory signify the culmination of a long running relationship between the biological sciences and economic thinking. The Darwinian inclinations of Adam Smith, and Friedrich Hayek's interest in psychology and cultural evolution theory are well known (Ulshöfer, 2008, p. 213). What human geography can offer is a sustained political critique of the evolutionary aspects of behaviour and the biological correlates of bounded decision-making. These are important but problematic developments in economics. The critique offered in the remainder of the chapter is based on an exposition of the cultural- and political-economic foundations of neural, psychological and behavioural explanation. Given the contemporary value ascribed to neuroeconomics and behavioural economics as a novel orthodoxy in public policy making and popular psychological thought, it is crucial to draw closer attention to their contested nature.

Work by economic geographers such as Clark (2010; 2011) and Strauss (2008) provides an important starting point for the development of a human geographical critique of neuromolecular capitalism. Such authors highlight the limitations of behavioural economics and cognitive science from a geographical point of view. Strauss (2008), for instance questions the way in which behavioural economics leaves intact the culturally specific and biologically essentialist ideology of the autonomously acting individual. She draws attention to the role of cultural and geographical context in decision-making, arguing for a far more sustained critique of the assumptions of behaviouralism (Strauss, 2008, p. 8). Similarly, Clark (2011) attends to the deficiencies, assumptions and methods of behavioural economics by again elaborating on the contextual determinants of decision-making, as well as better understanding the interaction between context and behavioural traits. This approach is applied to an analysis of the global financial crisis, specifically here the part played by myopic or short-term thinking in sustaining market volatility (Clark, 2011).

Clark does draw heavily on the new behavioural and neuroeconomic 'insights' toward which this chapter has remained sceptical, suggesting that geography can at times be drawn towards neuroscientific forms of explanation. To a certain extent, he attributes the global financial crisis to fundamental behavioural flaws amongst both bankers and regulators. These include: myopia, discounting the future, overconfidence, hubris and salience (Clark, 2011, p. 8), and this approach has been criticised from within geography (Lewis, 2011). However, Clark (2011, p. 6) does address economic geographers' concerns about universal or biologically determinist accounts of human nature and can therefore be understood as forwarding a context-sensitive account of economic decision making. It is therefore in identifying the behavioural geographies of the global financial crisis, that he is able to point toward the wider political and regulatory implications of this novel understanding of market instability. These geographies relate specifically to a global financial context which has exacerbated myopic predispositions. The three principal geographical factors highlighted by Clark (2011, p. 12) are: the bounded nature of markets; the role of spatially specific community norms in market valuation and risk assessment; and the (spatial and temporal) distance of investing agents (traders) from the companies on behalf of whom they invest. Clark notes that behavioural economists may have failed to pay sufficient attention to these contextual and interactional factors.

Hence for economic geographers like Strauss and Clark, behaviours are never wholly individual, neural or psychological, but are always in dynamic interaction with context. Notwithstanding this attention to the cultural and social determinants of behaviour, however, there may remain potential limits to this approach. The conclusion that the global financial crisis can be explained by the interaction of myopic predispositions and contextual factors still leaves intact the sense that the instability of global capitalism is a temporary, systems-based and thus soluble problem rather than one of inherent inequalities and injustices in economic, political and regulatory power. Furthermore, the appeal to universal human behaviours does not take account of the cultural specificity of norm-formation and indeed constructions of the human. In this way, the behavioural-contextual approach offered by Clark may be too optimistic about the possibility of correction, and by implication does not go far enough towards an understanding of how global financial capitalism is itself produced, performed and sustained. So too, the question of whether and how an economic hegemony might be culturally internalised in the biological human subject remains unresolved. A more wide-ranging critical geographical analysis of the implications of the neuroscientific economic orthodoxies for understanding governing practices, economic cultures and the cultural-political imagination itself is therefore of value.

Geographers have begun to make tentative forays into the complex social worlds of neuroeconomics and behavioural economics. The role of these novel economic orthodoxies in the geographies of public policies aimed at 'behaviour change' has been discussed at length by Gill and Gill (2012); Jones et al. (2011); Whitehead et al. (2011); Pykett et al. (2011) and their function in constituting dislocated and curiously disembodied feminised subject positions is considered by

Pykett (2012). Elsewhere, Gail Davies (2010) has drawn attention to the reductionist tendencies of neuroscience's experimental research methods and has questioned the applicability of 'mouse models' to explanations of human behaviour, in particular as justifications for pharmaceutical interventions. Meanwhile, Derek McCormack (2007, p. 360) provides an interesting account of how neurochemistry came to dominance as a way of mapping the "material economies of the human body" in the 1950s and 60s. His work is part of a vocal set of debates around the 'politics of affect' in human geography, which has implications for the kinds of questions that economic geographers might ask about neuroeconomics and behavioural economics. To provide a brief summary of these critical dialogues, the use of neuroscientific insights by human geographers promoting a turn to affect and/or non-representational approaches has recently been called into question by Papoulias and Callard (2010). The central insight used by affect theorists is that the brain and/or body acts before we can conceptualise, cognise, think or know what we are doing. Geographers such as Thrift (2004) and McCormack (2007) have sought a rapprochement between the social sciences and biological sciences through attention to the non-cognitive determinants of action. But Papoulias and Callard contend that this turn to affect has relied too heavily on the selective take up of certain lessons from certain neuroscientists. They take issue with both Thrift and McCormack's claim that a neuroscientific account is central to the very possibility of thinking, while others have pointed out a tendency for affect theorists to display a fundamental distrust of people's capacity to represent their own conscious thoughts (Barnett, 2008; Pile, 2010).

These debates within human geography raise some distinctive political and philosophical concerns which might usefully generate critical approaches to the "behavioural revolution" (Clark, 2010, p. 166) sweeping mainstream economic thought. The first concern is a call for a 'political geography' of neuromolecular capitalism, arguing that neuroeconomics and behavioural economics amount to much more than disciplinary developments. They are generative of a novel kind of "brain-world" (Malabou, 2008, p. 39), which requires further analysis in and of itself. The second further develops a critique of the behaviouralism found in neuroeconomics and behavioural economics, arguing that economic agents have been too easily conceptualised as decision-making actors as opposed to cultural subjects. The final concern is with the potential reductionism and biological determinism of neuroeconomics and behavioural economics' conceptions of human consciousness. While human geographers are arguably well-placed to question these "reductionist returns" (Davies, 2010), there are also signs that those geographers philosophically favouring materialist and/or non-representational positions resurrect these same old problems, with deleterious consequences for the political currency of the discipline as a whole. The following section examines these three concerns more closely.

Critiquing Neuromolecular Capitalism

Constructing the Brain-World

In an article picked up by *The New York Times* in February 2010[3], German authors Ewa Hess and Hennric Jokeit (2009) use the term "neuromolecular capitalism" to refer to the way in which the nineteenth-century capitalist concept of psychoanalytic neuroses has been replaced by a contemporary concept of libertarian self-improvement – whether through treating depressive illness, the development of neuro-enhancers or the increasing control of our states of attention. The contention here is that the burgeoning of neuroscientific research journals, conferences and institutes signifies much more than mere disciplinary, technological or methodological evolution. And as previously noted, the enthusiasm with which neuroscientific insights have been taken up by governments, educators, marketers and economists attests to the potential impact of such developments in everyday life.

An exciting area of academic interest has therefore come out of a sense of disquiet with the cultural, political, social and economic implications for this new relationship we have with our brains, changing how we interact with and act on the world. Critical neuroscience builds upon philosophical concerns for understanding subjectivity, mind-body consciousness and social and object relations in order to critically analyze the role of neuroscience in society – seeing "neuroscience itself as a cultural activity" (Choudhury et al. 2009, p. 63). These authors develop a broadly Foucauldian perspective which examines the social and cultural contexts in which neuroscientific 'discoveries' are constructed. This involves both close attention to laboratory methods and genealogical accounts which outline the historical contingency of the neuroscientific 'moment' and a molecular scale of explanation (Abi-Rached & Rose, 2010).

Others, too, see neuroscientific developments as intimately wrapped up with the late capitalist mode of production. In a study of the neuroscience of the 'brain at rest', geographer, Felicity Callard et al. (2010, p. 23), for instance, argue that even "the resting brain has been territorialized: it is conceptualized and materialized as a matrix that is constituted as perpetually productive ..." As part of a post-Fordist knowledge economy, neuroscience is thus mobilized to show the creative and productive capital of apparently aimless forms of inattention such as daydreaming. It is not too much of a leap, therefore, to see how the brain sciences are implicated in flexible capitalism; the kind of capitalism which requires emotionally intelligent, self-managing, risk-handling, relationship-managing, adaptive and entrepreneurial economic actors (Ulshöfer, 2008, p. 196; Boltanski & Chiapello, 2005).

It is not simply that neuroeconomics and behavioural economics have been shown to be driven by the commercial interests of the pharmaceutical industry, state imperatives for self-governing populations, or the late capitalist requirement of a flexible, adaptable, creative and emotionally intelligent workforce. There is also a circularity issue here. In popular science, media representations, and in the application of neuroeconomics and behavioural economics, ideal citizen-subjects are re-imagined through a market economic model of individual decision-making. This influences how we conceive of human nature, 'normal' behaviour and personal responsibility. For example, the arguably very social notion of trust gets framed as merely an expression of oxytocin levels (the hormone said to indicate trust) – with ovulating women being categorized as inherently untrustworthy due to raised levels of progesterone said to inhibit oxytocin uptake (Durante & Saad, 2010). Here political-economic issues around worker relationships are reframed as biophysical questions relating to hormone levels.

Behaviouralism: Constructing the Subject

The second problem with too readily accommodating neuroeconomics and behavioural economics is an insensitivity to the residual behaviouralism of these disciplinary knowledges. The shortcomings of behaviouralism have been well-rehearsed within geography (e.g., Walmsley and Lewis 1993). Despite having mounted a significant challenge to *Homo Economicus*, introduced new models of the perceptual environment, and foregrounded individual experience, behavioural geography was vigorously criticised as overly descriptive, voluntaristic, naïvely empiricist and insufficiently aware of the cultural, social, political and economic contexts which shape decision-making. In presenting mechanical and atomistic accounts of human cognition (in behavioural geography and repeated by neuroeconomics and behavioural economics), the constitutive role of the brain-world itself, interpretative schema and self-knowledge produced by the neurosciences is fundamentally ignored. Here we see the potential contribution of more cultural theoretical traditions to resolving the question of how neuroeconomics and behavioural economics are implicated in re-constructing the post-rational subject within both the popular imagination and in applications which shape our everyday experiences. This work also goes some way to outlining how despite an emphasis on systematic irrationality, we still act as if we are knowing, reflexive and rational subjects.

Similarly, while neuroeconomics and behavioural economics too reject the rational economic actor, the economic actor remains the key object of enquiry. It has been argued that this objectification of the human subject may be a result of the methodological limitations of experimental neuroscientific research. While people tested in neuroscience laboratories may be described as research 'subjects', their histories and biographies are not usually deemed to be important, their subjective experiences of having various tests exacted upon them can go unnoticed, and the cultural stereotypes to which reporting scientists sometimes resort may all be downplayed in the search for objectified and generalisable findings (Ulshöfer, 2008, p. 202). Challenges to both the abstraction of rational economic man and to behaviouralism are not unprecedented outside of a neurological or behavioural framework. Such challenges have been mounted from within economic theory, through feminist economics (at once sceptical of the masculinised *Homo Economicus* and biological determinism) and the French-based movement of 'Post-Autistic economics (PAE)' (Ferber & Nelson, 1993; Fullbrook, 2003). Neither field prioritises the brain in their analyses, instead drawing attention to the structural constraints on decision-making, relations of power within economic systems and the wider cultural embeddedness of economic behaviour. The power of their political critique is based on an attention to the constitutive role of economics itself in reproducing an autistic (read metaphorically rather than medically as an undifferentiated economics obsessed with mathematical modelling, socially irresponsible and without a theory of the mind) and "culturally sexist" epistemology (Nelson, 2001). Therefore, there are ample theoretical resources available from within heterodox economics and economic geography from which to further interrogate the political implications of neuroeconomics and behavioural economics – both as constitutive of the brain world and of neural forms of citizen-subjectivity.

Biologial Determinism: Constructing "Monkey Models" of Human Consciousness

Finally, it is important to further interrogate the biologism of neuroeconomics and behavioural economics, by which I mean both a tendency toward biological determinism, and the broader concurrence of biological thinking and economic thought (which as previously noted, travels in both disciplinary directions). Just as Davies (2010) has cautioned against the use of "mouse models" in developing neuroscientific applications for mental health, so too must we warn against the "monkey models" of human cognition sometimes forwarded by neuroeconomics and behavioural economics. For example, one of the architects of neuroeconomics, Paul Glimcher's lab research on the choice behaviours of monkeys found that "the behaviours of individual parietal neurons are well described by economic tools" (2004, p. 322). Not only can the world of monkeys be understood through an economic lens, but in turn, the conception of economic behaviour is one which is ultimately produced by neurobiology. In this sense, the social sciences would have little role to play in understanding behaviour, economics or indeed human consciousness. There is by no means universal agreement amongst proponents of neuroeconomics and behavioural economics as to the status of the social and of consciousness, yet there is much hyperbole about the value of neurobiological thinking, particularly in the more populist literatures. Glimcher, for example, is assured that any philosophical debate around free will and consciousness has now been solved:

> Free will may simply be the name we give to the probabilistic behaviours that are mixed strategy solutions. Our subjective experience of deciding may be what we experience when a mixed strategy solution requires the activation of a lawful [biophysical] neuronal randomizer.
>
> *(Glimcher 2004, p. 342)*

With the problem of free will, voluntary agency and conscious decision-making resolved, there would be little room for any notion of responsibility, ethical delib-eration or social and political debate. Indeed, proponents of neuroeconomics such as Ross et al. (2008, p. 10) consider themselves to ascribe to both a "sensible behav-iouralism" and a "pragmatic reductionism" (Ross et al., p. 121). They are explicitly dismissive of what they term the defeatist notion that seemingly irrational, addictive behaviours are a "complex social syndrome" best given over to (by implication 'mere') novelists and oral historians (Ross et al. 2008, p. 7). Ainslie (1992, p. 1) is more accommodating, stating that self-defeating behaviour may be symptomatic of modern industrial societies. But the general consensus is that "like all other known biological processes, consciousness is subject to natural selection and follows the physical laws of the universe" (Glimcher, 2004, p. 344). At its most basic, this mecha-nistic account of personhood requires unpacking.

As the previous section argued, there are resources from within geography which may contribute to this unpacking of the cultural subjects of neuroeconomics and behavioural economics, although there are equally warnings about naïvely 'reading off' subject positions from political rationalities, economic projects or the culture of neuroscience. More specifically, the lesson here is that much philosophical ground-work remains to be done within human geography to provide a normative critique of the neuromolecular capitalism arguably characteristic of contemporary West-ern economies. Moreover, there is a need to look beyond geography to emerging research in critical neuroscience to begin to find common grounds for political engagement of this nature.

Conclusions

The trend toward neuroscientific explanation appears unstoppable in its popularity and reach, with the 'neuro' prefix finding more and more endings and applica-tions. The neural agenda becomes enmeshed with other forms of knowledge, as seen in the development of neuroeconomics and behavioural economics. I have examined how the adoption of insights from neuroeconomics and behavioural economics signifies two important continuities: firstly, the ongoing dominance of economic orthodoxies in developing public policy strategies in Western economies, and secondly, the enduring concordance between biological and economic episte-mologies. Economic geography has begun to pay attention to these relatively new economic fields, but in some cases has over-estimated the extent to which they pose a genuine challenge to mainstream economic theory. There remains a need to find the means by which to investigate the wider cultural and political implications of conceptualizing economic practices, knowledges and actors in these neurosci-entific terms. Moreover, attempts to identity the biological correlates of economic decision-making within the confines of the brain – whether it be for the purposes of understanding the 'financial brain', the 'short-sighted brain', the 'emorational brain', the learning brain', the 'political brain', the 'responsible brain' or the 'anti-social brain' – point to a more concerted attempt to re-imagine the human subject in ways with which critics from the humanities and social sciences are well placed to explore and explain.

Within the wider discipline of geography, engagement with philosophies of the subject and of subjectification are well-developed, whether from humanistic, Marxist, feminist, psychoanalytic or post-structural approaches. And economic geography has been forthcoming in deriving novel perspectives from this cultural turn which make headway in rethinking the economic actor as cultural subject and the economy as performed. While substantial disagreement remains, the question of why we continue to act as if we are knowing subjects remains an important enigma. Why do we still act as if we are able to give form to the world, make decisions and judgments and partake in acts of refusal, when neurobiological explanations for consciousness and behavioural drivers of human action suggest otherwise? The widely presaged undoing of the human subject within human geography may therefore be premature (Thrift, 2008; Wylie, 2010), and there remains extensive work to be done in order to develop an adequate account of the cultural, political, philosophical and economic implications of the discernible advent of neuromolecular capitalism.

Not least, a human geography perspective has the potential to attend to not only the more obvious concerns of the neuromolecular capitalism, behaviouralism and biological determinism of neuroeconomics and behavioural economics, but also to the expertise ascribed to these disciplines, the methodological assumptions they make, and the ontological and epistemological claims advanced. Most crucially, perhaps, accepting that we do act as if we were knowing subjects, albeit 'plastic' ones, means that we should be all the more preoccupied with elucidating how neuroeconomics and behavioural economics change the way in which subjects are conceived, constituted, shaped and managed. This is not to resort to accusations of manipulation, brain control, subliminal intervention or straightforward accounts of subjectification – as if they are automatically effective and accomplished. Rather it is to pay closer attention to the use to which neuroeconomics and behavioural economics are being put in the fields of public policymaking, education and commercial marketing (amongst others), and to interrogate the justifications for so doing. In this way, it is possible to think more politically about how these biological-economic orthodoxies are mobilized in the prescription of (ir)rationality in decision-making and the legitimization of government regulation and deregulation in the new brain-world.

Notes

1. An earlier version of this chapter appeared in the *Journal of Economic Geography, 13* (5), 845–869 as "Neurocapitalism and the new neuros: using neuroeconomics, behavioural economics and picoeconomics for public policy" (DOI: 10.1093/jeg/lbs039), and some of the material is included here with thanks to the Oxford University Press.

2. Kim Kardashian is a celebrity.
3. "The Dawn of neuromolecular capitalism", at: http://ideas.blogs.nytimes.
   com/2010/02/17/the-dawn-of-neuromolecular capitalism/ 17th Feb 2010.

References

Abi-Rached, J.M., & Rose, N. (2010). The birth of the neuromolecular gaze, *History of the Human Sciences, 23* (1), 11–36.

Ainslie, G. (1992). *Picoeconomics: The strategic interaction of successive motivational states within the person.* Cambridge: Cambridge University Press.

Ariely, D. (2008). *Predictably Irrational. The hidden forces that shape our decisions.* London: HarperCollins Publishers.

Australian Public Service Commission (2007). *Changing Behaviour: A public policy perspective.* No Location: Commonwealth of Australia.

Barnett, C. (2008). Political affects in public space: normative blind-spots in non-representational ontologies, *Transactions of the Institute of British Geographers, 33* (2), 186–200.

Bell, V. (2013). "The unsexy truth about dopamine" *The Observer,* 3rd February 2013.

Boltanski, L., & Chiapello, E. (2005). *The New Spirit of Capitalism.* London: Verso.

Callard, F., Margulies, D.S., & Choudhury, S. (2010). The Restless Brain: Mind-wandering and the problem of the "default mode". Paper presented at the Human Science, Human Subjects Max Planck-University of Chicago Workshop, Chicago, Friday, April 2, 2010.

Camerer, C., Loewenstein, G., and Prelec, D. (2005). Neuroeconomics: how neuroscience can inform economics. *Journal of Economic Literature XLIII,* 9–64.

Choudhury, S., Nagel, S., & Slaby, J. (2009). Critical neuroscience: linking neuroscience and society through critical practice. *BioSocieties, 4* (1), 61–77.

Clark, G.L. (2010). Human nature, the environment, and behaviour: explaining the scope and geographical scale of financial decision-making. *Geografiska Annaler: Series B, Human Geography, 92* (2), 159–173.

Clark, G.L. (2011). Myopia and the global financial crisis: short-termism, context-specific reasoning, market structure and institutional governance. *Dialogues in Human Geography, 1* (1), 4–25.

Davies, G. (2010). Captivating behaviour: mouse models, experimental genetics and reductionist returns in the neurosciences. *The Sociological Review, 58* (1), 53–72.

Dolan, P., Hallsworth, M., Halpern, D., King, D., & Vlaev, I. (2010). *Mindspace. Influencing behaviour through public policy,* London: The Institute for Government and Cabinet Office.

Durante, K.M., and Saad, G. (2010). Ovulatory Shifts in Women's Social Motives and Behaviors: Implications for Corporate Organizations, in A.A. Stanton, M.Day and I.M. Welpe (Eds.) *Neuroeconomics and the Firm.* Cheltenham: Edward Elgar, 116–130.

Ferber, M. A., & Nelson, J. A. (1993). *Beyond Economic Man, Feminist Theory and Economics.* Chicago, IL: University of Chicago Press.

Fullbrook, E. (Ed.) (2003). *The Crisis in Economics, The post-autistic economics movement: the first 600 days.* Routledge: London.

Gill, N., Gill, M. (2012). The limits to libertarian paternalism: two new critiques, and seven best practice imperatives. *Environment and Planning C, 30*(5), 924–940.

Glimcher, P. (2004). Decisions, uncertainty, and the brain: the science of neuroeconomics. Cambridge, MA: MIT Press.

Glimcher, P., Camerer, C., Fehr, E., & Podrack, R. (Eds.) (2009). *Neuroeconomics. Decision Making and the Brain.* Elsevier: London.

Girgerenzer, G., & Brighton, H. (2009). Homo Heuristicus: why biased minds make better inferences, *Topics in Cognitive Science, 1*, 107–143.

Goldstein, W. M., & Hogarth, R. M. (Eds.) (1997). *Research on Judgment and Decision Making: Currents, Connections, and Controversies*. Cambridge: Cambridge University Press.

Haynes, L., Service, O., Goldacre, B., & Torgerson, D. (2012). *Test, Learn, Adapt: Developing Public Policy with Randomised Controlled Trials*. London: Cabinet Office Behavioural Insights Team.

Hess, E., & Jokeit, H. (2009). Neuromolecular capitalism, (translated from German, first published in Merkur). At: http://www.eurozine.com/articles/2009-11-24-jokeit-en.html (accessed 28-06-11).

Houser, D., & McCabe, K. (Eds.) (2008). *Neuroeconomics*. Bingley: Emerald Group Publishing Ltd.

John, P., Cotterill, S., Moseley, A., Richardson, L., Smith, G., Stoker, G., & Wales, C. (2011) *Nudge, Nudge, Think, Think: Experimenting with Ways to Change Civic Behaviour*. London: Bloomsbury Academic.

Jones, R., Pykett, J., & Whitehead, M. (2011). "Governing Temptation: changing behaviour in an age of libertarian paternalism", *Progress in Human Geography, 35*, 4, 483–501.

Jones, R., Pykett, J., & Whitehead, M. (2013). *Changing Behaviours: On the rise of the psychological state*. Cheltenham: Edward Elgar.

Kahneman, D. (2012). *Thinking Fast and Slow*. London: Penguin Books Ltd.

Lehrer, J. (2009b). The Decisive Moment: How the brain makes up its mind. Edinburgh: Canongate Books Ltd.

Lewis, N. (2011). Myopia and the global financial crisis: short-termism, context-specific reasoning and market structure. *Dialogues in Human Geography, 1* (1), 35–37.

Lindstrom, M. (2009). *Buy-Ology: How everything we believe about why we buy is wrong*. New York, NY: Broadway Books.

Low, D. (2011). *Behavioural Economics and Policy Design: Examples from Singapore*. Singapore: World Scientific Publishing.

Malabou, C. (2008). *What should we do with our brain?* New York, NY: Fordham University Press.

McCormack, D. (2007). *Molecular affects in human geographies: Environment and Planning A, 39* (2), 359–377.

Nelson, J.A. (2001). Why the PAE Movement Needs Feminism. *Post-Autistic Economics Newsletter* 9 (October). Available at http://www.paecon.net/PAEtexts/Nelson1.htm (accessed 24-06-11).

Oliver, A. (2013). *Behavioural Public Policy*. Cambridge: Cambridge University Press.

Oullier, O., & Sauneron, S. (2010). *Improving Public Health Prevention with Behavioural, Cognitive and Neuroscience*. Paris: Centre d'analyse stratégique.

Papoulias, C., & Callard, F. (2010). Biology's Gift: interrogating the turn to affect. *Body and Society, 16* (1), 29–56.

Pile, S. (2010). Emotions and affect in recent human geography. *Transactions of the Institute of British Geographers, 35* (1), 5–20.

Politser, P. (2008). *Neuroeconomics. A guide to the new science of making choices*. Oxford: Oxford University Press.

Pykett, J. (2015). *Brain Culture: Shaping policy through neuroscience*. Bristol: Policy Press.

Pykett, J. (2012). The new maternal state: the gendered politics of governing through behaviour change. *Antipode 44* (1), 217–238.

Pykett, J., Jones, R., Whitehead, M., Huxley, M., Strauss, K., Gill, N., McGeevor, K., Thompson, L., & Newman, J. (2011). Interventions in the Political Geography of 'Libertarian Paternalism'. *Political Geography, 30* (6), 301–310.

Ross, D., Sharp, C., Vuchinich, R.E., & Spurrett, D. (2008). Midbrain Mutiny: The pico-economics and neuroeconomics of disordered gambling. *Economic Theory and Cognitive Science*. London: MIT Press.

Schüll, N., & Zaloom, C. (2011). The shortsighted brain: neuroeconomics and the governance of choice in time. *Social Studies of Science* online, doi: 10.1177/0306312710397689.

Sent, E-M. (2004). Behavioral economics, how psychology made its (limited) way back into economics. *History of Political Economy, 36* (4), 735–760.

Simon, H. A. (1955). A behavioural model of rational choice, *Quarterly Journal of Economics 55*, 99–118.

Strauss, K. (2008). Re-engaging with rationality in economic geography: behavioural approaches and the importance of context in decision-making. *Journal of Economic Geography 8* (2), 137–156.

Sunstein, C.R. (2013). *Simpler: The Future of Government*. London: Simon and Schuster.

Thaler, R.H., & Sunstein, C. R. (2008). *Nudge: Improving decisions about health, wealth and happiness*. London: Yale University Press.

Thrift, N. (2004). Intensities of Feeling: Towards a Spatial Politics of Affect. *Geografiska Annaler 86B* (1), 57–78.

Thrift, N. (2008). I just don't know what got into me: where is the subject? *Subjectivity, 22 (1)*, 82–89.

Tversky, A., & Kahneman, D. (1974 [1982]). Judgment Under Uncertainty: Heuristics and Biases. *Science, 185*, 1124–1131. In Kahneman, Slovic and Tversky (Eds.) Judgment under uncertainty: heuristics and biases. Cambridge: Cambridge University Press, 3–22.

Ulshöfer, G. (2008), The economic brain: neuroeconomics and 'post-autistic economics' through the lens of gender. In N.C. Karafyllis and G. Ulshöfer (Eds.) *Sexualized Brains: Scientific modeling of emotional intelligence from a cultural perspective*. London: MIT Press, 191–271.

Walmsley, D.J., & Lewis, G.J. (1993). *People and Environment. Behavioural Approaches in Human Geography*, 2nd Edition. Harlow: Longman Scientfic and Technical.

Whitehead, M., Jones, R., & Pykett, J. (2011). Governing irrationality, or a more than rational government? Reflections on the rescientisation of decision making in British public policy. *Environment and Planning, A 43*, 2819–2837.

Wylie, J. (2010). Non-representational subjects? In B. Anderson and P. Harrison (Eds.) *Taking-Place: Non-representational theories and geography*. London: Ashgate, 99–114.

Zweig, J. (2007). *Your Money and Your Brain: How the New Science of Neuroeconomics Can Help Make You Rich*. London: Souvenir Press Ltd.

6

WHAT IS THE FEMINIST CRITIQUE OF NEUROSCIENCE?

A Call for Dissensus Studies[1]

Cynthia Kraus

"NeuroGenderings: Critical studies of the sexed brain" is a feminist and queer research program and network launched in 2009 with the aim to "elaborate a new conceptual approach of the relation between gender and the brain, one that could help to head gender theorists and neuroscientists to an innovative interdisciplinary place, far away from social and biological determinisms but still engaging with the materiality of the brain" (Dussauge & Kaiser, 2009).[2] The research agenda outlined in the first NeuroGenderings Call for Papers is reminiscent of an interdisciplinary project called "Critical Neuroscience: Linking Neuroscience and Society through Critical Practice" (Choudhury, Nagel, & Slaby, 2009). Both can be considered allied projects insofar as they promote interdisciplinarity as a critical practice, seeking to inform neuroscience with insights from the social and human sciences to contextualize and improve knowledge claims about the brain. At the same time, the alliance is complicated by the problematic ways in which critical neuroscientists conceive of their critical practices: they suggest that we work and talk across disciplines as if neuroscientists were from Mars and social scientists from Venus, assigning the latter to the traditional feminine role of assuaging conflict.

This chapter argues that brain science studies scholars in general, and not only the gender theorists in the field, must clarify how we are to frame our critical practices – a critique of what and for whom? The challenge is to articulate a critical perspective that cannot be domesticated for peacekeeping purposes. I suggest we shift focus: from enhanced communication to the study of conflicts and controversies (but also non-controversies, failed controversies, etc.). I illustrate the programmatic proposal I make for developing "dissensus studies" through two examples: the non-controversial notion of brain plasticity, and the controversial question of whether gender identity formation in intersex individuals is a function of their brains or their genitalia. "Socializing" neuroscience through the incorporation of insights from gender and science studies is good; highlighting the conflicting dimensions of social life in the same gesture is even better.

Critical Neuroscience: A Critique of What and for Whom?

Let us begin with this question: why do critical neuroscientists want to be critical towards neuroscience? And how is it that the call for reflexivity and critical practice emerges precisely in relation to neuroscience, sometimes from neuroscientists themselves and not from another professional group – say, dermatologists, ophthalmologists, or cardiologists? The fact that professionals engage in self-critical practices, challenging their peers with new issues or models, is not, per se, a remarkable event in the history of science and medicine (e.g., Engel, 1977). Critique from within the scientific and medical communities – sometimes from whistleblowers – tends to emerge in relation to crises or critical situations and controversies inside and outside expert circles, the laboratory, private practices or hospitals, which call into question research agendas or professional practices. Examples of this abound: nuclear research, genetic engineering, hormone replacement therapy, orphan diseases, diseases that cannot be cured through therapy or medication (such as schizophrenia or autism), the psychiatric etiology of transgender identities, genital surgery on intersexed newborns and so on.

In contrast, with the increasing legitimacy of neuroscientific knowledge claims regarding all living phenomena, social life included, the situation appears fairly good, and appears to be improving every day, it seems, since the '90s. This success story, however, should not obscure the fact that the revolutionary rhetoric of neuroscience also repeatedly dramatizes *its own crisis and critique*, taking as its audience the scientific community, healthcare professionals and citizens in a seemingly neurocentric world: advances in neuroscientific research "create new kinds of concerns", so that neuroscientists and society at large face new "social, cultural and political challenges" – *hence* the need for critical practice (Choudhury et al. 2009, pp. 61–64).

From a science studies perspective, it makes sense to argue that critical practice is constitutive of neuroscientific research – a sign of excellence and a distinctive feature/gesture – making it possible for neuroscientists to reconfigure knowledge spaces with brain issues and technologies, to question and assimilate other disciplines in "unprecedented and promising syntheses", expand on them and create new neuro-disciplines. In sum, promoting critical practice can be considered a self-promoting mode of interdisciplinary knowledge production, reconfiguration, expansion, proliferation and innovation, while interdisciplinarity can be considered an extensive research program, a means and a goal. As critical neuroscientists propose to occupy the forsaken space between "science studies and empirical neuroscience", and present this much needed interdisciplinary endeavor as a critical response to the "growing gulf" between the two (Choudhury et al. 2009, pp. 61, 63–64), one wonders whether criticalness and interdisciplinarity are not turned, in this manner, to the sole advantage of neuroscience, supporting (wittingly or not) its grandiose claim to become a "total science". If this argument is correct, social sciences are, then, enrolled as "subaltern studies" in the service of a brain-based master narrative.[3]

Are Neuroscientists from Mars and Social Scientists from Venus?

From a feminist and queer perspective, the Critical Neuroscience program raises further questions about the respective status and function allocated to neuro- and social scientists, but also to critical neuroscientists as "informed 'middle men [*sic*]' communicating between neuroscience and the public" (Choudhury et al. 2009, p. 67). Critical neuroscientists frame the question of a science gap between neuro- and social scientists, experts and the public, just as couples' guides for improving men and women's relationships conceive of the gender gap in terms of unawareness, misunderstanding, or ignorance, promoting the idea that all matters can be settled through enhanced communication and better knowledge of each other's distinctive language, culture, needs or concerns.

In the case of couples, emphasizing communication is obviously a convenient way to avoid talking about gender inequalities. In the area of critical neuroscience, this suggests that the so-called science gap might involve more than simple misconceptions or deafness. What about the increasing asymmetries in funding between the neuro- and social sciences? How does this contribute to weakening the explanatory power and truth-value granted to the social sciences in making sense of social life and relations? And, after all, is there really a "science gap" between the neuro- and social sciences, or is it rather that the very idea of a science gap is misleading, obscuring the existence of competing conceptions of humanness and styles of explanation within both fields, i.e., *intra*-disciplinary tensions (e.g., Ehrenberg, 2004)? Also, is it relevant to speak of a public misunderstanding of neuroscience and to seek to make it straight? What about the scientific understanding of the public, and all those forms of "lay expertise" (Epstein, 1995) developed by patients, relatives and activists, challenging expert and authoritative discourses not within the Critical Neuroscience communication framework or through critical practice as they conceive of it, but from a more confrontational perspective? Most importantly, why are social actors (individuals or collectives) and struggles – over competing truths, facts, entities, realities, categories, meanings, subjectivities and ways of being and living in an unequal society – kept out of the Critical Neuroscience picture? In this respect, I argue that the Critical Neuroscience framework prevents politics, or rather, engages in preventive politics in a specific and gendered manner: by assigning social scientists to the typically feminine and most political job of assuaging dissensus – tensions within and between disciplines, scientific controversies, political struggles, social conflicts and so on – in the name of interdisciplinarity. The peacekeeping function of the social sciences in relation to neuroscience and the public not only circumvents political matters. One major contribution of science studies scholars has been to help us consider controversies and conflicts "not only as typical and common but […] normal (perhaps even desirable)" phenomena (Jasanoff, 2008, 391). If controversies and conflicts are indeed constitutive of good science, peacekeeping may also preclude the possibility of doing better empirical research.

It is not my intention, of course, to advocate disciplinary separatism or purity. Quite to the contrary, I believe that the social sciences – gender and science studies in particular – are relevant in relation to empirical neuroscience. But let us not forget that "interdisciplinarity" is a relatively recent affair. It would not have made much sense, say, to Pierre Janet (1859–1947), a neurologist and a philosopher. If social scientists today have a responsibility to advance the normative dimensions of their work, it is also because most of the normative talking so far has been on the part of neuroethicists, and in ways, as certain feminist neuroethicists have pointed out, that have tended to "make the job of 'preempting the critics' easier for scientists" (Roy, 2010). For these reasons, it is worthwhile and important to develop interdisciplinary projects such as "critical studies of the sexed brain" or even Critical Neuroscience to address this matter. However, in contrast to a preemptive critique of neuroscience but consistent with a feminist/queer agenda in the field of neuroethics, science studies and beyond, I also believe that our critical and normative tasks as social scientists are to exacerbate political matters, rather than to absorb or prevent them. In the discussion that follows, I would like to suggest a possible means of linking neuroscience, gender and society with a critical framework, in which analytical precedence is given to controversies and conflicts over enhanced communication. This shift in focus opens up the possibility of reconsidering and redefining the ways in which we want to implement interdisciplinary dialogue and collaboration between neuro- and social scientists.

Controversy and Conflict Studies for What?

> In order to advance towards problem resolution, what is needed is not conflict resolution, but *conflict exacerbation.*
>
> *(Martinez-Alier, 2002, p. 68, emphasis in original)*

Scientific and sociotechnical controversies constitute a major object of inquiry in the broad field of science studies: the social studies of knowledge (SSK), the studies of the social construction of technology (SCOT), science and technology studies (STS) or the actor-network theory (ANT). We can even argue that controversy studies have been paradigmatic in articulating a constructionist perspective, distinct from positivist, internalist and indigenous accounts of scientific progress and knowledge by traditional philosophy/epistemology or by scientists themselves. The so-called 'science wars' in the '90s launched a controversy over science studies' constructionist approaches, pitting constructionism against realism and social sciences against the life sciences. It was also in this controversial context, during a moment when sciences studies had begun to be established as an academic field, that the question of an interdisciplinary dialogue and collaboration – and "cooperation for what?" (Jasanoff, 1995) – was raised by both natural scientists and science studies scholars. Furthermore, critiques from within the field of science studies regarding problems inherent to controversy studies began to emerge. Among the problems discussed, two are of particular interest in relation to a NeuroGenderings project. First, some feminist scholars have argued that controversy studies, particularly when conducted from an ANT perspective, are not a gender-neutral framework but one that conceives of science-in-action in terms of a masculine battlefield (Haraway, 1996). Secondly, authors such as Sheila Jasanoff (1996) suggested that the narrative of winners and losers was not the best explanatory style to capture the ambivalent outcomes of scientific controversies, nor of constructionist arguments about knowledge production in relation to political or legal issues. She called attention to the fact that science studies scholars were being increasingly pressured to take sides in sociotechnical controversies, and proposed an alternative framework centered on co-production and reflexivity:

> "co-production" – the simultaneous production of knowledge and social order – provides a more satisfying conceptual framework than "controversy" for understanding the relationship between science and society, and the scholar's role in that relationship. Political engagement is better achieved through reflexive critical scholarship than through identification with apparent "winners" or "losers" in well-defined but contingent controversies. (p. 393)

While I agree with both the nature of her critique and her effective articulation of the critical and normative tasks of science studies scholars, I suggest that her conception of controversy studies as a theoretical and practical obstacle to a reflexive and normative intervention needs to be updated in light of today's repeated calls for (self-)critical interdisciplinarity. My suggestion is that we need not abandon an agonistic politics of explanation to achieve reflexivity with the aim of making science studies relevant to political matters; quite to the contrary, we should enrich it with the study of social conflicts inherent to processes of knowledge and world making.

To be more precise, we need to understand how knowledge production regarding the brain is situated not just in time (to be studied historically) and space (to be studied by sociology or anthropology), but also, most importantly, in relation to the production of a social order – indeed, co-production. But what we mean by co-production needs to be specified as well. I suggest that we can take as a privileged site of research all brain questions that are a matter of struggles for a better life, linking matters of fact and matters of concern, discursive frames and frames of action, description/perception of a situation and a prescription for changing or coping with it through a "moral grammar of social conflicts" (to borrow an expression from Honneth [1992/1995]). Or, to put it in a more sociological vein, people come to speak the language of the brain, not only because it has become a prominent truth-discourse about the self in contemporary Western societies where concerns, complaints, claims and struggles for recognition are increasingly expressed in terms of mental health issues;[4] they do it to come to terms with conflicting life situations. Not unlike scientists from both the life and social sciences, or healthcare professionals for that matter, who also advance cerebral arguments in a confrontational context – sometimes referred to as the "subject wars", opposing competing conceptions (rather than disciplines) of human beings, defined in primary reference either to their brain/body or to their society (see Ehrenberg, 2004).

Brain Plasticity: The Right Tool for the Job?

What does it mean and take to analyze and intervene through the study of controversies and conflicts? First of all, it involves considering what is not (or hardly) a matter of controversy – typically the very attractive notion of brain plasticity and the related argument pertaining to individual idiosyncrasy in relation to the singular and variable ways in which one materializes a sexed/gendered/sexualized brain of one's own according to one's life history and experience in a given society.

> "[N]euronal plasticity is a crucial factor in elucidating the question of sex/gender differences in the brain. [...] The concept of neuronal *plasticity* describes the experience-driven modification of neuronal networks. [...] Based on such assumptions, sex/gender differences [...] appear as not fixed and immutable in the cerebral organization but rather open to any kind of experience during life. [...] In other words, sex differences in the brain themselves are not evidence of a pure material dimension, but reflect gendered behavior as learned and incorporated in a social context. Once incorporated into the brain, gender differences become part of our cerebral biology (Fausto-Sterling, 2000). This is how gender comes into the brain and why it is appropriate to use the term of *sex/gender* rather than *sex or gender* in the context of language processing".
> *(Kaiser, Haller, Schmitz, & Nitsch, 2009,*
> *pp. 56–57, emphases in original)*

The authors here argue for the relevance of the notion of brain plasticity to account for the ways in which gendered behaviors are being brained, i.e., sexed, through the experience of growing up in a gendered society. Learning and socialization have, thus, material effects on the phenotype through a process of incorporation, to use these authors' term. This process is, however, an open-ended one that works in a 'paradoxical' manner: it produces both sex/gender differences (group differences) *and* individual differences, i.e., as many sexed/gendered brains as there are individuals. In other words, the same process of incorporation that sexes/engenders brain differences between men and women (as social groups) *unsexes/de-genders* their brains at the same time. The notion of brain plasticity assumes some continuity among brain, self and society, but what matters, what is first and foremost materialized (as the above quote indicates) are singular differences, incommensurable between individuals and irreducible to nature/culture dichotomies or determinist explanations.

Plasticity arguments are extremely interesting, as they reject both biological and social determinism, reductionism, essentialism and other –isms. For this very reason, they are currently promoted across the disciplines as being an acceptable peace agreement for all parties in the 'subject wars', but also for making a new alliance between a gender perspective on neuroscience and the pervasive scientific endeavor of sexing the brain from nineteenth-century phrenology to contemporary brain sex research. Now, is the notion of brain plasticity the right tool for "counteract[ing] neuro-sexism, -heterosexisms, and -racisms?" Could it be that we already have the key term with which to "elaborate a new conceptual approach of the relation between gender and the brain" (Dussauge & Kaiser, 2009)? Further, if it makes sense to speak of sex/gender instead of sex or gender in the article quoted above (Kaiser et al. 2009), how does this work as a political argument? That is, what kinds of cerebral subjects/identities of sex, gender and sexuality are being produced (or not) through the notion of brain plasticity and the related sex/gender term?

As we are well aware, plastic and other biosocial (nature-culture) arguments that conceive of the many intricate, productive and feedback processes among the self, the body and society, underscoring individual variations rather than group differences, have been deployed for "all biological levels" (and not just the brain) by feminist critics precisely against deterministic, reductionist and fixed versions of the human body in a gendered society (Bleier, 1986; Birke, 1992; Fausto-Sterling, 1992). In fact, biological plasticity can be considered a key idea and a long-lasting trope in the critical history of feminist science studies – and not an unproblematic one. Indeed, feminist critics have tended to subsume most issues of sex under the category of gender (sex, they have argued, is sexed/engendered/incorporated in our bodies, ourselves), while assuming at the same time that the stuff composing sex (typically the sex-determining genes) would draw the material limit to biological plasticity *and social construction* (Kraus, 2000; Kraus, 2005). Today, with regards to the neuroscience hype, it is more imperative than ever, I suggest, to reflect critically on the undercurrents of arguments regarding brain plasticity, individual variations, idiosyncrasies and the like. At the very least, we should not simply presume that this discourse innocently advances strategic/critical engagements with neuroscience.

The language of plasticity and the related subject-centered discourses have become particularly attractive inside and outside neuroscience: it is spoken equally by neurophiles and critics of brain sex research, whether they be biologists, psychoanalysts, psychiatrists and other healthcare professionals, feminists, queer and transgender scholars, 'normal people', patients, or pro-gender and sexual diversity activists, to name a few. In this regard, brain plasticity and plasticity-related notions, such as biological variations or continuums can be analyzed as "boundary objects" (Star & Griesemer, 1999). The very plasticity of the notion of brain plasticity, one could argue, makes it the ideal candidate for linking neuroscience, gender and society and even more so as the notion is already circulating between various communities of practice and in social worlds. From this perspective, we may want to use it to increase traffic between the existing "trading zones" (Galison, 1999), or differently to meet the requirements of a feminist-inspired research.

The success and self-evidence of plasticity arguments in the contemporary debate are of particular interest for "critical studies of the sexed brain". Indeed, what does it mean and take to develop a critical stance when biosocial, plastic and idiosyncratic arguments are, it seems, so attractive and promoted both inside and outside of neuroscience? In what ways do we want "critical studies of the sexed brain" to bring together neurobiology and feminism? What would be the purpose and research program of such "neurofeminism"? Should feminist-informed critiques contribute to increasing the robustness of the neuroscientific endeavor – in addition to more? After all, are the brain sciences relevant to feminist concerns and projects? Which ones, to what extent and at what price, if any?

With these questions in mind, I argue that the boundary notion of plasticity is part of the problem to be tackled, rather than a preferred tool for increasing the robustness of the neuroscientific endeavor. First of all, it is unclear whether this notion is actually able to bring some gender trouble to problematic identity categories, because it can be – and is – used in two ways: either to undermine (Fausto-Sterling, 2000; Kaiser et al. 2009; Vidal & Benoit-Browaeys, 2005) or to stress the very idea of brain sex/gender (Moir & Jessel, 1991; Hines, 2005). At issue, therefore, is less biological determinism per se (e.g., biological invariance/fixity or a 'hardwire theory') than *tensions* within plasticity arguments, and unresolved (perhaps unresolvable) tensions between the brain, the body, the self and society, but also between sex and gender.

At this point, it is worth recalling that brain plasticity has not always been taken for granted as a neuroscientific fact, or even a fact of any kind for that matter: the notion as we understand it has come a long way – from nineteenth-century psychology to histology to anatomopathology to the so-called new brain sciences – and has involved significant degree of translation work and persuasion to attract and hold the interest of scientists, as well as new visual technologies to evidence the reality of the notion (Droz Mendelzweig, 2010; Rubin, 2009). The idea that the human brain is plastic, not only malleable, but also capable of generating new neurons from early embryonic development till death, is a recent achievement that can be dated to the '90s. It became a core neuroscientific notion and a research priority in the life sciences only at the beginning of the twenty-first century.[5] Since then, neuroscientists have increasingly framed their research questions in terms of plasticity, while individuals have begun making sense of their personal identities and life histories through this most meaningful matrix. The kinds of subjects and identities produced through the notion of brain plasticity today are, then, not only *cerebral* subjects (Ehrenberg, 2004; Vidal, 2005) but more and more *plastic* ones: "the twenty-first-century human subject will be plastic or won't be at all" (Droz Mendelzweig, 2010, translation mine).

This raises a crucial methodological question for "critical studies of the sexed brain": isn't it problematic to acknowledge, as critical neuroscientists do, that "in advanced capitalist and highly medicalized societies [...] citizenship and personhood are increasingly constituted by notions of individual choice and autonomy", and that "neuroscientific explanations of behavior fit well with cultural focus on the individual and interiority" (Choudhury et al. 2009, pp. 62–63) *while promoting at the same time the integration of brain plasticity into neuroscientific research questions and explanations* as an "orthopedic" style of explanation in order to incorporate complexity, nature-culture and sex/gender feedback processes in the making of brain facts? Today, in an emerging 'plastic' era, how does this strategy work?

Another approach to the problem is to ask in return what kind of social order and conceptions of human agency are being co-produced through knowledge claims about brain plasticity. A 2008 foresight study entitled "Mental Capital and Wellbeing: Making the Most of Ourselves in the 21st Century", commissioned by the UK government, is a telling example of the ways in which plasticity arguments are sometimes used to reframe imperatives of performance and flexibility, thereby enforcing managerial values in times of economic crises and lasting unemployment. If we have lost the prospect of a long-term job, the good news is that we have earned a lifelong plastic brain. Today's discourses about brain plasticity, individual variations and idiosyncrasy involve not only an ambivalent politics of self-realization and optimization but also a problematic theory of action. Indeed, the question of agency for the plastic subject is framed in terms of a "biology of freedom" (Ansermet & Magistretti, 2004, 2007). In this framework, it is assumed that individual variability, novelty and the unexpected will come from biological plasticity and related processes, rather than from social practices, norms or interactions that mold individuals in conformity with gender and heterosexual expectations towards traditional gender/sexual roles and identities. Discourses about brain plasticity work here as a political argument, as they figure the cerebral plastic subject they are actively producing as the agent capable of resisting, or even subverting, social determinisms. It is in this light that discourses advocating neurodiversity (such as that by Asperger's; for a discussion, see Ortega, 2009) or gender and sexual diversity (for example, by intersex and trans' activists, to which we will now turn) may appear to subvert socio-medical categories.

Am I My Brain or My Genitals? Anatomy of a Social Conflict

Initially, I suggested that we develop dissensus studies – and organize dissensus (rather than consensus) conferences[6] – in relation to my work on the clinical management of intersex and the ongoing debates about best practice issues in this area, with the aim to improve the existing standards of care. I made the suggestion in response to a plain fact: the International Consensus Conference on Intersex held in 2005 and the resulting "Consensus Statement on Management of Intersex Disorders" (Lee, Houk, Ahmed, & Hughes, 2006) did not resolve the most controversial issues for the persons concerned, and, a fortiori, for the clinicians.

It is not just the very definition of intersex, renamed "disorders of sex development" (DSD) by the Consensus group, that is disputable (see, e.g., Diamond & Beh, 2006; Hinkle, 2006). The supposed novelty and improvement of the consensus recommendations in terms of healthcare that caters to the specific needs of intersex individuals are equally debatable. In retrospect, even some experts involved in the process concede that the "existing consensus recommendations are uncomfortably nonspecific" (Byne et al. 2012, p. 789). Further, these recommendations are not always very different from the now controversial treatment plan outlined by John Money and colleagues that defined standard practice from the 1950s until recently (Money, Hampson, & Hampson, 1955a; Money, Hampson, & Hampson, 1955b; American Academy of Pediatrics AAP, 2000). Genital surgery in particular remains the most contentious issue from the perspective of the persons concerned and biomedical ethics (see, e.g., Karkazis, 2006; Swiss National Advisory Commission on Biomedical Ethics, 2012).

Although it is a top-down process – typically, only two intersex activists were invited to join the expert group – the consensus conference model for public participation in science, technology and medicine is, of course, not an uninteresting process. But we need to bring up for discussion that it is not rare that consensus conferences and statements result in dissensus, and, even sometimes, more dissensus. However, the consensus framework denies this possibility, because it presumes that we can come to an agreement that would not be contested, that objections can be contained upstream, and once for all. And of course, any matters of fact and concern that are unquestioned prior to consensus conferences are not put on the table.

Among these is the assumption that brain sex research offers new insights into the "true gender" of intersex newborns, and could, therefore, lead us to a more scientific and compassionate medicine (e.g., Dennis, 2004; for critical discussion, see Kraus, 2011). This obscures the fact that the clinical promises of brain sex research make sense, and are advanced, in the context of a crisis and a critique of medicine: the critique of a normalizing medicine initiated by intersex activists during the decade of the brain (see Chase, 1998). Slowly, healthcare professionals began to express some reservation about the case management protocols developed by Money and colleagues. It is in this controversial context that the question of which is the most important sex organ (is it the brain or the genitalia?) in the psychosexual development of intersex newborns became instrumental in professional struggles over best practice issues. But, as feminist science studies scholars are well aware, brain sex research offers no real data to answer this question (see e.g., Bluhm, Jaap Jacobson, & Maibom, 2012; Dussauge & Kaiser, 2012; Fausto-Sterling, 2012; Fine, 2010; Jordan-Young, 2010; Kraus, 2011). Rather, the question itself suggests an either neuro- or genital-centric framework, a framing that needs precisely to be interrogated.

And yet, we also know that the ideas of a gay brain, of a transsexual brain or that the true gender of intersex newborns cannot be altered by genital surgery, because it depends on their fetal brain sex – have sometimes been mobilized by the persons concerned to claim for normality, or a more open access to sex change surgeries and hormonal treatments, or, to the contrary, the end of unwanted medical treatments, when an intersex condition is diagnosed. These claims are entirely justified, but they raised for me the question of how and why intersex and trans' activists with a feminist and queer political agenda have sought to challenge standards of care and the very definition of their 'disorders' by mobilizing plastic and idiosyncratic knowledge claims from studies of the transsexual or intersexed brains.

The reasons are neither accidental nor incidental. Intersex and trans' activists were able to enroll the discourse of fetal brain sex in feminist-informed projects of subverting identity categories, gender and heterosexual norms, precisely because this appropriation is consistent with – in fact an extension of – the ways in which feminist, queer and transgender scholars have been refuting biological determinism with plasticity arguments, as earlier discussed. However, the affinities between neuroscientific and feminist-inspired discourses are not only epitomized, but also fundamentally produced through intersex struggles for recognition in the context of a nature-culture controversy, in which two developmental sciences (neurobiological and psychosexual) of gender identity formation have been pitted against each other since the mid-'60s.

In 1965, Milton Diamond, a neurobiologist trained at William Young's laboratory, the founder of behavioral neuroendocrinology, proposed a sexuality-at-birth according to which hermaphroditism (as it was called at the time) involved atypical brain development (Diamond, 1965). This theory is explicitly presented as a biological refutation of the so-called neutrality-at-birth theory and of the treatment plan developed by Money and colleagues. Diamond's thesis is that *one becomes the man or woman one is born as*, and one is born with an innate sexual identity, i.e., with predispositions that are tied up to the fetal development of a brain sex. At the time, however, his sexuality-at-birth was not grounded in any human evidence, but inferred from animal studies on sex development (i.e., Phoenix, Goy, Gerall, & Young, 1959; Young, 1961; Young, Goy, & Phoenix, 1964). The developmental antagonism between the brain and the genitalia outlined in these animal studies underwrites Diamond's opposition to early genital surgery in the late 1990s: *braining* intersexuality involves *degenitalizing* sex development, sexual identity and orientation altogether. In retrospect, it seems obvious that Diamond would have been an ideal candidate for an alliance with intersex activists seeking to put an end to unwanted genital surgery. In 1965, however, it is as a biologist trained in behavioral neuro-endocrinology that Diamond responds to theories that privilege family and social conditioning over our mammalian heritage. His intervention in the hermaphrodite debate appears in this regard as a professional statement against psychology and sexology on its way to institutional recognition. But despite Diamond's polemical tone, his blow did not strike home, and for long time, he would be rather lonely in the battlefield.

From a controversy and conflict-centered perspective, it matters that we analyze why and when some controversies catch on, but also why and when others do not, i.e., failed controversies. I suggest that Diamond's attempt (in fact, several attempts) at creating a controversy were unsuccessful in the absence of a social conflict. Diamond remained a minor figure in the hermaphrodite debate until intersex adults got political during the Decade of the Brain. The Intersex Society of North America (ISNA) has been the most influential in defining the intersex agenda over the past two decades, the most present in the media, the most cited in medical literature, and the first to take an overtly political stance. Indeed, intersex activists got political in explicit reference to feminism and other feminist-inspired social movements existing or emerging at the time (see Chase, 1998).

However, the primary item on the intersex agenda was not to change society, but to put an end to unwanted genital surgery and non-consensual treatments. During the '80s and '90s, intersex adults and activists were confronting professionals with patient dissatisfaction with medical care and liability for the treatment plan outlined by Money and colleagues. Early professional reactions to intersex activism were rejections. In response, ISNA's modes of action were rather confrontational, e.g., by picketing in 1996 in front of the conference building where the annual meeting of the American Academy of Pediatrics took place (see Beck, 1997, 1998). During the first decade of intersex activism, there was a social conflict between the activists and the medical community, but still no biomedical controversy.

Two professional events were of particular significance for changing medical views. In 1997, Diamond and psychiatrist Keith Sigmundson (1997a) published an article in which they reevaluated the case management by Money and colleagues of the boy (pseudonym John) who accidently lost his penis and was surgically made into a girl (pseudonym Joan). Even if John was not born with any hermaphroditic condition, the John/Joan case can be considered a "foundational story" in neurobiological discourse about intersexuality and in the growing public awareness about this clinical issue (see in particular Colapinto, 2000). The second significant event took place in 1999 in Texas. A multidisciplinary conference sponsored by the National Health Institute brought together "basic scientists, endocrinologists, surgeons, psychiatrists, psychologists and ethicists WHERE THE PARTICIPANTS DISCUSSED the management of the neonate with ambiguous genitalia" in order to reflect critically on the long-term outcomes of past practice and to allow "for better medical and emotional management of these patients in the years ahead".[7] Diamond views the Texas Conference as a historical event not just for intersex advocacy, but also for the advancement of a more scientific medicine. Finally, "the brain was to be recognized as a sexual organ" (Diamond, 2004, p. 599).

These two major events contributed to creating a biomedical controversy where there was previously an overall consensus over standards of care. In the case of both events, critiques of past practice are "indigenous" critiques, i.e., from experts, researchers and healthcare professionals. Intersex activism is not mentioned in the 1997 reevaluation of the John/Joan case; no intersex people were invited to speak at the Texas Conference. In sum, the conflict and the controversy are now coexisting, but somehow in parallel. The two will converge by presenting a common front against early genital surgery, but not always on the same grounds. As intersex activists became more vocal about the damage of past practice on their bodies and lives, calling for the end of unwanted early genital surgery and the right of bodily integrity, neurobiology became instrumental in promoting a more compassionate and evidence-based medicine.[8] Supporting and building on intersex activism, neurobiologists such as Diamond found an opportunity to assert, theoretically and professionally, the relevance of brain sex research for the clinical management of intersexuality (e.g., Diamond & Sigmundson, 1997b; see also and again Dennis 2004). In the latest AAP guidelines, biological factors, and not the least the brain, are given ontogenetic precedence over psychosexual factors and socialization (Lee et al. 2006, p. 489). A decade earlier, the AAP's guidelines made explicit reference to Money and colleagues' theoretical and practical framework (see AAP, 1996, p. 590).

So What?

At the core of this debate is what I call an "anatomy of social conflict". This expression seeks to capture the critical focus I have argued for throughout this chapter: an analysis of the co-production of knowledge claims regarding the brain/body and social order in controversial and conflicting terms. In the former section, I proposed a selective analysis of cerebral arguments in the so-called hermaphrodite debate to ground my programmatic proposal to work with a dissensus framework. This framework seeks to articulate two questions that I have addressed through a constructive critique of "Critical Neuroscience" and of the consensual notion of brain plasticity: what is the usefulness of a social science critique of (neuro-)science, technology and medicine, and in particular of gender studies? And how is this practical question related to the question of critical practices?

I have argued that the task of clarifying how we want to frame our critical practices is a prerequisite for articulating normative positions, making it possible to reconsider and redefine the conditions under which interdisciplinarity – or other interesting ways of shaping dialogue across different social worlds, of confronting perspectives, of cooperating, etc. – could be valued as a theoretical and practical solution. I have further argued that it is a solution that would seek not to prevent, absorb, nor even resolve controversies and social conflicts, but rather to exacerbate them through critical analysis. If we want to make science and gender studies relevant to social science interventions, what is needed is not preemptive critiques, e.g., a peacekeeping communication framework for social scientists from Venus, but critical practices framed from a strong social science perspective centered on controversy and conflict analysis.[9]

Notes

1. Parts of this chapter appeared previously in Kraus (2012a) and Kraus (2012b), and are reprinted here with permission from Springer and from Palgrave Macmillan, respectively.
2. Since the kick-off event held in March 2010 in Uppsala, the NeuroGenderings network has organized two more conferences: one in Vienna (http://neurocultures2012.univie. ac.at/); the other in Lausanne (www.unil.ch/neurogenderings3).
3. To put it differently, one could speak of the proleptic function of critique and of interdisciplinarity (as defined in the Critical Neuroscience manifesto and in the heterogeneous field of neuroscience itself in reference to Hagner and Borck's argument about the proleptic structure of neuroscience as a defining and long-lasting feature of brain research since the eighteenth century (Hagner & Borck, 2010). Pidoux (2012) drew my attention to this reference and documents nicely, in my opinion, the more conceptual point I made at the time.
4. In this context, it would be rather odd not to mobilize such a discourse. Also, let's not forget here that in people's everyday life and language, brain talk coexists with other scientific discourses about the body, the self and society, in particular genetics and biochemistry (especially in the case of psychoactive drugs).
5. In this regard, psychiatrist and 2000 Nobel laureate, Eric R. Kandel seems to have played a prominent role in promoting the notion, see (Ehrenberg, 2004; Droz Mendelzweig, 2010).
6. See "NeuroGenderings III: The first international dissensus conference on brain and gender" www.unil.ch/neurogenderings3.
7. I draw the quotes from the documents distributed to the conference attendees. I thank Dr Blaise-Julien Meyrat, pediatric surgeon at the University Hospital CHUV in Lausanne, Switzerland, for passing them to me.
8. This does not mean that intersex activists are necessarily buying into the whole discourse related to brain sex. Some do, but at least in their public statements, most support and advocacy groups are either agnostic (ISNA), ambivalent (Organization Intersex International), or rather silent on this issue (Androgen Insensitivity Syndrome Support Group in the UK, The UK Intersex Association).
9. The advantages of a controversy and conflict-centered perspective for inquiring into the relations between neuroscience, medicine, gender and society, and the normative commitments involved in my dissensus framework with consequences for research, training and action, are discussed in more details in Kraus (2012b).

References

American Academy of Pediatrics [AAP] (1996). Timing of elective surgery on the genitalia of male children with particular reference to the risks, benefits, and psychological effects of surgery and anesthesia. *Pediatrics*, 97(4), 590–594.

Ansermet, F., & Magistretti, P. (2007). *Biology of freedom: Neural plasticity, experience, and the unconscious.* (S. Fairfield, Trans.) London: Karnac Books. (Original work published 2004).

Beck, M. (Fall 1997/Winter 1998). Hermaphrodites with Attitude Take to the Streets. *Chrysalis: The Journal of Transgressive Gender Identities, 2*(5), 45–50.

Birke, L. (1992). In pursuit of difference: Scientific studies of women and men. In G. Kirkup & L. Smith Keller (Eds.), *Inventing women: Science, technology and gender* (81–102). Cambridge, U.K.: Polity Press.

Bleier, R. (1986). Sex differences research: Science or belief? In R. Bleier (Ed.), *Feminist approaches to science* (147–164). New York, NY: Pergamon Press.

Bluhm, R., Jaap Jacobson, A., & Maibom, H. (Eds.) (2012). *Neurofeminism: Issues at the intersection of feminist theory and cognitive science* (New Directions in Philosophy and Cognitive Science). Basingstoke, UK: Palgrave Macmillan.

Byne, W., Bradley S. J., Coleman E., Evan Eyler, A., Green, R., Menvielle, E. J., … Tompkins, D. A. (2012). Report of the American Psychiatric Association Task Force on Treatment of Gender Identity Disorder. *Archives of Sexual Behavior, 41*, 759–796.

Chase, C. (1998). Hermaphrodites with Attitudes. Mapping the emergence of intersex political activism. *GLQ: A Journal of Lesbian and Gay Studies, 4*(2), 189–211.

Choudhury, S., Nagel, S. K., & Slaby, J. (2009). Critical neuroscience: Linking neuroscience and society through critical practice. *BioSocieties, 4*(1), 61–77.

Colapinto, J. (2000). *As nature made him: The boy who was raised as a girl.* New York, NY: HarperCollins Publishers.

Dennis, C. (2004). Brain development: The most important sexual organ. *Nature, 427*, 390–392.

Diamond, M. (1965). A critical evaluation of the ontogeny of human sexual behavior. *The Quarterly Review of Biology, 40*(2), 147–175.

Diamond, M. (2004). Sex, gender, identity over the years: A changing perspective. *Child and Adolescent Psychiatric Clinics of North America, 13*(3), 591–607.

Diamond, M., & Beh, H. G. (2006, July 27). Variations of sex development instead of disorders of sex development [Electronic Letter to Hugues, I. A. et al. (2006). Consensus Statement on Management of Intersex Disorders], *Archives of Disease in Childhood.*

Diamond M., & Sigmundson, H. K. (1997a). Sex reassignment at birth: Long term review and clinical implications. *Archives of Pediatrics and Adolescent Medicine, 151*, 298–304.

Diamond, Milton, & Sigmundson, H. Keith. (1997b). Management of intersexuality: guidelines for dealing with persons with ambiguous genitalia. Retrieved from http://www.ukia.co.uk/diamond/diaguide.htm.

Dreger, A. (Ed.) (1998). Intersex in the age of ethics. *Journal of Clinical Ethics, 9*(4).

Droz Mendelzweig, M. (2010). La plasticité cérébrale de Cajal à Kandel: cheminement d'une notion constitutive du sujet cérébral. *Revue d'histoire des sciences, 63*(2), 331–367.

Dussauge, I., & Kaiser, A. (2009). NeuroGenderings: Critical studies of the sexed brain. Call for papers. Retrieved from http://www.genna.gender.uu.se/themes/bodyembodiment/news/CFP_NeuroGenderings/.

Dussauge, I., & Kaiser, A. (Eds.) (2012). Neuroscience and Sex/Gender. *Neuroethics, 5*(3).

Ehrenberg, A. (2004). Le sujet cérébral. *Esprit, 11*, 130–155.

Engel, G. L. (1977). The need for a new medical model: A challenge to biomedicine. *Science, 196*(428), 129–136.

Epstein, S. (1995). The construction of lay expertise: AIDS activism and the forging of credibility in the reform of clinical trials. *Science, Technology & Human Values, 20*(4), 408–437.

Fausto-Sterling, A. (1992 [1985]). *Myths of gender: Biological theories about women and men* (2nd ed.). New York, NY: Basic Books.

Fausto-Sterling, A. (2000). *Sexing the Body: Gender politics and the construction of sexuality.* New York, NY: Basic Books.

Fausto-Sterling, A. (2012). *Sex/gender. Biology in a social world*. NY & London: Routledge.

Fine, C. (2010). *Delusions of Gender: How Our Minds, Society, and Neurosexism Create Difference*. New York, NY: W. W. Norton.

Galison, P. (1999 [1997, abridged 1998]). Trading zone: Coordinating action and belief. In M. Biagioli (Ed.), *The science studies reader* (137–160). New York, NY: Routledge.

Gray, J. (2012). *Men are from Mars, women are from Venus: A practical guide for improving communication and getting what you want in your relationships* (Paperback edition). New York, NY: Harper Collins.

Hacking, I. (1998). *Mad travelers: Reflections on the reality of transient mental illnesses*. Charlottesville, VA & London, VA: University of Virginia Press.

Hagner, M., & Borck, C. (2001). Mindful practices: On the neurosciences in the twentieth. century. *Science in Context*, *14*(4), 507–510.

Haraway, D. (1996). Modest witness: Feminist diffractions in science studies. In P. Galison & D. J. Stump (Eds.), *The disunity of science: Boundaries, contexts, and power* (428–441). Stanford, CA: Stanford University Press.

Hines, M. (2005). *Brain gender*. New York, NY: Oxford University Press.

Hinkle, C. (2006, August 16). Thank you very much Dr. Diamond, [Electronic Letter to Hugues, I. A. et al. (2006). Consensus Statement on Management of Intersex Disorders], *Archives of Disease in Childhood*.

Honneth, A. (1995). *The struggle for recognition: The moral grammar of social conflicts*. (J. Anderson, Trans.). Cambridge, U.K.: Polity Press. (Original work published 1992).

Jasanoff, S. (1995). Cooperation for what?: A view from the sociological/cultural study of science policy. *Social Studies of Science*, *25*(2), 314–317.

Jasanoff, S. (1996). Beyond epistemology: Relativism and engagement in the politics of science. *Social Studies of Science, 26*(2), 393–418.

Jasanoff, S., Markle G. E., Peterson J. C., & Pinch T. (Eds.) (2008). *Handbook of. science and technology studies* (revised ed.). Thousand Oaks, CA: Sage Publications.

Jordan-Young, R. (2010). *Brain storm: The flaws in the science of sex differences*. Cambridge, MA: Harvard University Press.

Kaiser, A., Haller, S., Schmitz, S., & Nitsch, C. (2009). On sex/gender related similarities and differences in fMRI language research. *Brain Research Reviews*, *61*(2), 49–59.

Karkazis, K. A. (2006). Early genital surgery to remain controversial. *Pediatrics, 118*(2), 814–815.

Kraus, C. (2000). Naked sex in exile: On the paradox of the "sex question" in feminism and in science. *The Science and Politics of the Search for Sex Differences: A Special Issue of The National Women's Studies Association Journal*, *12*(3), 151–177.

Kraus, C. (2005). Of "Epistemic Covetousness" in Knowledge Economies: The Not-nothing of Social Constructionism. *Social epistemology, 19*(4), 339–355.

Kraus, C. (2011). Am I my brain or my genitals? A nature-culture controversy in the hermaphrodite debate from the mid-'60s to the late '90s. *Gesnerus. Swiss Journal for the History of Medicine and Sciences, 68*(1), 80–106.

Kraus, C. (2012a 2011 Online First™). Critical studies of the sexed brain: a critique of what and for whom? *Neuroethics, 5*(3), 247–259.

Kraus, C. (2012b). Linking neuroscience, medicine, gender and society through controversy and conflict analysis: A "dissensus framework" for feminist/queer brain science studies. In R. Bluhm, A. Jaap Jacobson, & H. Maibom (Eds.), *Neurofeminism: Issues at the intersection of feminist theory and cognitive science* (193–215). Basingstoke, UK: Palgrave Macmillan.

Lee, P. A., Houk, C. P., Ahmed, S. F., & Hughes, I. A. (2006). Consensus statement on management of intersex disorders. *Pediatrics, 118*(2), e488-e500.

Martinez-Alier, J. (2002). *The environmentalism of the poor: A study of ecological conflicts and valuation*. Cheltenham, UK: Edward Elgar.

Moir, A., & Jessel, D. (1991). *Brain sex: The real difference between men and women* (2nd ed.). New York, NY: Dell Publishing.

Money, J., Hampson, J. G., & Hampson, J. L. (1955a). Hermaphroditism: Recommendations concerning assignment of sex, change of sex, and psychological management. *Bulletin of Johns Hopkins Hospital, 97*, 284–300.

Money, J., Hampson, J. G., & Hampson, J. L. (1955b). Examination of some basic sexual concepts: Evidence of human hermaphroditism. *Bulletin of Johns Hopkins Hospital, 97*, 301–319.

Ortega, F. (2009). The cerebral subject and the challenge of neurodiversity. *BioSocieties, 4*(4), 425–445.

Pidoux, V. (2012). *Cerveaux, sujets et maladies: contribution à une épistémologie historique. de l'étude de l'activité cérébrale en psychiatrie*. Thèse de Doctorat en sciences sociales, Université de Lausanne.

Phoenix, H., Goy, R. W. Goy, Gerall, A. A., & Young, W. C. (1959). Organizing action of prenatally administered testosterone propionate on the tissues mediating mating behavior in the female guinea pig. *Endocrinology, 65*, 369–82.

Roy, D. (2010, March). *Brain tease: Feminist neuroethics and the search for a cosmopolitical brain*. Paper presented at NeuroGenderings: Critical studies of the sexed brain, University of Uppsala, Sweden.

Rubin, B.P. (2009). Changing brains: The emergence of the field of adult neurogenesis. *BioSocieties, 4*(4), 407–424.

Star, S. Leigh, & Griesemer, J. R. (1999 [1989, abridged 1998]). Institutional ecology, "translation", and boundary objects: Amateurs and professionals in Berkeley's museum of vertebrate zoology, 1907–39. In M. Biagioli (Ed.), *The Science Studies Reader* (505–524). New York, NY: Routledge.

Swiss National Advisory Commission on Biomedical Ethics. (2012). *On the management of differences of sex development. Ethical issues relating to 'intersexuality'. Opinion No. 20/2012*. Bern: Author.

van den Wijngaard, M. (1997). *Reinventing the sexes: The biomedical construction of femininity and masculinity*. Bloomington, IN: Indiana University Press.

Vidal, F. (2005). Le sujet cérébral: Une esquisse historique et conceptuelle. *Psychiatrie, Sciences Humaines, Neurosciences, 3*(11), 37–48.

Vidal, C., & Benoit-Browaeys, D. (2005). *Cerveau, Sexe et Pouvoir*. Paris: Belin.

Young, W. C. (1961). The hormones and mating behavior. In W. C. Young (Ed.), *Sex and Internal Secretions* (1173–1239). Baltimore, MD: Williams & Wilkins.

Young, W. C., Goy, R. W., & Phoenix, C. H. (1964). Hormones and sexual behavior. *Science, 143*(3603), 212–218.

7

BRAIN IN THE SHELL

Assessing the Stakes and the Transformative Potential of the Human Brain Project

Philipp Haueis and Jan Slaby

Introduction

The Human Brain Project (HBP) is a large-scale European neuroscience and computing project that is one of the biggest funding initiatives in the history of brain research.[1] With a planned budget of 1.2 billion € over the next decade and building on the prior Blue Brain Project, the project initiated by Henry Markram pursues the ambitious goal of simulating the entire human brain – all the way from genes to cognition – with the help of exascale information and communication technology (ICT). The HBP hopes to thereby produce new, brain-like computing technologies, so-called neuromorphic computers, which would be both highly energy-efficient and usable by the general public.

Despite the potentially enormous significance for both brain research and computer technology – as well as society and culture – the ambition and approach of the HBP has been a matter of substantial controversy from the beginning, both in the scientific community and the general public. Critics have claimed that the model-based bottom-up approach of the project is scientifically wrong-headed, have accused the project of not being managed transparently, and have attested that the aims of the HBP are too ambitious, such that the project is likely to waste valuable resources for research and infrastructure in Europe. It is currently – in mid-2015 – still a debated question whether the HBP in its current format and direction should be pursued *at all* (Bartlett, 2015). The controversy was fuelled in early 2014 by an open letter to the European Commission (EC) signed by over 750 European neuroscientists urging a reform of the HBP even before its operational phase was set to begin. They threatened to boycott the project if no independent review panel was put in place to assess whether the HBP would meet the standards of excellence required for a Future Emerging Technologies (FET) flagship program

(Open message to the EC, 2014; Nature, 2014; Marcus, 2014).The exclusion of the experimental cognitive neuroscience strand from the core project and the emphasis on building ICT infrastructures furthermore raised the question whether – despite the project's name – the human brain and neuroscience are actually at the center of HBP research (Frégnac & Laurent, 2014, Nature 2014). As a result, the HBP now increasingly risks losing support from the very scientific community it purports to serve. Most recently, the HBP board of directors responded to this criticism and to the report of a subsequent mediation committee by taking over the responsibilities of the project's three executive directors Henry Markram, Richard Frackowiak and Karlheinz Meyer (Abbott, 2015; Enserink, 2015).

Taking a broader, more critical perspective on the controversy surrounding the HBP, we ask the following questions: What is at issue and at stake in this controversy with regard to the project's potential mid- to long-term impacts on the field of neuroscience and on neuroscience's role in society? How does the use of ICT and simulation in the HBP reconfigure the brain as a research object? By analysing the project's impact beyond its initial scientific or translational agenda, we argue that what is at stake in the HBP is not whether it is about the brain or ICT, but whether it can show how to create a 'brain in the shell', by extending the neural domain beyond biological brains and into the computer. Hence our allusion to the society of 'cyberbrains' in the science fiction manga "Ghost in the Shell".

Analytical Perspective and Source Material

The concept of "experimental systems" (Rheinberger, 1997; Rouse, 2011) figures in the background of the first three sections of this chapter. Experimental systems consist of technologies, scientific methods and institutional settings that allow scientists to study the unknown properties of the entity under investigation – the human brain in the case of the HBP. The discussion of several proposed changes to neuroscientific practice, medicine and ICT will elucidate what kind of experimental system the HBP is planning to build. This analysis is valuable regardless of the actual success of the HBP in implementing its envisioned research architecture. As we will outline below, many of the proposed changes to neuroscience practice have far wider ramifications than those pertaining to this single large-scale project. If it doesn't happen at this particular juncture and in the context of the HBP as currently constructed, many of the proposed measures will quite likely spring up elsewhere sooner rather than later.

The second analytical concept that we employ is that of an "experimental microworld" (Rouse, 1987). It is used to assess the larger transformative potential of a project like the HBP. Constituted by experimental systems, such microworlds allow entities to show orderly patterns of behaviour that lead researchers to new scientific insights. To successfully extend these insights beyond the isolated circumstances in which they were established, it is often necessary to change the material configurations of the world outside the laboratory so that the world itself begins to resemble the isolated circumstances of the experimental microworlds. Only then can scientific insights be used successfully in non-scientific contexts, and only then do they provide their non-scientific users with new possibilities of action—think of electrical power grids, light bulbs, batteries or power outlets that are available and usable for an ever-increasing portion of the public (Rouse, 1987, pp. 199, 226ff.). We discuss below how the HBP's aim of building neuromorphic technologies may put such far-reaching material transformations on the agenda, and what impact these transformations could have on society and culture if the HBP comes remotely close to fulfilling some substantial parts of its projected research plan.

The primary sources for our analysis are the "Overall Vision for the Human Brain Project" document (HBP, 2013) and the "Framework Partnership Agreement" (HBP, 2014a, hereafter FPA document), which to date are the most detailed, publicly available documents about the HBP that have been authored by the members of the project committee themselves (for the earlier official report to the EC see HBP, 2012). We discuss the most important of several proposed changes to neuroscientific practice, medicine and ICT. We furthermore amend our analysis with scientific research and overview articles from or on the HBP, official websites, newspaper articles and blog-post commentaries. It needs to be noted, however, that there is to date rather little concrete information – let alone independent scholarly analysis – on how the HBP is supposed to operate, which and how many of the proposed plans of the Vision and FPA document are actually being pursued at the moment, and whether some of the issues we discuss in the following are even on the current internal agenda of the project or not. In fact, from what can be gleaned from recent reports, much in the organizational structure of the HBP seems to be in flux as a result of encompassing internal and external reviewing (see e.g., Nature, 2014; Bartlett, 2015; Abbott, 2015; Enserink, 2015). The available body of source material therefore limits our ability to draw more than preliminary conclusions, which is why some of the following considerations have a slightly speculative flavour. We therefore chose to take a descriptive and analytical (instead of an overly normative and critical) approach to the sources available, which we hope can serve as a starting point for further critical analyses of the changing landscape of big-scale neuroscience in the years to come.

Scientific Practice

A good starting point for discussion is the neuroscientific research agenda of the HBP, since one of its main goals is to "change the way neuroscience is done" (Markram, 2013, p. 146). The following five focal topics delineate the methodological approach and scientific practice that initiates the required infrastructure projects, motivates the forms and domains of future applications and indicates the larger societal implications of the HBP – and potential other projects with comparable agendas – discussed in the rest of the paper.

Scaling Up

Big Science projects investigating the brain move away from the common model of small, investigator-driven research groups that study the brain at one or a few levels of description and with one or a few instruments. Single-cell studies, for instance, investigate action potentials at the chemical level of ion channels, Ca^+ molecules and neurotransmitters. Functional MRI studies in humans correlate changes in blood oxygenation within whole cortical areas or networks to the level of cognitive tasks (e.g., counting numbers). These different levels are usually assumed to be parts of multi-level mechanisms (Craver, 2007), a view that the HBP also embraces with its multi-scale modelling approach (cf. HBP, 2013, p. 37; HBP, 2014a, pp. 14–15). But instead of studying each level individually, the HBP is planning to use most (if not all) laboratory-scale approaches (e.g., molecular, genetic, physiological or computational methods) simultaneously and on an industrial scale. It, therefore, attempts to bridge the enormous gap between microscopic and macroscopic neuroscientific evidence (such as from single-cell and fMRI studies), a task that is also tackled by other, small- and large-scale projects (Bohland et al. 2009; Grillner, 2014; Siero et al. 2014). The potential virtue of scaling up the existing approaches is expected to be a better *integration* of data from the many levels of brain organization (cf. HBP, 2013, p. 56; HBP 2014a, p. 187). Better integration can then be seen as the presupposition for a better understanding of the brain, which is why good neuroscience *ought* to become a large-scale and integrative effort.

It is this normative impetus of the agenda that in part stirred the recent controversy surrounding the HBP. The critics argue that although multi-level integration and stronger funding is needed to better understand human brain organization, an industrial-scale project with a relatively fixed agenda may not be the best way to achieve such goals. Instead, they support a 'mechanism of individual investigator-driven grants', which would foster the analytic and creative capacities of small research groups with the overall funding level of the HBP (Open message to the EC, June 7 2014). Even some advocates of the HBP stress that developing new concepts or formulating interesting, specific questions about human brain organization will remain the task of small groups or individual neuroscientists (cf. Mathews in Kandel et al. 2013, p. 663; Grillner, 2014, p. 1211). Although the exact utility of the HBP for later research remains an open question, its initiation is already reshaping the global neuroscience landscape: since 2013, projects of a similar scale – although with different agendas – have been installed or pronounced in the US, Japan, China and Australia (Grillner, 2014, p. 1211; HBP, 2014a, p. 16).

Fewer Experiments, More Models

While the HBP plans to scale up and integrate existing approaches, it simultaneously moves away from acquiring experimental data. The HBP asserts that previous neuroscientific research has already generated most of the data necessary for understanding the human brain from genes to cognition (cf. HBP, 2014a, p. 2; HBP, 2013, p. 6). Besides the strategic collection of mouse and human data in the starting phase, the project therefore focuses on *multi-scale modelling, prediction* and *simulation* of brain structure and function (cf. HBP, 2014a, pp. 3–5; HBP, 2013, p. 19ff.). Through data-mining of existing studies and by using their own or data from other large-scale projects, the HBP aims to identify general principles of brain organization (cf. HBP, 2013, p. 6–17, Kandel et al. 2013, 662ff.). Unifying the data and principles in multi-scale models would then allow researchers to predict, for instance, connectivity patterns at different spatial scales, plasticity changes at different time scales or putative neural mechanisms of organismic behaviour. The predictions generated by these models could then be tested by simulating the brain on the HBP supercomputing platform (cf. HBP, 2013, p. 21; HBP, 2014a, pp. 20, 191–94).

Whether such model-based predictions will be of scientific value, however, crucially depends on the biological data put into the simulations. It is here where the HBP's vision to create biologically meaningful whole-brain simulations within a decade has been criticized as premature and overly ambitious. Despite large-scale projects mapping human brain connectivity (e.g., Bohland et al. 2009), community consensus suggests that, so far, the data required to properly constrain the multi-scale models or simulation-based hypotheses is largely missing (Denk et al. 2012; Frégnac & Laurent, 2014).

Despite the questionable turn away from data acquisition, the HBP proposes several strategies for validating brain models against experimental data. By mining data in common atlases, or using strategic imaging and behavioural data, researchers could validate 'knowledge gaps' about brain organization or multi-scale simulations of neural function (cf. HBP, 2013, p. 12, 61; HBP, 2014a, pp. 186–90). One-level 'snapshot models' could also be initially validated against biological data, before they are trained to display behaviour and cognition (cf. HBP, 2013, p. 21). This co-existence of biological and computational validation strategies indicates that the HBP does not principally distinguish between the brain as being materially realized in biological tissue or within a computer (see also Parker, 2009). Nevertheless, the methodological primacy of simulation and modelling over experimentation seems to imply that the *focus* of the HBP is not the biological brain *per se*. Rather, invasive or non-invasive laboratory experiments on actual biological brains would only be the occasion for enabling various theoretical, mathematical and computational scientific activities, which can be pursued independently within the fully operating HBP. Since the majority of neuroscientists regard experimentation with biological brains as the key procedure toward understanding the brain, it comes as no surprise that the computational focus of the HBP deeply challenges current neuroscientific practice.

Virtualizing the Lab – Cerebral Technoscience Goes in Silico

The HBP plans to implement or develop a number of technological innovations that, if successfully realized, would move the entire neuroscientific experimental practice into the ICT domain. Once the first principles are identified from the data and the first predictions can be inferred from the models, the Brain Simulation Platform of the HBP would allow researchers to perform *in silico* experiments. The final outcome would be a closed loop between brain models in virtual bodies (or virtual neurorobots) that are interacting with a virtual environment, which can in turn be manipulated by the scientists in their *virtual laboratories* (cf. HBP, 2013, p. 32; HBP, 2014a, pp. 8, 11). Such laboratories would include virtual versions of instruments like fMRI or EEG, or eDrugs for simulating the mechanisms of brain diseases.

The virtue of virtualization is that researchers might gain access and control over the biological processes of the brain which are difficult to manipulate in material laboratories. By stressing these virtues, the HBP approach defines the main role of *in silico* experiments as providing computational manipulations of multi-scale brain models. In contrast, the comparison of simulation results to *in vivo* or *in vitro* experiments seems to be of less interest, especially since the limited experimental data acquisition is unlikely to produce laboratory counterparts to all virtual experiments over the course of the project. This change in priority also provides the HBP with a productively provocative answer to those who criticize its simulations as insufficiently constrained by biological data: if computational manipulations trump laboratory manipulations, the lack of comparison with experimental data can be reinterpreted as a *success* over the limits of access and control in traditional experiments.

Standardization

One apparent drawback of current neuroscientific practice is the enormous variety of experimental protocols, data analysis methods and modelling algorithms. The outcome is that results are only partially comparable, or even worse, that the high number of possible choices leads to false positive results, independently of the quality of the individual experimental design (for the case of imaging, see Carp, 2012). Current efforts to standardize neuroscientific research tools (e.g., the Allen Brain Atlas) will likely allow neuroscientists to compare results across different laboratory sites more accurately. The HBP's specific contribution to that effort would be six remotely accessible ICT platforms (Neuroinformatics, Brain Simulation, Medical Informatics, High-Performance Computing, Neuromorphic Computing, and Neurorobotics, cf. HBP, 2013, p. 17; HBP, 2014a, 4, pp. 3–9).

If the ICT platforms can be sufficiently developed in the thirty-month ramp-up phase, researchers are expected to use them during the operational phase to mine experimental or clinical data, build brain models and interact with them in real time via a human-supercomputer interface, build virtual robots based on the insights of the models and implement some version of these robots into neuromorphic computing systems (cf. HBP, 2013, pp. 17, 53ff.; HBP, 2014a, p. 23ff.). In order to make the platforms accessible for non-expert scientific users, the HBP also plans to provide standardized versions of experimental protocols, data pipelines and modelling algorithms (cf. HBP, 2013, pp. 19, 29, 37ff.; HBP, 2014a, pp. 184, 196). While it would increase access and comparability, the encompassing standardization of the platforms also comes with a loss of experimental flexibility. Many proponents of open science, for instance, do not only share their data but also share their code for data analysis, so that other researchers can further develop it according to their own needs, geared to their specific experimental situation.[2] It is currently unlikely that scientists from outside the project will have that option, since the use of the HBP platforms is allocated via a partnering project mechanism (initially: a Competitive Calls programme, cf. HBP, 2013, p. 36) based on the milestone-driven approach of the HBP core project (HBP, 2014a, pp. 13, 212). Although the HBP publicly supports open source and community-driven approaches to scientific inquiry (cf. HBP, 2013, pp. 19, 61; HBP, 2014a, pp. 9, 25–29, 184), its current institutional and funding structure places strong constraints on experimental flexibility.

Iteration

Another essential feature of the HBP could be its ability to switch iteratively between many modes of scientific inquiry. The idea is that principles extracted from the gathered data can be used for new model algorithms, and by using the models for predictions which are themselves tested in *in silico* experiments, new principles might emerge which can in turn be used to create more powerful algorithms, leading to better predictions, and so on. This methodological iteration is ideally accompanied by the coevolution of neuromorphic computers that implement the principles of brain organization identified so far, and thereby accelerate the iterative process through an increase in computing power. The ultimate vision of the HBP is to let methods and technology evolve into an exascale supercomputer which is capable of simulating the entire human brain. The iterative approach therefore raises the question whether the real goal is to understand the human brain (technology being the proxy) or to build the next generation of supercomputers (the brain being the proxy).

In response to the aforementioned controversy, the EC and the HBP directors stressed that the project is primarily concerned with the development of new ICT infrastructure (HBP, 2014b; Madelin, 2014a). According to some commentators, the HBP now appears to be a "costly expansion of the Blue Brain Project, without any further evidence that it can produce further [neuroscientific] insights" (Frégnac & Laurent, 2014, p. 28; Bartlett, 2015). For reasons that will be elaborated on in the section "world making" below, we believe that it is inappropriate to contrast ICT development with the neuroscientific research conducted within the HBP. The iterative approach that the project pursues blurs the distinction between computer and brain, making them effectively inseparable in practice.

The push towards hybridization is already apparent in the active collaborations between the HBP and European exascale computing projects (e.g., CRESTA in the UK, DEEP in Germany and Mont-Blanc in France) to create ICT that meets the specific demands of whole brain simulations (cf. HBP, 2013, p. 25; HBP, 2014, p. 193). Independently of specific simulation outcomes, these collaborations could turn neuroscience into the next major player in a series of simulation-focused research programs – from nuclear weapons research to climate science – that shaped the development of supercomputing technologies (Elzen & MacKenzie, 1994). Somewhat parallel to the limited flexibility created by the standardized ICT platforms, the goal of building a neuromorphic supercomputer furthermore indicates that the HBP approach works with a *closed* type of iteration. Whereas interactions among the elements of the iterative chain (modelling, algorithms, predictions, simulations) are possible, interaction with elements from the outside (e.g., exploration and conceptual development, question generation, see O'Malley et al. 2010) is only possible *insofar* as they contribute to the overall goal of the HBP. *Open* iteration within HBP's own methodology seems not to be possible, or is at least not explicitly intended in a milestone-driven approach.

These five projected and expected changes that the HBP is set to bring to neuroscientific practice can be summed up in the following slogan: *The HBP sets out to standardize iterative modelling and virtual experimentation on a large-scale, thereby aspiring to move neuroscientific practice successively away from interacting with actual biological brains.*

Infrastructure

A goal that is perhaps even more fundamental than simulating the human brain – and certainly also more likely to be achieved – is to "build a completely new ICT infrastructure for neuroscience […] medicine and computing" (HBP, 2013, p. 3). Building (Big Science) infrastructures is more fundamental than specific scientific goals because the platforms, institutions and facilities will outlast the project's relatively short duration of ten years, even if the goal of simulating the entire human brain will not have been achieved by then.[3]

From Experiment to Database, From Laboratory Bench to Remote Access

The common training as a neuroscientific practitioner requires students to learn principles of data acquisition, experimental design and how to skilfully use laboratory instrumentation (Harrington, 2010). The ICT platforms of the HBP would instead provide *databases* as the initial starting point of neuroscientific inquiry. While the standard interfaces of the platforms can be also used to upload further experimental data from different levels of brain organization, the main task of an HBP practitioner would be to use the existing evidence to create a new *kind* of data, describing simulated brain behaviour on multiple levels. The use of such data within virtual laboratories also implies that in principle, no *material* laboratory would be required to conduct a wide range of neuroscientific activities (e.g., generating and testing hypotheses, designing *in silico* experiments or identifying causal mechanisms, cf. HBP, 2013, pp. 5, 28, 56; HBP, 2014a, pp. 3, 11, 22, 170, 168, 187). The same logic also applies to neurologists working within the HBP, for the Medical Informatics platform allows them to federate clinical data, i.e., to mine them for biological disease patterns without physically removing them from the hospital site of recording (cf. HBP, 2013; HBP, 2014a, p. 195). Here, too, medical scientific inquiry (e.g., disease classification, drug testing or personalized diagnosis) would be possible in principle without requiring researchers to actually enter a material clinic (cf. HBP, 2013, p. 38ff.).

The computer with a remote internet access to the ICT platforms could, therefore, become the actual workplace of the next generation of neuroscientists working in the HBP, even if most or all efforts to build neuromorphic supercomputers fail. In that case, there would still remain a less encompassing database for experimental and clinical data, accessible via conventional computers. Finally, the existence of new simulation facilities implies that the HBP is also a massive data *generation* project (cf. HBP 2013, p. 57), albeit of a different sort: the data are the outcome of computer simulations, not of invasive or non-invasive studies of biological brains. Big Science projects often produce more data than the scientists working on them are able to analyse immediately, and at times further retrospective analysis leads to surprising discoveries.[4] Here, another novel possibility of working as a neuroscientist emerges, perhaps closer to archaeological research than to experimental laboratory practice. Scientists trained on the ICT platforms of the HBP could specialize in large-scale data analysis using different parameter values and pattern recognizers without having to conduct their own (laboratory or virtual) experimental work, and again independently of whether the HBP goal of building a working human brain simulation is ever achieved.

User Environments for Neuroscientists

A broader infrastructural change follows from the creation of multiple interfaces to make the supercomputing and simulation technology of the HBP accessible to the broader scientific community (e.g., the Brain Simulation and the Neurorobotics Cockpit, cf. HBP, 2013, pp. 22, 34; called Virtual Neurorobotics Laboratory in the FPA document, cf. HBP, 2014a, p. 206). Moving neuroscientific practice onto ICT platforms thereby creates two types of researcher that are not specific to any particular subdiscipline. The first type is the *developer*, i.e., a researcher, engineer or technician who builds, develops and maintains the platforms themselves (including, besides technical apparatuses, the interfaces, data pipelines, implemented algorithms, standard models and so on). The second type is the *user*, i.e., a neuroscientific or medical practitioner who conducts, tests and compares her research through the ICT platforms provided by the developer.

How separate these two roles will be within the HBP will depend on the feedback loops built into the project's institutional structure during the operational phase (the iterative approach already indicates that a dynamic feedback model would be easily possible). The separation seems to be quite sharp, however, once researchers outside the project will access the platforms, for they will neither have the knowledge nor the skills to maintain supercomputers or large databases.[5] The user-developer distinction furthermore runs orthogonal to more traditional divisions of scientific labour such as experimenter-theoretician or basic and applied scientist. What unites both the developer and the user, however, is that the ICT platforms establish the computer as the primary object of interaction with the neuronal domain, both in the form of commercial devices and specific (neuromorphic) supercomputers.

The two infrastructural changes, then, can be again summarized in a slogan: *The HBP developer generation aspires to create remotely accessible databases and user environments for scientist-supercomputer interactions.*

Application

Given that the success of the HBP's ambitious aim to simulate the entire human brain from genes to cognition cannot be guaranteed, there are two kinds of potential application outside neuroscientific practice but within the project. *Immediate* applications are independent of simulating human brains with (neuromorphic) supercomputers, while *intermediate* applications are dependent on at least a partial success of this endeavour. Although not sharp, this distinction allows us to assess the likelihood of whether certain transformative potentials of the HBP will be actualized over the next decade(s).

Healthcare and Medical Diagnosis

The HBP considers improvements in diagnosing and treating brain diseases (i.e., neurogenerative diseases, but also anxiety or mood disorders, etc.) to be "the most immediate impact [...] for European society" (HBP, 2013, p. 60; HBP, 2014a, p. 199). The likelihood of fairly quick changes in medical practice initiated by the HBP is comparatively high, because the Medical Informatics Platform and its data federation system are set to function independently of other advances in the project. A central access point to physically remote clinical data could indeed provide new ways to tackle the challenge of developing novel and potentially more effective diagnoses of Alzheimer's, Parkinson's or clinical depression. Even if the HBP will not produce an exascale supercomputer or a new powerful paradigm for predicting biological disease signatures in the next decade, the large-scale nature of the clinical database alone could still substantially transform neurology. To date, case-based reasoning and individual syndromic and histopathological tests constitute the most common practice for treating patients in this domain of medicine (cf. HBP, 2013, p. 38; HBP, 2014a, p. 195).

It is peculiar that the proposal for a new, federated clinical database and nosology is repeatedly justified with the economic argument that brain diseases cost the

European health economy 800 billion € per year (HBP, 2013, p. 55; Markram, 2013, p. 148; Kandel et al. 2013, p. 659). The attempt to tackle this economic burden scientifically implies a strong medical strand within a Big Science project like the HBP. Significantly, it is also said to require science and society to consider "clinical data as a public good, rather than the proprietary information of health insurers and providers" (HBP, 2013, p. 56). Together with stressing the economic burden of disease, the HBP is *ex negativo* construing the Medical Informatics Platform as an *investment in the public*, a rhetorical figure known from the presentation of previous large scale biomedical databases, such as the UK Biobank (Petersen, 2005).

The rhetoric of contrasting the health industry's private data policy with the open data policy of the HBP somewhat conceals that ultimately, the same logic is at work in both cases. Like health insurers and providers, the HBP's economic argument configures 'health' to be primarily a commodity. Clinical data, then, are just the quantified, scientifically objective indicators for individual health, and clinical data can therefore be most easily traded in the health market. Biologically valid classifications of the data into disease categories are then also the most (cost-)effective way of treating personal suffering caused by neurological disorders. The suffering or the disorders themselves, however, are secondary to the goal of commodifying health more effectively, in about the same sense as the biological brain may be secondary to the goal of building neuromorphic computers.

Although the economic and social or personal effects of 'health' cannot be neatly separated in contemporary societies, the bioinformatics approach of the HBP medical platform reflects how the current EU research agendas increasingly focus on the application of technological fixes to societal problems. Further sociological and anthropological studies need to critically investigate this linear policy approach from technological innovation to the expected increase in the well-being of citizens (Levidow & Neubauer, 2014).

Neuromorphic Computers for the Life World?

In the vision document of 2013 the HBP claims, in a characteristic display of its self-aggrandizing proposal rhetoric, that the development of neuromorphic computers for general purpose use could represent a "disruptive technology with a potential social and economic impact comparable to that of the first commercial computer" (HBP, 2013, p. 59).[6] To construct such a 'disruptive' technology as an intermediate application, HBP researchers would need to (i) identify organizational principles from mouse or human brain data, (ii) incorporate the principles into multi-scale brain models, (iii) validate the models and principles by successfully simulating known brain processes and finally, (iv) export a simplified version of the validated model into the neurorobotics platform, where it can be run as the control architecture of a virtual neurorobot on a supercomputer. If the supercomputer itself is neuromorphic, then implementing a brain-inspired hardware system with a brain-inspired control architecture into a standard size commercial device becomes an engineering problem.

Although mutual adjustments between (i) to (iv) are possible within the HBP methodology, the outcome of one of the elements is also interdependent upon the success of the others. Consider the case of building a neuromorphic device with the ability to "predict the likely consequences of [its] decisions, and to choose the action most likely to lead to a given goal" (HBP, 2013, p. 58; cf. HBP, 2014a, p. 165). The HBP would first have to produce a top-down model of this ability, validate the model through simulation and then export a simplified version of it into the neurorobotics platform. In view of the currently uncertain future of the cognitive neuroscience subproject within the HBP (Frégnac & Laurent, 2014; Madelin, 2014b), it seems unlikely that human decision-making will be the first template for a neuromorphic control architecture (cf. also HBP, 2013, p. 54).

Given that there are no commercial applications of neuromorphic computers so far, and given that the interdependencies between the iterative elements make the complexity of a first application highly unpredictable, the disruptive nature of these technologies most likely does not lie in their immediate scientific, economic or societal impact.[7] It would rather lie in showing that it is *possible* to extend the neural domain – i.e., the principles governing the behaviour of neural entities – beyond the biological brain into a silicon-based computer.[8] The disruptive potential of the HBP itself, its immediate impact, then, would derive from concretely exploring this space of possibilities over the next decade.

The proposed immediate and intermediate applications can be summarized in the following slogan: *The HBP medical database and nosology sets out to foster the commodification of personal health as a public good, while the successful construction of a neuromorphic device would show that it is possible to extend the neural domain beyond biological brains.*

World Making

Combining these prospective changes to neuroscientific practice, infrastructure and domains outside of science, we now analyse a number of potential intermediate effects of the HBP (and/or comparable present and future initiatives) on the material, socioeconomic and perhaps even political configurations within which human beings live. The process that is likely to lead to these larger implications can be described in three steps, roughly corresponding to the three slogans at the end of the previous sections.

The De-Organ-ization of the Brain

As described above, the HBP moves away from small-scale invasive animal studies, and from the correlational paradigm of imaging studies in cognitive neuroscience. By attempting to change the normative standards of neuroscience to multi-scale modelling, predictive neuroinformatics, simulation and large-scale integration, the HBP also attempts to overcome currently unresolvable issues such as individual variability (Miller et al. 2012), measurement artefacts (Horton & Adams, 2005, p. 843) and identifying causal mechanisms in the human brain (Logothetis, 2008).

The HBP approach could in principle resolve these issues because the new norms of good neuroscientific practice also reconfigure the object of investigation, i.e., the brain *itself*. The move away from working on biological tissue de-*organ*-izes the brain: that is, it shifts the scientific significance away from characteristics typical for *biological organs*, such as their evolutionarily contingent organization, the variability of cells and areas, or the biochemical nature of signal transmission. What is highlighted instead are the brain's characteristics that become salient from the outlook of predictive informatics, modelling and simulations, such as the statistical connectivity of neurons with different morphologies (Hill et al. 2012) or the electrical signatures around cells which can be simulated in a large-scale model (Reimann et al. 2013). While certainly biologically *informed*, these studies produce a non-biological kind of data (i.e., simulation results), which is then taken as evidence for the behaviour of the entities in question. In other words, the de-organ-ized brain is given the *possibility to behave in new ways*, if the neuroscientist studying it is able to "monitor and control all states and parameters of the [*in silico*] experiment" (HBP, 2013, p. 33; HBP, 2014a, p. 187). Once the HBP moves into its operational phase the biological characteristics would drop out of the iterative chain step by step, until models could be refined entirely by referring to the rapidly accumulating simulation data. But that implies that the new ways of brain behaviour enabled by the iterative simulation method of the HBP are themselves – in a strict sense – not biological, but *computational*, in the sense of computer processing steps run on silicon chips. The ICT platforms of the HBP, therefore, not only provide the neuroscientists with a virtualized experimental system to work with, but also create a *virtual microworld* for the de-organ-ized brain to live in. This world is also populated by virtual neurorobots and environments, or eDrugs, whose behaviour is governed by mathematical algorithms, and is scaffolded by, and probably ultimately built into, (neuromorphic) supercomputers.

The Cerebralization of the Computer

It can now be shown why the respective aims of human brain simulation and building an exascale supercomputer are in fact inseparable in the practice of the HBP. Evolving multi-scale brain models and ICT into a neuromorphic supercomputer also changes the ability of computers to process data (in the same way that virtualization changes the space of possibilities for conceivable brain behaviour). In order to implement such changes, the HBP proposes to build neuromorphic computers by using heterogeneous and highly diverse parts, which behave stochastically, can switch between synchronous and asynchronous communication, individually 'interpret' received inputs and are organized in a hierarchical and highly recurrent structure (cf. HBP, 2013, p. 56ff.).

The outcome of changing hardware and software architecture would be that the computer gets *cerebralized*, which is just the flipside of de-organizing the brain as described above. By providing a virtualized microworld for it, the HBP computers need to become more like the brain in order to fulfil their purpose of running multi-scale simulations. In the more mature stages of the HBP, then, the cerebralized computer and the de-organ-ized brain would become practically indistinguishable for neuroscientists who simulate brain processes on the ICT platforms.

One possible effect of this indistinguishability is that the HBP reshapes the metaphor of "the brain as computer". Whereas it initially enabled neuroscientists to describe brains as serial or parallel information processors, hard-wired circuits and so on (Borck, 2012), the metaphor now implies that computers have to become more like brains, via an iterative convergence upon neuromorphic devices. It also implies that the brain *is* the better computer, since traditional computing reaches its technological limits without the ability to compute processes that match the complexity of neural behaviour. Therefore, one might expect that retroactively, what the history of computing was *about* is changed once the first neuromorphic device can be built.[9] The HBP's major initiator and former spokesperson Henry Markram already wrote in 2006 that "Alan Turing [...] started off 'wanting to build a brain' and ended up with a computer" (Markram, 2006, p. 153). In the context of brain simulation and neuromorphic computing, Turing's aim gains the semantic force of a *factual* claim about the prospects of computer science which were back then technically impossible to achieve. From the perspective of the HBP today, it was already conceivable back then that computing as a field would progress into a stage where it becomes part of the neural domain itself.

Extending the Microworld Beyond the Human Brain Project

The final step of the transformative process beyond the initial HBP agenda involves the material transformation of the world outside the project's ICT infrastructure. Here, the history of computer development is again instructive. Initially a highly specific tool for academic and military purposes, the computer gradually evolved into a commercial device in the late 1980s and became the primary point of accessing information through the Internet in the 1990s. The widespread accessibility of the latter via Wi-Fi or smartphone technology coincided with the (material) transformation of public places (cafés, airports, libraries, classrooms), social and political issues (privacy in social networks, WikiLeaks, NSA surveillance), the economy (online shopping and banking, Dotcom Bubble, The Internet of Things), and of course, scientific research itself.

Processes of the kind just described are often inevitable because the material conditions in question were simply non-existent before the relevant scientific practice was established. Extending knowledge beyond the laboratory is therefore usually not an application to (applied to *what?*) but rather a *reconfiguration* of the world according to the principles embodied in experimental microworlds. As elaborated in the last two sections, the HBP is planning to build a virtual microworld that simultaneously enables new possibilities of action for neuroscientists, and new ways of behaviour for brains and computers. This microworld can be extended outside the HBP by reconfiguring the material conditions – and furthermore the economic, social, cultural and political conditions – so that they resemble the order maintained in the HBP itself. Needless to say, the commercial cerebral computer would be the primary interface between the virtual microworld that is materially realized in the ICT platforms, and the material macroworld of hospitals, family homes, offices, factories or sports stadiums.

The reconfiguration of the macroworld is indicated by the intermediate applications of neuromorphic devices to non-scientific contexts. Here, the promise is that such devices could contribute to the automation of labour in "sectors requiring non-repeated actions that are difficult to standardize: for instance the construction industry, services and the home" (HBP, 2013, p. 60; cf. HBP, 2014a, p. 165). Promising such potential economic benefits falls firmly into the agenda of the FET program of the EU. The FET's focus on ICT is itself connected to the Digital Agenda for Europe within the EU's Horizon 2020 funding initiative launched in 2014. Crucial objectives of the Digital Agenda are the creation of a single digital market in Europe, maintaining European competitiveness in R&D of ICT and fostering ICT-based economies, health and public services, as well as the Digital Science movement. Given that the EU-funded HBP obviously shares many of the aims with these larger policy initiatives, the crucial question is not *whether* the project aims to extend its insights from the micro- into the macroworld, but *how* it attempts to do so.

A possible model for interacting with general-purpose neuromorphic devices would be the neuroscientific user of the ICT platforms, albeit in a technically less sophisticated form. Such an 'ordinary' user would have new possibilities of interacting with neuromorphic devices in the workplace (manufacturing neurorobots, neuromorphic controllers), through communication (mobile devices) or at home (neuromorphic computers or household appliances, cf. HBP, 2013, p. 40; cf. HBP, 2014a, p. 202). Of course, it seems highly unlikely that any of these devices will be built and developed into a marketable commodity in the near future, but the HBP puts at least the *possibility* of doing so on the horizon. It remains to be seen whether and how that possibility will get realized over the course of the project. But the preceding remarks should have made clear that Big Science projects like the HBP are *world making projects*: that is, they are in the business of materially reconfiguring the world we live in. They might have the potential to affect our lives in ways that are more profound, sustained and potentially also less reversible than the isolated 'application' of this or that novel device.

The final slogan that summarizes this section is as follows: *The HBP is a world making project, because it plans to build a microworld for de-organ-ized brains and cerebral-ized computers, and shows how it is possible to extend this microworld through reconfiguring the macroworld via non-scientific neuromorphic devices and a new type of ordinary user.*

Ethics and Society

A project division that requires particular critical attention is the HBP's Ethics and Society Programme, whose level of funding with about 3 per cent of the overall budget roughly mirrors the proportion of relevance accorded to ethics and society in the Human Genome Project. Given such a massive section dealing with foresight, social impacts, ethics and public engagement (HBP, 2013, p. 43ff.; HBP, 2014, p. 208ff.), it might be objected that the kind of external analysis we conduct here is superfluous, as the project's own researchers might be considered to be in a better position to analyse and evaluate the initiative. We reject both parts of this objection, because the available vision and perspective documents are not putting any relevant emphasis on the issues we have addressed in this chapter. Besides the usual programmatic of scientific research ethics, the documents mostly raise rather classical (neuro-)philosophical questions – such as freedom of the will, the biological basis of consciousness or psychiatric illness and so on – questions that are considerably less relevant when it comes to understanding the impacts *specific* to the HBP's agenda. The issues regarding the potential formatting effects exerted by novel technologies and research procedures, medical practice, personal computing or various data management policies do not figure prominently in the documents. What has been slightly modified between the 2013 and 2014 versions, however, is the ratio of emphasis between narrowly ethical and broader societal and public acceptance issues, where the latter have gained increasing prominence. This can be considered a step in the right direction – particularly given the fact that the Ethics and Society Programme initially seemed at risk of adopting little more than a standard neuroethics approach to brain research. This would have amounted to little more than unabashed advertising campaigns for specific lines of research (cf. de Vries, 2007). Refocusing on issues of technology assessment, foresight and public participation, while taking into account normative factors tacitly at work in those sectors of society into which potential innovations are set to be introduced (HBP, 2014, p. 209), are steps that should be welcomed, although not without critical caution.

While the potential for forms of intensified critical engagement within the project might also be gleaned from a recent paper by HBP Foresight Lab leader, Nikolas Rose (Rose, 2014), project initiator and former spokesperson, Henry Markram had a quite different vision for this segment of the HBP. To Markram, the task of the Ethics and Society program was chiefly one of "building public support" (Markram, 2013, 150). Apparently, he construed the public's understanding of the HBP as one of entirely ungrounded fears that arise with regard to the project's impact on matters diffusely perceived as relevant to our humanity. Accordingly, the task of a neuroscience initiative would be to "recognize these fears, lay them to rest and actively build support for neuroscience research": for instance through education and trust building (ibid.). Drawing on the our analysis above, it almost seems like Markram wanted the HBP's Ethics and Society Programme to prepare and condition the wider public for future transformations of the macroworld to come, rather than to engage in critical studies that would have the potential to impact the HBP's agenda, let alone unsettle it in as of yet unforeseeable ways.[10] In stark contrast to this perspective, our assessment here should have made clear that further independent and critical analyses by STS and "neuroscience-in-society" scholars are needed in order to prevent the HBP agenda from influencing or worse, even monopolizing scholarly assessments of the project's likely impacts on neuroscience and society.

However the future of the HBP will play out, it is crucial that the potential impacts of the projected agenda on the technical and informational infrastructure of science, medicine, education and personal computing are subjected to thorough independent scrutiny from multiple perspectives. This being said, it must also be noted that this task calls for a certain amount of patience and also for a dose of hermeneutic charity in one's assessments of some aspects of the scientific agenda, including those that may at first glance seem fantastically exaggerated. Before us appear the initial stages of what will likely be a long game of piecemeal restructuring of several sectors of science and society, with far wider implications than those pertaining to the fate of this one particular project. We risk missing out on relevant issues if we jump on the first opportunity to enter the familiar reflex currents of academic critique. What is called for instead is the more difficult task of staying closely attuned to a large number of developments in order to grasp what will likely remain a highly complex and fluid situation. In the present paper we could do no more than outline the very first steps of what will hopefully become a sufficiently broad and informed assessment of transformations whose full extent and full range of consequences have only just appeared on the horizon.

Conclusion

How does our analysis help understand the larger stakes of the current controversy about the place of neuroscience in the HBP? To date, it seems like the critics' demands are going to be fulfilled, since the EC announced an independent review of the project in early 2015 and promised to biennially evaluate the scientific and organizational agenda before approving further funding (Madelin, 2014b). With the decision to not publish the complete first interim report, however, the HBP continues its restrictive information policy (Abbott, 2015).[11] Thus, there are very good reasons to remain cautious, since the project's basic institutional structure of an EU-funded core project and regionally funded partnering projects, as well as the scientific direction of ICT infrastructure building and whole brain simulation, will likely remain unchanged. Based on our analysis, we would add that the construction of standardized ICT infrastructures – perceived as a positive development by the majority of the neuroscience community – could have wide-reaching impacts on neuroscientific practice independently of the HBP's aim of whole-brain simulation. With regard to the disciplinary effects of integration, standardization and iteration, paired with the HBP's potential impact on society and culture that we call 'world making', one could speak of a massive *lateral agenda* of the HBP which demands critical scrutiny.

Perhaps the most persistent force contravening these expected effects remains the currently fragile support for the HBP by the neuroscientific community. Even in disciplines where standardization is widely supported, heated debates remain over the reliability and proper use of the shared methods and tools (Leonelli, 2012). It is here where neuroscientific practitioners critical of the HBP could remain an active force of resistance that reaches beyond the current dispute over transparency and scientific excellence. With regard to the prospects of reform, however, it is crucial to see that the power relations between the HBP and its critics are asymmetric. The HBP has now gained a material and intellectual *gravitas* – with hundreds of researchers, collaborators, buildings, an education programme and so on – which could make it 'too big to fail', even if the bottom-up simulation approach towards the brain turns out to be scientifically unfruitful (Schatz, 2013).

Besides the analysis of the current issues and future stakes of the HBP, our remarks should also be seen as first steps towards more encompassing critical studies of the HBP. They could serve as outlines for various questions that might be investigated from different science studies perspectives:

- *HPS and STS of computer simulation:* How does the large-scale, standardized, multi-level simulation practice of the HBP bear on discussions about the relationship between experiments, simulations and theories (Winsberg, 2003)? More specifically, what are the epistemological and ontological implications of the aim to create a non-biological target system for human brain simulation in the form of a neuromorphic supercomputer (Parker, 2009)? More broadly, what are the (institutional and economic) implications of the simulation- and ICT-based approach for neuroscientific research culture, and how do they differ from simulation in astrophysics, meteorology and nanotechnology (Johnson, 2006; Sundberg, 2010) or in silico experimentation in molecular biology (Moretti, 2011)?
- *Medical anthropology and medical humanities:* How could the data-federation system and clinical database of the HBP transform local and global medical practice and healthcare? How does the commodification of "health" as a public good (in the form of clinical data) relate to the concept of "venture science" and capitalized biopower (Sunder Rajan, 2006; Cooper, 2008)? How do medical clinical databases relate to the discussions surrounding E-health and the Patient 2.0 (Jensen, 2005; Langstrup et al. 2013)?
- *History and philosophy of neuroscience and technology:* How will large ICT platforms in the HBP impact the relation between users and developers in scientific practice (Millerand & Baker, 2010)? More generally, how does it relate to the historical emergence of "the user", i.e., the type of person interacting with

a computer (Stadler, 2014)? Moreover, how does neuromorphic computing reconfigure the long history of technomorphic metaphors of the brain – from the telegraph to the network (Borck, 2012)? And finally, how does the need for computing power for whole-brain simulations reshape the socio-technological development of supercomputers (Elzen & MacKenzie, 1994)?

• *Historical ontology/political theory of future technologies*: Perhaps less emphasized in our paper is how the notions of de-organ-ized human brains and cerebralized computers relate to the question of what it means to be human in the twenty-first century. Do policy agendas about the use of "converging technologies" that aim to increase human performance (or public science reports about the impact of neuromorphic technologies on society) make it legitimate for scholars to announce the dawn of a "trans-human" society (Fuller, 2011, 2012), or are such announcements premature? At stake here is an assessment of the intensifying debates about issues such as human enhancement, life extension, or technological singularity in the context of the political, economic and social orientations that inform them.

Obviously, this list is incomplete and just points to some of the links between our analysis of the HBP and prevalent themes in science studies that strike us as potentially fruitful for further investigation. Our hope is that we can thereby motivate researchers from disciplines including, but not restricted to the ones mentioned above, to consider the HBP as a significant research topic for critical inquiries into contemporary science, technology and society.

Acknowledgments

Philipp Haueis is a collaborator of Hubbub, and this work was supported by the Wellcome Trust 103817/Z/14/Z.

Notes

1. See the official website of the project: http://www.humanbrainproject.eu.
2. A good example is the community driven, open-source software development system NeuroDebian (Halchenko & Hanke, 2012).
3. For reasons of space we have to omit a discussion of the large-scale educational programme of the HBP (cf. HBP, 2013, p. 44ff.). We would note, however, that the plan to educate 5,000 PhD students within a decade could foster the simulation-based approach to neuroscience independent of the specific outcomes of the HBP (the precise number of PhD's is not provided in the FPA document, cf. HBP 2014a, p. 28ff.). The education programme also represents a form of institutional reproduction commonly found in Big Science projects – see also the analysis of the remote access site Nanohub within the US Network for Computational Nanotechnology by Johnson (2006), p. 46ff.
4. An example of such a discovery is provided by the Fermi National Accelerator Laboratory, where the decay pattern of Higgs bosons was identified in the data long after the Tavatron particle accelerator had already been shut down (Fermilab, 2012).

5. Depending on the project phase, the HBP could also exemplify aspects of Sundberg's (2010) organizational typology of simulation code collectives. In the ramp-up phase, the HBP seems to function internally like a "code of the centre collective", where development (and use) of the ICT platforms is tied to HBP membership. During the operational phase, it could resemble a "code spread all around collective", where HBP members are internally split into "core developers" and periphery developers or users respectively, while nonmembers could take up the position of external developers in the Competitive Calls program or to maintain the community driven Wiki "Brainpedia" (HBP, 2013, pp. 19, 34).

6. Neuromorphic computing was developed by Caltech electrical engineer and computer scientist Carver Mead in the 1980s as an alternative to ICT that relies on Moore's law, i.e., the conjecture that the number and density of transistors doubles roughly every two years. Neuromorphic computers could therefore provide a promising, low-energy alternative to meet the increasing demands for computing power in the future. Only recently, it has become possible to build large-scale neuromorphic systems (e.g., in the SpiNNaker group, UK, the EU FACETs program, or the DARPA SyNAPSE program, USA), although these systems currently do not meet the desired energy efficiency of 10 million Multiply Accumulate Operations per second and Watt (Hasler and Marr, 2013, 19f). The HBP crucially builds upon further improvements of these technologies in order to run its multi-level human brain simulations on exascale supercomputing technology (cf. HBP 2013, p. 23ff., HBP, 2014a, p. 191ff.). Note that the use of the word 'disruptive' was derived from the initial call for the FP7 program of the EC, but has been subsequently dropped in later official reports of the HBP.

7. In August 2014, the SyNAPSE team built the first neuromorphic chip that could be used for commercial application, called "IBM TrueNorth" (Merolla et al. 2014). It runs with 769 times less energy than the SpiNNaker microprocessor. While this energy reduction seems to be an enormous step forward for neuromorphic computing, it remains to be seen how quickly IBM can transfer this prototype into applicable commercial devices, and how TrueNorth may influence the neuromorphic agenda of the HBP.

8. We consider the extension of inquiry beyond an initial domain to be an integral aspect of scientific research (Rouse, 1987, 2011). As a comparison, consider how in nineteenth century physics, electricity and magnetism were considered two independent phenomena, until the laboratory practices of Oersted, Ampère, Faraday and others established new concepts to study the interaction between electrical wires and magnets (Steinle, 1997). It is similarly a trademark of how the HBP understands the brain conceptually that it recognizes a shared boundary between the neural domain and the domain of computing. Implementing ICT platforms that serve as interdisciplinary "trading zones" (Galison, 1996) between both domains is, therefore, a practical consequence of that conceptual understanding.

9. Our claim here draws on Rheinberger (1997), who argues that the initial target of scientific inquiry – what it is 'about' – can retroactively change depending on the further directions an experimental system subsequently takes. Rheinberger's example is Peyton Rous' chicken sarcoma system, which initially seemed to be about the link between viral entities and cancerous cell growth, but subsequently became a means to study normal cell physiology with the help of ultracentrifuges. Only after WW II (in part through the introduction of electron microscopy into molecular cell biology) did viruses re-appear as a determinate entity within the sarcoma system. Rous' conjectures about the viral origin of cancer were therefore retroactively supported, after being largely ignored by the research community for forty years (Rheinberger, 1995, p. 56ff., 76ff.).

10. The HBP therefore neatly follows the Horizon 2020 research agenda, which for the most part diminishes the role of the social sciences and humanities in the guidance – if

not reinforcement – of "capital-intensive technoscientific solutions" to the "grand challenges" of European society (Levidow & Neubauer, 2014).

11. Abbot's claim that the report was not published is not entirely true, since a summary of it is available (Digital Agenda for Europe 2015). Many of the recommendations made in this summary resemble the critical points that we mentioned above (e.g., stronger involvement of the neuroscientific practitioners outside the HBP in the early use and adjustment of the ICT platforms, and a more open exchange between experimental and computational subprojects, cf. ibid., 2, 4). Note, however, that the summary of the report mainly concerns issues of transparent communication and the better integration of the subprojects within the overall structure of the HBP. It therefore does not deal with what we have called above the *lateral agenda* of the HBP. For the different kinds of rhetoric surrounding the report, compare the above document to Van der Pyl (2015).

References

Abbott, A. (2015). Human Brain Project votes for leadership change. *Nature,* March 4 2015, doi: 10.1038/nature.2015.17060 (accessed April 16 2015).

Bartlett, T. (2015). Can the Human Brain Project be saved? And should it be? *The Chronicle of Higher Education*, February 20, 2015, A6 (accessed at April 16 2015). Available at: http://chronicle.texterity.com/chronicle/20150220a?folio=A6#pg6.

Borck, C. (2012). Toys are Us: Models and Metaphors in the Neurosciences In: Choudhury, S. and Slaby, J. (eds.), *Critical Neuroscience: A handbook of the social and cultural contexts of neuroscience.* (London: Blackwell-Wiley, 113–133).

Bohland, J.W., Wu, C., Barbas, H., Bokil, H., Bota, M., et al. (2009). A proposal for a coordinated effort for the determination of brainwide neuroanatomical connectivity in model organisms at a mesoscopic scale. *PLOS Computational Biology, 5*(3), e1000334. doi: 10.1371/journal.pcbi.1000334.

Carp, J. (2012). On the plurality of (methodological) worlds: estimating the analytic flexibility of fMRI experiments. *Frontiers in Neuroscience, 6*(149). doi: 10.3389/fnins.2012.00149.

Craver, C.F. (2007). *Explaining the brain. Mechanisms and the mosaic unity of neuroscience.* Oxford: Clarendon Press.

Cooper, M. (2008). *Life as surplus: biotechnology and capitalism in the neoliberal era.* Seattle, WA: University of Washington Press.

De Vries, R. (2007). Who guards the guardians of neuroscience? Firing the neuroethical imagination. *EMBO Reports, 8*(S1), 1–5.

Denk, W., Briggman, K.L., & Helmstaedter, M. (2012). Structural neurobiology: missing link to a mechanistic understanding of neural computation. *Nature Reviews Neuroscience, 12*, 351–358.

Digital Agenda for Europe (2015). 1st Technical Review Human Brain Project (HBP): Main conclusions & recommendations. March 6 2015 (accessed April 16 2015), available at: http://ec.europa.eu/digital-agenda/en/news/1st-technical-review-human-brain-project-hbp-main-conclusions-recommendations.

Elzen, B., & MacKenzie, D. (1994). The social limits of speed: The development and use of supercomputers. *IEEE Annals of the History of Computing, 16*(1), 46–61.

Enserink, M. (2015). Europe's Human Brain Project needs urgent reforms, panel says. *Science*, March 6 2015 (accessed April 16 2015). doi: 10.1126/science.aab0285.

Fermilab (2012). Tevatron scientists announce final results on the Higgs particle. 2 July. Available at http://www.fnal.gov/pub/presspass/press_releases/2012/Higgs-Tevatron-20120702.html (accessed 15 July 2014).

Fuller, S. (2011). *Humanity 2.0. What it means to be human, past present and future*. London: Palgrave MacMillan.

Fuller, S. (2012). *Preparing for Life in Humanity 2.0*. London: Palgrave Pivot.

Frégnac, Y. & Laurent, G. (2014). Neuroscience: Where is the brain in the Human Brain Project? *Nature, 517*, 27–29.

Galison, P. (1996). Computer simulations and the trading zone. In Galison, P. and Stump, D.J. (eds.), *The Disunity of Science: Boundaries, Contexts, and Power*. Stanford, CA: Stanford University Press, 118–157.

Grillner, S. (2014). Megascience efforts and the brain. *Neuron, 82*, 1209–1211.

Halchenko, Y.O., & Hanke, M. (2012). Open is not enough. Let's take the next step: an integrated, community-driven computing platform for neuroscience. *Frontiers in Neuroinformatics, 6*(22). doi: 10.3389/fninf.2012.00022.

Harrington, M. (2010). *The design of experiments in neuroscience*. 2nd ed. London: Sage.

Hasler, J., & Marr, B. (2013). Finding a roadmap to achieve large neuromorphic hardware systems. *Frontiers in Neuroscience, 7*(118). doi: 10.3389/fnins.2013.00118.

HBP (2012). The Human Brain Project. A report to the European Commission. Available at http://cordis.europa.eu/fp7/ict/programme/fet/flagship/6pilots_en.html (accessed 15 July 2014).

HBP (2013). "Appendix 1: Overall Vision of the Human Brain Project" August 16, Available at https://www.humanbrainproject.eu/documents/10180/17646/Vision%2B Document/8bb75845-8b1d-41e0-bcb9-d4de69eb6603+&cd=1&hl=en&ct=clnk&gl=de (accessed 15 July 2014).

HBP (2014a). "Proposal: Human Brain Project. Framework Partnership Agreement" 29 July. Available at https://www.humanbrainproject.eu/documents/10180/538356/HBP_ FPA_PRINT_29-07-14.pdf (accessed 08 April 2015).

HBP (2014b). The vital role of neuroscience in the Human Brain Project. 9 July. Available at: https://www.humanbrainproject.eu/documents/10180/17646/HBP-Statement.090614. pdf (accessed 14 July 2014).

Hill S.L., Wang Y, Riachi, I., Schürmann, F., & Markram, H. (2012) Statistical connectivity provides a sufficient foundation for specific functional connectivity in neocortical neural microcircuits. *Proceedings of the National Academy of Sciences, USA, 109*(42), E2885–2894. doi: 10.1073/pnas.1202128109.

Horton, J.C., & Adams, D.L. (2005). The cortical column: a structure without a function. *Philosophical Transactions of the Royal Society London: B. Biological Sciences, 360*(1456), 837–62.

Johnson, A. (2006). Institutions for simulations: the case of nanotechnology. *Science Studies, 19*(1), 35–51.

Jensen, C.P. (2005). An experiment in performative history. Electronic patient records as a future-generating device. *Social Studies of Science, 35*(2), 241–267.

Kandel, E., Markram, H., Mathews, P.M., Yuste, R. and Koch, C. (2013). Neuroscience thinks big (and collaboratively). *Nature Reviews Neuroscience, 14*(9), 659–664.

Langstrup, H., Iversen, L.B., Vind, S., & Erstad, T.L. (2013). The virtual clinical encounter. Emplacing patient 2.0 in emerging care infrastructures. *Science and Technology Studies, 26*(2), 44–60.

Leonelli, S. (2012). When humans are the exception: Cross-species databases at the interface of biological and clinical research. *Social Studies of Science, 42*(2), 214–236.

Levidow, L., & Neubauer, C. (2014). EU Research Agendas: Embedding what future? *Science as Culture, 23*(3), 397–412.

Logothetis, N.K. (2008). What we can and cannot do with fMRI. *Nature, 453*(7197), 869–78.

Marcus, G. (2014). The trouble with brain science. *The New York Times*, July 11. Available at: http://www.nytimes.com/2014/07/12/opinion/the-trouble-with-brain-science.html?_r=0 (accessed 14 July 2014).

Markram, H. (2006). The Blue Brain Project. *Nature Reviews Neuroscience, 7*(2), 153–160.

Markram, H. (2013). Seven challenges for neuroscience. *Functional Neurology, 28*(3), 45–151.

Madelin, R. (2014a). No single roadmap for understanding the human brain, 18 July. Available at: https://ec.europa.eu/digital-agenda/en/blog/no-single-roadmap-understanding-human-brain (accessed 21 July 2014).

Madelin, R. (2014b). Preparing the next steps of the Human Brain Project in, Digital Agenda for Europe, blog of the European Commission, 16 September. Available at: https://ec.europa.eu/digital-agenda/en/blog/no-single-roadmap-understanding-human-brain (accessed 22 September 2014).

Merolla, P.A., Arthur, J.V., Alvarez-Icaza, Cassidy, A.S., Sawada, J., et al. (2014). A Million Spiking-Neuron Integrated Circuit with a Scalable Communication Network and Interface. *Science, 345*(6197), 668–673.

Moretti, S. (2011). *In silico* experiments in scientific papers on molecular biology. *Science Studies, 24*(2), 23–42.

Miller, M.B., Donovan, C.L., Bennett, C.M., Aminoff, E.M., & Mayer, R.E. (2012). Individual differences in cognitive style and strategy predict similarities in the patterns of brain activity between individuals. *NeuroImage, 59*(1), 83–93.

Millerand, F., & Baker K.S. (2010). Who are the users? Who are the developers? Webs of users and developers in the development process of a technical standard. *Information Systems, 20*(2), 137–161.

Nature (2014). Brain Fog. Editorial, *Nature, 511*(125). 10 July 2014. Available at: http://www.nature.com/news/brain-fog-1.15514 (accessed 14 July 2014).

O'Malley M.A., Elliott, K.C., & Burian, R.M. (2010). From genetic to genomic regulation: Iterativity in microRNA research. *Studies in History and Philosophy of Biological and Biomedical Sciences, 41*(4), 407–417.

Open message to the European Commission concerning the Human Brain Project. 7 July 2014, Available at: http://www.neurofuture.eu/ (accessed 8 July 2014).

Parker W.S. (2009). Does matter really matter? Computer simulations, experiments, and materiality. *Synthese, 169*(3), 483–496.

Petersen, A. (2005). Securing our genetic health: engendering trust in UK Biobank. *Sociology of Health and Illness, 27*(2), 271–91.

Rose, N. (2014). The Human Brain Project: Social and ethical challenges. *Neuron, 82*(6), 1212–1215.

Rouse, J. (1987). *Knowledge and power: towards a political philosophy of science*. (Ithaca, NY: Cornell University Press).

Rouse J. (2011). Articulating the world: experimental systems and conceptual understanding. *International Studies in the Philosophy of Science, 25*(3), 243–254.

Reimann, M.W., Anastassio, C.A., Perin, R., Hill, S.L., Markram, H., & Koch, C.A. (2013). Biophysically detailed model of neocortical local field potentials predicts the critical role of active membrane currents. *Neuron, 79*(2), 375–390.

Rheinberger, H.J. (1995). From microsomes to ribosomes: 'Strategies' of 'representation'. *Journal of the History of Biology, 28*(1), 49–89.

Rheinberger, H.J. (1997). *Toward a history of epistemic things: synthesizing proteins in the test tube*. Stanford, CA: Stanford University Press.

Schatz, G. (2013). Human Brain Projekt ist too big to fail. 29 January. Available at: http://www.srf.ch/player/radio/srf-4-news-aktuell/audio/gottfried-schatz-human-brain-project-ist-too-big-to-fail?id=542beb04-43ae-463b-b4c7-d894c720d741 (accessed 23 September 2014).

Siero, J.C.W., Hermes, D., Hoogduin, H., Luijten, P.R., Ramsey, N.F., & Petridou, N. (2014). BOLD matches neuronal activity at the mm scale: A combined 7T fMRI and ECoG study in human sensorimotor cortex. *NeuroImage*, *101C*, 177–184.

Stadler, M. (2014). Neurohistory is bunk? The not-so-deep history of the post-classical mind. *Isis*, *105*(1), 133–144.

Steinle, F. (1997). Entering new fields: exploratory uses of experimentation. *Philosophy of Science*, *64*(4), S65–S74.

Sundberg, M. (2010). Organizing simulation code collectives. *Science Studies*, *23*(1), 37–57.

Sunder-Rajan, K. (2006). *Biocapital: The constitution of postgenomic life*. Chicago: University of Chicago Press.

Van der Pyl, T. (2015). Human Brain Project at its First Buoy! February 9 2015 (accessed April 16 2015). Available at http://ec.europa.eu/digital-agenda/en/news/1st-technical-review-human-brain-project-hbp-main-conclusions-recommendations.

8

CONFESSION OF A WEAK REDUCTIONIST

Responses to Some Recent Criticisms of My Materialism

Adrian Johnston

For better or worse, my ongoing theoretical labors are associated now with what has become yet another journalistic-style branding label in the marketplace of contemporary philosophy, namely, "transcendental materialism". I readily admit to bearing no small part of the blame for this, given my frequent reliance upon this label as quick-and-easy shorthand for the constellation of ideas and arguments I seek to explore and develop. If nothing else, convenient economies are all too often well nigh irresistible.

What I have accepted and employed as a self-identification originated in a naming and characterization of Slavoj Žižek's distinctive philosophical project (as per my 2008 book *Žižek's Ontology: A Transcendental Materialist Theory of Subjectivity*). In his 2012 magnum opus, *Less Than Nothing: Hegel and the Shadow of Dialectical Materialism*, Žižek (2012, pp. 906–907) adopts the phrase "transcendental materialism" and further clarifies precisely what it involves (Johnston, 2014a, pp. 13–22; Johnston, 2015b, pp. 7–42). However, in 2014's *Absolute Recoil: Towards a New Foundation of Dialectical Materialism*, arguably a sort of sequel to *Less Than Nothing*, he forcefully repudiates – predictably, I am tempted to say "absolutely recoils" from – this designation, expressing his preference for a dialectical rather than a transcendental materialism (2014, pp. 223–226). He does so in the context of responding to a recent article critical of him (and also of me) by Ed Pluth entitled "On Transcendental Materialism and the Natural Real" (Pluth, 2012b, pp. 95–113). I soon will discuss at greater length in what follows Pluth's thought-provoking interventions.

Putting Žižek largely aside for the immediate time being, my own version of transcendental materialism, especially its generally positive engagements with the empirical, experimental sciences of nature, has drawn certain criticisms from several quarters. In particular, my insistence that being a proper materialist also entails commitments to a (carefully qualified) naturalism and corresponding responsibility *vis-à-vis* the natural sciences has elicited reservations and objections by those wary of granting these sciences any authority in the special explanatory jurisdictions claimed by what are broadly called in France the "human sciences" (or, for post-war French anti-humanists and their followers, the inhuman sciences). The (anti-) humanistic fear, of course, is that a proverbial inch given will result swiftly and inevitably in much more than a mile taken. For those perceiving themselves as the ideologically and institutionally embattled enemies of purportedly megalomaniacal bulldozing scientists and their legions of slavish academic and media minions, the (in)human must be defended against this barbarous onslaught without voluntarily ceding the slightest bit of ground.

To be even more exact, my syntheses of, on the one hand, philosophy and psychoanalysis and, on the other hand, neuroscience tap into old, deeply entrenched conflicts clustering around the perpetually contested distinctions between, for lack of better terms, nature and culture, matter and mind, objectivity and subjectivity. Additionally, my extensive and intensive reliances upon both the Continental philosophical tradition as well as Lacanian analytic metapsychology in these engagements of mine with (neuro)biology unsurprisingly and understandably tend to provoke others sharing my Continentalist and/or Lacanian leanings to protest against these very engagements. Such protesters always end up voicing permutations of the seemingly rhetorical questions: Is not one of the lowest common denominators uniting the otherwise disparate (and not infrequently disagreeing) movements and factions of the past two centuries of post-Kantian European thinking implacably fierce opposition to any and every naturalism as being essentially crude and vulgar, as necessarily mechanistic, reductive, reifying, leveling, eliminative and the like? Is not one of the major legacies of this thinking the lesson that the natural sciences of modernity conceptually cannot and politically should not – the latter is, next to the former, a possibly revealing and perhaps superfluous prohibition – contribute substantially to renditions of subjects, psyches, societies and so on?

In various prior texts, I repeatedly have elaborated theoretical and exegetical arguments maintaining that Hegelianism, Marxism and Lacanianism (three of my [and Žižek's] main sources of inspiration) are compatible with and, indeed, cry out for something along the lines of what I aim to articulate under the heading of transcendental materialism – and this *contra* many interpretations of these orientations according to which they are unwaveringly hostile to any sort of science-informed naturalism. Although I will not exhaustively rehearse here the details of these earlier-made arguments of mine, I nevertheless must rely upon aspects of some of them in the present context of responding primarily to Pluth. In tandem with these transcendental materialist reinterpretations of my acknowledged philosophical and psychoanalytic sources of inspiration, I also newly will reinforce my extant insistences to the effect that the images and impressions of the sciences of nature pervading and purveyed by my critics are somewhat outdated, inaccurate and misleading. However, at the same time, this exercise in counter-criticism will not amount to a mere reiteration of previous claims and conclusions on my part. Instead, it contains refinements and even modifications of my position in light of Pluth's insightful, inspiring and probing observations.

My engagement with Pluth specifically is the continuation of an already-underway dialogue, with me here responding to Pluth's response to a text by me on Lacanianism and neuro-psychoanalysis (Johnston, 2013e, pp. 48–84; Pluth, 2013, pp. 85–93). I also will be referring in this intervention to two contemporaneous pieces by Pluth closely related to the contents of our discussion: the aforementioned "On Transcendental Materialism and the Natural Real" (i.e., Pluth's article addressed by Žižek in the latter's *Absolute Recoil*) as well as an essay in a volume on *Badiou and Philosophy* entitled "The Black Sheep of Materialism: The Theory of the Subject" (2012a, pp. 99–112). In these three texts, taken together, Pluth brings up a host of crucial issues and apprehensions about the intersections between philosophy, psychoanalysis and the sciences as these feature in my work (as well as in that of Žižek and Alain Badiou).

Employing a 'first the good news, then the bad news' format, I will begin by remarking upon the multiple points Pluth makes with which I am in profound agreement. First of all, I concur with his choice to see Sigmund Freud's foundational accomplishments as amounting to something on the order of a Bachelardian-Althusserian 'epistemological break' and/or Badiouian 'event' (he directly makes these French theoretical references) (2012b, p. 99; 2013, p. 86). Although I have reservations about Pluth's labelling of psychoanalysis as a new 'science' – and, insofar as Pluth himself takes great pains to distinguish strictly between analysis and natural science (2012b, pp. 100–103; 2013, pp. 87, 92), he would have to share these reservations – I too recognize the birth of the Freudian field a little over a century ago as a transformative seismic upheaval of gargantuan historical proportions. Similarly, I do not disagree when, speaking of psychoanalysis, Pluth (2013, p. 87) says, "its objects are not identical to natural-scientific objects". In other words, there is a consensus between us that any strongly reductive or eliminative naturalist materialism would be unwilling and unable to acknowledge and do justice to the entities and events, structures and dynamics uniquely captured by the peculiarities of psychoanalytic theory and practice. Likewise, Pluth and I indeed share the *desideratum* that, within a science-compatible yet non-reductive/eliminative materialism, "the autonomy of psychoanalysis and its region of influence is preserved" (as Pluth [2013, p. 88] himself puts something he and others suspect I, with my turns to the natural sciences, might not truly want or care about sufficiently). We are on the same page when he maintains that philosophy and psychoanalysis, as disciplines irreducible to exclusively empirical dimensions, cannot simply be falsified, invalidated, nullified or the like by the natural sciences (2012b, p. 102). Let me be as clear and unambiguous as possible right up front: As an adamant materialist and quasi-naturalist, I nevertheless come to praise philosophy and psychoanalysis, not to bury them (with the sciences as undertakers).

Furthermore, and as a flip-side to the immediately preceding, Pluth (2012b, p. 97) avows that one of his motivations is to defend the thesis that, as he articulates it, "truths are indeed available to us in natural human languages". By this, he means that the formal languages of mathematics and logic arguably underpinning the post-Galilean natural sciences of modernity do not enjoy an exclusive monopoly on what can be asserted with ontological validity and epistemological legitimacy apropos "the really real" (2012b, pp. 104, 112). Whereas these sciences of nature favor intrinsically meaningless but maximally rigorous formal languages, psycho-analysis, both metapsychologically and clinically, relies upon the meanings of living tongues actually used (and using) human beings individually and collectively (and this notwithstanding Jacques Lacan's extensive, protracted efforts at the formaliza-tion of analytic theory). I subsequently will return from critical angles to what lies behind Pluth's contrast between formal and natural languages. For the time being, I want to underscore that I endorse his complementary insistences that there is more to "the really real" than merely what can be quantified, formalized and so on and that non-mathematical discourses can and do (at least sometimes) truthfully articulate these other really reals.

In "On Transcendental Materialism and the Natural Real" (2012b), Pluth addresses Žižek and me along these just-sketched lines. For instance, he states therein:

> The sciences have a right to reductionism. It is difficult to imagine a material-ist philosophy that would reject this. What they are not entitled to – at least, what does not follow from their reductionism – is the philosophical view that the order to which everything reduces (the natural real) is alone the really real. Whatever human reality is built up out of non-human components; but it does not thereby follow that these components, on which human reality depends, qualify exclusively as the really real. This is a philosophical point, and not a sci-entific one. The question is: does Žižek's transcendental materialism, which he also wishes to be a dialectical materialism, get us to this point? (p. 104)

Then, he concludes this article with the following proposal:

> … I would suggest that arguments for reductionism be embraced but also reconsidered: does the claim that every being reduces down to more simple constituents – a claim that does need to be defended – necessarily entail the claim that those constituents are the really real, the ontologically fundamental level? While spiritualisms and dualisms may not be able to put up with such a vigorous reductionism, a version of dialectical materialism should be able to, when it is drawing on the legacy of Hegel, Marx, Freud, and Lacan. (p. 112)

Taken together, these two block quotations from the same text seem to be calling for a pluralistic yet simultaneously flat ontology encompassing both certain onto-logical regions within which efficient-causal and/or mereological reductions are appropriate and correct (the set of these domains constituting what Pluth dubs "the natural real") as well as other ontological regions in which such reductions are out of place and order (i.e., everything really real that nonetheless does not belong and is irreducible to the natural real). Earlier in this article, Pluth comments that, "an ordering or ranking of beings is one of the hallmarks of idealism, whereas one of the hallmarks of materialism is its ontological egalitarianism" (p. 104). Correspondingly, in Pluth's essay "The Black Sheep of Materialism" (2012a), which defends Badiou against me (Johnston, 2013b, pp. 81–107), he repeatedly insists, on the basis of his interpretation of Badiou's 1982 *Theory of the Subject*, that the most important tenet for a materialist is the insistence on a radical equalization of the weight of being assigned to any and every entity and happening (with Pluth here expressing concerns to the effect that I prioritize the objects and processes dealt with by the empirical, experimental sciences of nature as more real than the subjects, structures and dynamics not addressed by these sciences) (pp. 102, 105–106, 108–109, 112).

Despite Pluth's association of idealism and materialism with vertical/hierarchized and horizontal/de-hierarchized ontologies respectively (basically, anti-monism versus monism), he nonetheless displays in his various essays an acknowledgment of the untenability of this fashion of distinguishing between idealisms and materialisms, at least in the cases of dialectical (and transcendental) versions of the latter. For instance, he stipulates that any palatable ontological egalitarianism "equalises apparently distinct regions of being without collapsing them into a monistic unity" (2012a, p. 108), adding a sentence later that: "… what the desired materialist theory of the subject needs to do is level down two different regions – here, let's say, thought, languages and formal codes, on the one hand, and bodies and organisms on the other – without risking monism" (p. 108).

Elsewhere, Pluth (2012b) relatedly maintains:

> … the sciences, as sciences, can only ever be reductive … Žižek (along with Adrian Johnston on this) points out that contemporary sciences actually give us a different, non-deterministic, non-mechanistic, and indeed indefinite, model of nature, such that while a reductionism to constituent parts may still be part of what the sciences do, this is no longer a reductionism that entirely eliminates topics such as freedom, the negative, and the subject from the picture … This is what Žižek's call to situate psychoanalytic insights within the brain sciences should accomplish: rather than relying on an account of how what psychoanalysis says and does is true because it is, or can be, grounded in the neurosciences, instead the basic structures psychoanalysis reveals will also be seen to be structures unveiled by the neurosciences themselves. (p. 106)

It now has become clearer exactly what Pluth has in mind as regards a proper, satisfying dialectical and/or transcendental materialism (in his own previously quoted words, "a version of dialectical materialism … drawing on the legacy of Hegel, Marx, Freud, and Lacan"): On the one hand, such a materialism ought to be ontologically egalitarian (i.e., de-hierarchized) specifically in the sense of refusing for philosophical reasons to privilege one identifiable region or (sub-)set of regions of being as of greater or ultimate reality as compared with all other regions (the latter thereby would be rendered in principle, if not also in practice, reducible or eliminable *vis-à-vis* the former); on the other hand, such ontological egalitarianism should not itself be entirely 'flat' or 'horizontal' insofar as, in order not to be reductive (or 'leveling') in its own manner, it must allow and account for (relatively) autonomous layers and tiers of entities and events emerging out of other strata of beings and occurrences – with, for any truly materialist materialism, the layers and tiers of 'the natural real' (Pluth mentions 'bodies and organisms') still enjoying some sort of grounding or explanatory priority. I am not sure precisely how Pluth envisions squaring egalitarianism with materialism along these lines. However, I both agree with the bulk of what is indicated by Pluth's criteria for dialectical/transcendental materialism as well as simultaneously anticipate that he nevertheless will not be comfortable with what I will propose below in terms of my own rapprochement between egalitarianism and materialism.

As seen here, Pluth adamantly alleges that, ontologically speaking, the modern sciences of nature are inherently anti-egalitarian, hierarchizing beings and events such that all of them are reduced down to or eliminated in favor of 'the natural real' as the one-and-only 'really real' ('the sciences, as sciences, can only ever be reductive'). He writes of "their intrinsic reductionist tendencies" (2012b, p. 110). His extended reply to my sketches of a Lacanian neuro-psychoanalysis in the *Southern Journal of Philosophy* closes with the warning that, "if the sciences are given a reductionist inch, they will take everything" (2013, p. 93). As Pluth already knows, this posit of the sciences necessarily bringing with them reductionism is where the 'bad news' of my disagreements with him gets underway.

Žižek already formulates a rebuttal of Pluth's assertions about scientific reductionism in *Absolute Recoil*. In the article to which Žižek is responding here, Pluth gestures in passing at Žižek's psychoanalytic engagements with the neurosciences (2012b, p. 106) (most extensively in 2006's *The Parallax View* [Žižek, 2006, pp. 201–250; Johnston, 2008, pp. 203–209, 269–287; Johnston, 2014a, pp. 111–138; Johnston, 2015e, pp. 121–152]). But, for both the Žižek of *Absolute Recoil* and Pluth's article "On Transcendental Materialism and the Natural Real", the topic of Lacan with quantum physics is the real bone of contention. Like Pluth, I have criticized (albeit differently) Žižek's forays into physics elsewhere at length; and, unlike Žižek, I consider biology rather than physics to be the provider of the key natural-scientific ingredients for an anti-reductionist-yet-materialist theory of the subject (Johnston, 2014a, pp. 111–183; Johnston, 2015d). That said (and without rehashing my objections to Žižekian quantum physics), Žižek (2014) argues against Pluth that:

> … insofar as our human reality is characterized by the irreducible gap between imaginary-symbolic experience and the Real, where the two levels

are inextricably mediated (i.e., the 'symbolic Real' is the Real of this human reality), *it is this very gap which is present in the quantum universe*, in the guise of the gap between the virtual pre-ontological quantum universe and ordinary physical reality that emerges through the collapse of the wave function, and this collapse has to be mediated (if not by subjectivity proper then) by some kind of perceptive/registering agency. In other words, what quantum physics discovers 'in nature' is another version of the very gap between 'objective mechanisms' and 'subjective experience' that we usually take as specifically human. In this precise sense, quantum physics is not simply and directly 'reductionist': its lesson is not that there is a natural 'real Real' independent of our experience, reducing this experience to a mere appearance, but that this very gap between the Real and its appearing is already out there, 'in nature.' Or, to put it in yet another way, the lesson of quantum physics is that 'nature itself' is already 'non-reductionist': *already 'in nature,' appearance matters, is constitutive of reality*. (p. 225)

For reasons spelled out on another occasion, I think that Žižek's recourses to the physics of the extremely small carry reductionist risks not easily defused by considerations such as those contained in this block quotation (Johnston, 2014a, pp. 165–183). Nonetheless, quantum physics aside, I agree, *contra* Pluth, with this passage's broader "lesson … that 'nature itself' is already 'non-reductionist': *already 'in nature,' appearance matters, is constitutive of reality*". Given Pluth's tethering of the sciences to reductionism plus the synonymy he implies between the non-reductive and the dialectical, it follows for him, as he emphasizes several times, that the sciences are devoid of any spontaneous dialectical materialist (*qua* anti-reductive) tendencies whatsoever (Pluth, 2012b, pp. 96, 110–111; Pluth, 2013, pp. 87, 89). Both Žižek and I dissent from this view, instead seeing such natural scientific disciplines as particle physics, evolutionary theory and/or the biology of the human to be implicitly (*an sich*), if not also explicitly (*an und für sich*), anti-reductionist. But, in tension with Žižek as well as contrary to Pluth, I consider the life sciences generally and the neurosciences particularly to be the precise indispensable disciplines for a dialectical/transcendental materialism constructed around an anti-idealist and non-dogmatic account of subjectivity.

Žižek, right on the heels of responding to Pluth's "On Transcendental Materialism and the Natural Real" in *Absolute Recoil*, expresses some critical reservations with respect to a recent article of mine on 'weak' (*ohnmächtig*) and 'rotten' (*pourri*) nature *à la* Hegel and Lacan respectively (Johnston, 2012a, pp. 23–52; Žižek, 2014, pp. 225–226). He states:

My counter-argument here is that this line of thought should nonetheless be further developed in (at least) two directions. While 'rotten nature,' the failure and dysfunctionality of animal life opens up the space for the symbolic, the entry of the symbolic still cannot be causally explained in this way – it does indeed occur as a 'miracle,' *ex nihilo*. In other words, there is no teleology here, the symbolic only retroactively renders its natural (pre)conditions readable as such, as its (pre)conditions. But how is this 'miraculous' entry *ex nihilo* possible? How should the 'pre-human Real' be structured so that the symbolic can explode in its midst? A possible answer is indicated by speculations in quantum physics about the virtual Void out of which (particular) reality emerges through the collapse of the wave function: negativity materialized in the symbolic process is not something that magically cuts into positive nature; it rather (re)actualizes at the specific level a negativity immanent to the 'pre-human Real' as such. So while it is true that the emergence of (human) negativity can take place only against the background of certain biological (pre)conditions, the pre-human Real itself *does* emerge *ex nihilo*. (Stephen Hawking makes this point nicely when he claims that, although within an established order of things, nothing – no particular element – can emerge *ex nihilo* without violating the laws of nature, an entire universe paradoxically *can* emerge *ex nihilo*.) (p. 226)

Whatever Žižek's intentions, I consider these reflections to constitute less a 'counter-argument' than a set of friendly amendments largely compatible with my position. My friendly amendments in turn to these remarks begin with the stipulation that I do not posit weak/rotten nature as a 'causal explanation' *qua* sufficient condition (instead, only as a necessary condition) for everything more-than-natural (as, I would claim, Žižek himself does too [Žižek, 2012, pp. 185, 263–264, 283–284, 744; Žižek, 2014, pp. 18, 21, 27–28, 96, 107–109, 202–205, 240, 396]). Additionally, like both Charles Darwin and Žižek, I too deny the existence of any deep, archaic teleology preordaining the immanent genesis of denaturalization out of nature (i.e., for Darwinians, the evolution of human beings in their distinctiveness, the natural history of their rise as itself the rise of human history). Furthermore, I seek to answer Žižek's question "How should the 'pre-human Real' be structured so that the symbolic can explode in its midst?" at the level of the transition specifically from non-human biology to properly human life-forms (in the *Realphilosophie* of Hegel's mature encyclopedic system, the stretch running from the last third of the *Naturphilosophie* ["Organics"] to the first third of the *Geistesphilosophie* ["Subjective Mind/Spirit"]).

As for the recourse to theoretical physics in the second half of the preceding block quotation, I will limit myself in the present context to two remarks. First, as Žižek himself indicates ("it is true that the emergence of (human) negativity can take place only against the background of certain biological (pre)conditions"), there is no *prima facie* mutual exclusivity whatsoever, at least in principle and insofar as neither Žižek nor I are strong reductionists, between my focus on biology and his on physics. Second, and as I already noted, I elsewhere have articulated what I see as problematic (and even, perhaps, non-Žižekian) in Žižek's appeals to quantum realities. Related to this second remark, one should pause to ponder the fact that physics is a science which, since the toppling of Newtonianism in the early 1900s, has been in a state of permanent crisis for the past century, a crisis still yet to be resolved to this day. Apart from the rift between general relativity and quantum mechanics, the position of string theory and its permutations, as mathematically promising to mend this rift, in (or out) of physics *qua* science/scientific per se continues to be a matter of heated controversy. Considering that variants of string theory call into question the picture Žižek relies upon of a universe emerging *ex nihilo* via a Big Bang (with these variants postulating instead an alternate picture of an eternal multiverse perpetually spawning different universes), Žižek's "speculations … about the virtual Void out of which (particular) reality emerges" might have to remain, for some time to come, just that, namely, speculations as intra- and extra-scientifically contestable and con-tested guesses, hunches, musings and the like.

Anyhow, both Žižek and I are committed not only to Hegelian dialectical-speculative approaches generally, but also specifically to the spirit (if not always the letter) of Hegel's *Naturphilosophie* as well as, relatedly, *Naturdialektik à la* dialectical materialism (although Žižek and I differ in our interpretations and criticisms of this tradition running from Friedrich Engels through V.I. Lenin and onward primarily within non-Western Marxisms) (Žižek, 2012, pp. 461, 907–908; Žižek, 2014, p. 93; Johnston, 2011, pp. 141–182; Johnston, 2013a, pp. 103–136; Johnston, 2015a; Johnston, 2015c; Johnston, 2015d; Johnston, 2016). Pluth voices two main objections to these commitments: First, Hegelianism and materialism are fundamentally incompatible (2012b, pp. 108–109); second, neither nature nor the natural sciences can be qualified as properly dialectical-speculative (2012b, p. 109; 2013, p. 87). As regards the first objection, it hinges on Pluth's assertion that Hegel's philosophy is "(badly) idealist" (2012b, p. 109). I take Pluth to mean by this that Hegel is, at a minimum, an anti-materialist who, being a mental monist positing as the be-all-and-end-all Absolute. A God-like, cosmic, mega-Subject, mirrors reductive materialism in an oppositely but equally reductive spiritualism, thereby inverting a mechanistic "all is matter" into an animistic "all is mind". To cut a long story short, both Žižek and I (as well as various other Hegel specialists) consider this picture of Hegel's philosophy to be plain wrong as factually incorrect textually and historically (Žižek, 2012, pp. 141, 149, 237–239, 285–286, 291, 380, 386, 389–390, 400–401, 459, 536–539, 740, 924–926; Žižek, 2014, pp. 96–97, 106–109, 140–141, 153, 192, 202–205, 227; Johnston, 2012b, pp. 103–157; Johnston, 2014a, pp. 23–25, 37–46; Johnston, 2014b, pp. 371–418; Johnston, 2014d, pp. 204–237; Johnston, 2015b, pp. 7–42; Johnston, 2016).

Succinctly summarized, the lamentably commonplace image of Hegel as a deludedly grandiose 'spirit monist' is plagued by four interrelated shortcomings divisible into two major oversights and two false conflations. In terms of over-sights: one, this caricature neglects the profound early influence on Hegel's (and F.W.J. Schelling's) thinking of Friedrich Hölderlin's 1795 critique in "*Über Urtheil und Seyn*" of the transcendental idealism of J.G. Fichte's 1794 *Wissenschaftslehre* as excessively, indefensibly subjectivist (Hölderlin, 1972, pp. 515–516); And, two, this image unjustly eclipses moments in Hegel's corpus (such as, among many other moments, the "Remark on Idealism" appended to the end of the discussion of the finite-infinite distinction in "The Doctrine of Being" of the *Science of Logic* [1969, pp. 154–156]) when he take great care to explain how and why his absolute idealism is a holistic metaphysics taking as its antagonist not mind-independent objective reality and/or physical matter but, instead, (false) absolutizations of the finite *qua* atomistic, self-identical and sufficient unto itself (i.e., absolute idealism is diametrically opposed to finitism, not realism, materialism and the like). In terms of conflations: One, Pluth's rendition of Hegel as "(badly) idealist" mistakes absolute idealism for subjective idealism, with the latter (unlike the former) essentially involving the anti-realist/materialist insistence that everything counting as 'really real' ultimately depends for its existence on the immaterial mental mediations of perceiving and/or conceiving subjectivity (whether that of individual human beings or some divine, transcendent[al] macro-Mind); and, two, it equivocates between panlogicism (to which Hegel subscribes) and pantheism/panpsychism (to which he definitely does not), erroneously assuming absolute idealism's anti-Kantian claim that mind-independent objective reality already is formed in and of itself along categorically and conceptually delineable lines (rather than [in]consisting of formless things-in-themselves) to be tantamount to claiming that this reality is metaphysically reducible to categories and concepts in the narrow mentalistic/psychologistic sense of subjective idealism. Given the combination of an absolute idealism properly construed as non/anti-subjectivist and a philosophy of nature sublating (*als Aufhebung*) the polar extremes of hylozoism-pantheism/panpsychisim-vitalism (as per Aristotle, neo-Platonism, Baruch Spinoza and Schelling at certain moments in his youth) and atomism-determinism-mechanism (as per Isaac Newton, Pierre Simon Laplace and aspects of Immanuel Kant's theoretical philosophy), Hegel facilitates instead of impedes the development of dialectical and transcendental materialisms.

Now, what about Pluth's second objection to Žižek and me (in addition to the first objection asserting the incompatibility between Hegelianism and materialism) according to which neither nature nor the natural sciences can be qualified as properly dialectical-speculative? Although Pluth spends some time in this vein on Žižek's philosophical appropriations of quantum physics, I will not be defending this Žižek, given both that I too am critical of these Žižekian appropriations as well as that I rely on biology rather than physics (with accompanying arguments to the effect that biology is far from fully reducible to physics). That noted, the fundamental thrust of my answer to Pluth's second objection is the contention that organic nature and the life sciences are self-limiting on a speculative-dialectical interpretation explicitly raising them to the dignity of their implicit notions. That is to say, this nature and its scientific disclosures include within themselves, at least as nascent potentials capable of fitting theoretical activations, intraregional capacities for interregional auto-limitings, namely, intra-natural grounds immanently critiquing scientistic (i.e., non/extra-scientific) reductionist ambitions *vis-à-vis* more-than-natural regions.

My resistances to treating biology as reducible to physics (ultimately inspired by the interrelated historical root sources of the Kant of the *Critique of the Power of Judgment*, Hegel's *Naturphilosophie* and encyclopedic system overall, plus Marxian-Engelsian historical and dialectical materialisms) already go a long way toward allaying Pluth's fears of rabid, unchecked and excessively austere reductionism of a mechanistic and/or eliminative sort. But, moreover, Pluth has even less to fear in that, analogously to Žižek with respect to quantum physics, I maintain that the life sciences of the human organism have begun to reveal a spontaneously non/anti-reductive (living) nature, namely, a self-denaturalizing nature *qua* a biology already in and of itself blocking unqualified naturalist identifications of the biological as exhaustively determinative of everything (apparently) in excess of things biological. If nothing else, the epigenetics of the human organism generally and the related neuroplasticity of this organism's central nervous system specifically – these recently established and exemplary life-scientific facts are central to my, Catherine Malabou's and Žižek's overlapping yet distinct efforts toward early-twenty-first-century reactivations of the legacies of the dialectical materialist tradition – are paradigmatic instances of intra-scientific grounds for indicting as scientifically indefensible scientistic reductions of non/extra-scientific subjects and disciplines (those of the humanities and social sciences) as epiphenomenal, fictional, illusory, unreal and so on.

To gesture back to when Pluth warns that "if the sciences are given a reductionist inch, they will take everything", I hence am tempted to rebut this by very loosely paraphrasing it: If the sciences are given enough inches of rope, they sooner or later will hang themselves. To be more precise, they auto-reflexively will self-limit and de/in-complete themselves in relation to other ontological regions and disciplinary jurisdictions and schemas. To refer again to epigenetics and neuroplasticity as quintessential instances here, these are structures and dynamics situated "extimately" (to adverbialize a Lacanian neologism for the intimately exterior, the internally external [Lacan, 1992, p. 139; Lacan, 2006c, pp. 224–225, 249]) within the natural sciences and, thus, signal these sciences' needs for non/extra-scientific explanatory complements and supplements (including those concerned principally with the historical, the social, the cultural, the linguistic, the conscious, the unconscious and so on). Like the figures/shapes of consciousness in Hegel's *Phenomenology of Spirit*, with "Observing Reason" being the figure/shape most relevant in this precise context, the natural-scientific *Weltanschauung* can be trusted eventually to "do violence to itself at its own hands" (Hegel, 1977b, pp. 51–52, 145–210; Johnston, 2012b, 103–157).

Pluth (2013) maintains that "the sciences are currently in a particularly pernicious ideological position", and recommends countering this with "some kind of philosophical move, which I can only think of now in terms of a humbling of the sciences' ambitions to give us both the best ontologies and the best explanations" (p. 93). How and why Pluth and I each think differently about this situation marks one of the (if not the) fundamental points of divergence between us. I view the 'ideological position' of the natural sciences as at least as much of an opportunity to be welcomed and utilized (as a kind of Trojan horse for ideology critique) as a 'pernicious' threat or disaster to be combatted and repelled. Pluth counsels preserving anti-reductionism through counter-offensives against the sciences and their conjunctural hegemony (i.e., "a humbling of the sciences' ambitions to give us both the best ontologies and the best explanations") mounted from a site of philosophical resistance completely outside scientific edifices. In short, he prefers a strategy of external critique (for reasons I have spelled out at length on other occasions [2011, pp. 141–182; 2013a, pp. 103–136; 2013f, pp. 91–99; 2014a, pp. 139–164; 2015a], I consider this strategy not only to be likely to go down in vain to not-entirely undeserved ideological and intellectual defeats, but even to bring with it a host of its own ideological dangers associated with idealist, religious and spiritualist structures continuing to enjoy a hegemony easily rivaling that of the sciences). By contrast, I counsel preserving anti-reductionism (while, at the same time, not risking compromise on or betrayal of materialism) through, as Hegel would put it, sublationally (*als Aufhebung*) raising these same sciences to the dignity of their arguably anti-reductive notions. This amounts to allowing the sciences internally to delineate and display from within themselves (however wittingly or not) their own epistemological and ontological limitations and correlative (co-)dependencies upon other disciplines. In short, I prefer a strategy of immanent critique.

Pluth's earlier-underscored insistences on nature and the natural sciences being completely non-dialectical and essentially, inevitably reductive force him to defend a non/anti-reductionist materialism (if it still can be qualified as properly materialist) via purely external (rather than immanent) critiques of these sciences. Recalling Pluth's enthusiastic appeals to "Hegel, Marx, Freud and Lacan", I consider my immanent-critical maneuvers with respect to the sciences to be much more in the spirit of both the procedures and concepts forwarded by these four thinkers (among many others), including their subtle, nuanced appreciations of nature and the natural sciences. However, my somewhat abstract philosophical assertions in this and the four preceding paragraphs call for additional clarifications on my part in tandem with further engagements with Pluth's ideas and arguments.

Žižek's above-quoted response to Pluth in *Absolute Recoil* mentions "a natural 'real Real' independent of our experience". This is an allusion to Pluth's distinction between a natural Real and a philosophical and/or psychoanalytic Real (Pluth, 2012b, p. 103), with this binary opposition serving as the load-bearing central pillar of his criticisms directed at Žižek and me. The soundness and plausibility of the cases Pluth makes apropos dialectical and transcendental materialisms ultimately depend upon the solidity and justness of his avowedly non-dialectical fashion of distinguishing between these two Reals. So, obviously, everything hinges here on the question of whether or not this *Verstand*-type distinction of Pluth's is, in fact, solid and just.

Pluth contrasts the Real of natural science with that of philosophy/psychoanalysis in a cluster of closely interconnected ways. To begin with, he maintains that, "natural-scientific objects, unlike psychoanalytic ones, do not change with our theories of them", immediately equating this with his already-discussed thesis according to which "the natural sciences are necessarily undialectical" (2013, p. 87). He then employs these contentions so as to suggest, *contra* what he takes to be my position, that the "objects" of neurobiology and psychoanalysis are different-in-kind, with the former as unchanging and the latter as changing. Hence, Pluth maintains, neurobiological and psychoanalytic objects are not to be confused or identified with each other (2013, p. 87).

Already at this juncture, I want to pause so as to challenge Pluth's fashion of distinguishing between the natural Real and the philosophical/psychoanalytic one. In particular, his suggestion that human central nervous systems "do not change with our theories of them" strikes me as scientifically out of date and debunked. Its falsification starts with such life-scientific watersheds as Donald O. Hebb's work on learning mechanisms (as per his 1949 *The Organization of Behavior: A Neuropsychological Theory* [pp. 63, 70]) as well as Stephen Jay Gould's proposals related to "punctuated equilibrium" (beginning with a 1972 article co-authored with Niles Eldredge [pp. 82–115]). The new basic tendency in the life sciences represented by the likes of Hebb and Gould rapidly gains momentum in the 1990s thanks to research related to evolutionary theory, epigenetics, neuroplasticity, mirror neurons, affective neuroscience and neuro-psychoanalysis. This fundamental thrust of biological investigations into human beings over the course of recent decades up through the present has been increasingly to reveal just how (self-)changeable human organisms generally and their brains specifically are in relation to such enveloping milieus as larger natural environments (with their periodic natural disasters), historical inheritances, social institutions, cultural practices, linguistic structures and so on (milieus including, among myriad other things, natural-scientific theories about humans propagated by humans).

In Pluth's own Lacanian terms, a distinctive peculiarity of human (neuro)biology is that its own natural Real (as arguably far from entirely reducible without remainder to the natural Real[s] of inorganic chemistry and/or particle physics) is in and of itself also something more-than-natural inextricably intertwined with Real (*qua* other material levels and layers within and beyond the individual organism), Symbolic (*qua* structural) and Imaginary (*qua* phenomenal) dimensions. When Pluth (2013) comments in his detailed response to my article "Drive Between Brain and Subject" that, "I suspect Johnston is not saying that the drive is somehow located *in* the thalamus, which would be very strange" (p. 91), his suspicion is correct. I would say instead that any and every *Trieb* as per psychoanalytic metapsychology, although having such biological and neurobiological necessary (albeit not sufficient) conditions as the thalamus, is both widely distributed within the central nervous system itself and body as a whole as well as even more widely distributed between this complex bodily system of systems and the extra-bodily mediating dimensions, with which this body is inseparably entangled, of the natural, the historical, the social, the linguistic, the cultural and so on. All of this entails the upshot that the (auto-) transforming and spontaneously self-denaturalizing natural Real specific to the life sciences of human beings involves a dialectical short-circuiting of Pluth's admittedly undialectical dichotomy partitioning a purportedly static natural Real from a kinetic non/anti-natural one. As Lacan (1977) would put it, there is something in (human) nature more than nature itself (p. 268). Or, through a deliberate misappropriation of some of Jean-Paul Sartre's language, I would say that a hallmark feature of the natural Real proper to human beings is to be a not-wholly essential essence, namely, an essence essentially opening up to the predominance of existence over essence (Johnston, 2013b, pp. 90–91, 103–104, 107) (with Pluth's opposition between his two Reals echoing the contrast central to both the younger and older Sartre between essence and existence [Pluth, 2013, p. 92]). In yet other words, and to employ the simplistic nature-nurture pair, the human natural Real is a nature naturally inclined toward the dominance of nurture over nature – evolutionarily pushed into pushing back against evolutionary pushes, genetically pre-programmed for epigenetic reprogramming and neurally hard-wired for more-than-neural rewiring.

To connect directly my line of counter-argumentation immediately above with the origins of what both Pluth and I agree is on the order of magnitude of a Badiouian event – I am referring to Freud founding psychoanalysis through his discovery of the unconscious – Freud's early essay "Some Points for a Comparative Study of Organic and Hysterical Motor Paralyses" (*SE* 1, pp. 155–172) is one of many pieces from the Freudian corpus with which my proposals dovetail (additionally, this 1893 essay looms large in the background of Lacan's account of the mirror stage, especially as he encapsulates it in his first text in English, the 1951 presentation and 1953 article "Some Reflections on the Ego" [1953, pp. 11–17]). For this Freud as well as the Lacan who follows him – and, I follow both of them here – at the level of things bodily, there is more than one body of interest to psychoanalysis. In addition to the anatomy and physiology of the organic body of concern to biology and somatic medicine (a body Pluth would situate within his register of the natural Real), there also are (in Lacan's parlance) Imaginary and Symbolic bodies formed out of imagistic and linguistic ideational representations (i.e., Freud's *Vorstellungen* and Lacan's signifiers). Some of the most fundamental networks constituting foundational formations of the unconscious are grounded upon the associative trellises of these virtually-real, non-organic, more-than-natural bodies of representations of things bodily.

Freud, in the same pioneering period of the mid-1890s during which he unprecedentedly paves the way for his invention of psychoanalysis, also brings to the fore (starting in 1895's *Project for a Scientific Psychology*) the life-scientific fact of the prolonged prematurational helplessness (*Hilflosigkeit*) distinctive of human beings (*SE* 1, p. 318; *SE* 20, pp. 154–155, 167; *SE* 21, pp. 17–19, 30). This ontogenetic material bedrock (as anything but solid, with its fissures and fragility) of human nature likewise becomes lastingly pivotal within Lacan's theorizing too (Lacan, 2001a, pp. 33–35;

Lacan, 2001b, p. 427; Lacan, 2006a, pp. 76, 78; Lacan, 2006b, pp. 92; Lacan, 2013, pp. 27–30). Both via this biological reality and the not-unrelated theme (with myriad variations) of conflict so absolutely central to analysis (Johnston, 2013b, pp. 13–38), Freud (somewhat more implicitly relative to Lacan) and Lacan (somewhat more explicitly relative to Freud) hypothesize that, to refer back to 1893's "Some Points for a Comparative Study of Organic and Hysterical Motor Paralyses", deficiencies and tensions internal to the organic body are the intra-organic necessary conditions of possibility for this same organic body coming to be affected and even overwritten by more-than-organic 'bodies' composed of *Vorstellungen* and signifiers drawn from surrounding experiential and socio-symbolic matrices of mediation (including, at least always potentially, *Vorstellungen* and signifiers drawn specifically from medical, scientific, philosophical and/or psychoanalytic discourses – *contra* Pluth, and here on psychoanalytic, in addition to biological, grounds, the natural Real of soma can be impacted and altered by theories of soma). For Freudian-Lacanian analysis, the help-less, unharmonized body-in-pieces (*corps morcelé*) of the invariably premature human infant thrown into being, this baseless base of a bio-material facticity, is the pre-cise endoskeletal opening within living first nature for this nature's transformative symbioses with any and all exoskeletal denaturalizing second natures (Johnston, 2012a, pp. 23–52). This specific Real, crucial for Freud's and Lacan's purposes, has the status of being a third something neither-nor/both-and in relation to Pluth's non-dialectical division between the natural Real and the philosophical/psychoana-lytic Real. It is this Real dialectically-speculatively subverting Pluth's *Verstand*-level dichotomy between his two Reals that I seek to delineate throughout my work under such different-yet-interrelated headings as, for instance, the "barred Real", "weak nature" or the "weakness of nature" (Hegel's *Ohnmacht der Natur*), "kludginess" and the "anorganic" technically defined as distinct from the merely inorganic.

Furthermore, Lacan himself (not only for me, but also for the Badiou Pluth tries to employ as a foil against me) pointedly would take issue with Pluth's move of strictly quarantining the natural Real in the ways he does in the process of criticizing Žižek and me. Much earlier here, I quoted Pluth as stating that, "truths are indeed available to us in natural human languages". He says this in the course of maintain-ing that the artificial formal languages of the post-Galilean sciences of nature, with their meaningless mathematized descriptions of material beings and happenings, do not enjoy an absolute monopoly over truths apropos "the really real". This implies, among other things, that he associates "natural human languages", by contrast with artificial formal languages, with meaning rather than meaninglessness (an implica-tion explicitly corroborated when Pluth [2012b] declares that, "the kind of under-standing we allegedly get from the sciences … is what I'm calling a theoretical understanding, which needs to be taken as one that is deprived of *sense*" [p. 100]).

However, for Lacan, Freudian psychoanalysis, unlike, for example, Jungianism and contrary to popular (mis)perceptions of analysis, is anything but a depth psychological hermeneutics concerned with uncovering eclipsed meanings and bringing to light submerged, subterranean profundities. The Symbolic status of the Lacanian unconscious is, when all is said and done, precisely that of a Real Symbolic, namely, a web of structures and dynamics ultimately (un)grounded upon the accidental, the arbitrary, the contingent, the factical, the given, the gratuitous, the nonsensical and the like. This Real-Symbolic status of the unconscious is conveyed over the arc of Lacan's teachings by his theories of material-rather-than-meaningful pure signifiers-separate-from-signifieds, letters, *jouis-sens*, *lalangue* and so on. Relatedly, and specifically because the object of psychoanalysis (i.e., the unconscious) is fundamentally Real-Symbolic as just outlined, Lacan regularly emphasizes that the Galilean contribution to the early-seventeenth-century birth of modern natural science (i.e., the mathematization of the study of nature) is a crucial historical condition of possibility for Freud's later creation of psychoanalysis; Galileo Galilei's (mathematized) natural Real foreshadows the Freudian unconscious *qua* network of senseless structures nonetheless amenable to rigorous, rational description and delineation via formal, mathematical-style analytic accounts and interpretations. Similarly, Lacan's career-long relations with various formalisms (including game, set and knot theories, structural anthropology, cybernetics, symbolic logics and topology), intensifying in the 1960s and, especially, 1970s, culminates in the doctrine of the 'matheme', with Lacan seeking (however successfully or not) to get beyond, behind or beneath Pluth's "natural human languages" so as to distill the truths of analysis's "really real" (i.e., the Real-Symbolic unconscious) into meaningless-yet-exact(ing) elements of an artificial formal language for metapsychology. These particular core features, among others, of Lacan's thinking make Pluth's partitioning of the natural from the psychoanalytic Real appear to be utterly un-Lacanian (Johnston, 2008, pp. 85–90; Johnston, 2009, pp. 118–124; Johnston, 2013b, pp. 32–58; Johnston, 2013c, pp. 141–147; Johnston, 2014a, pp. 248–294).

Lacanian linguist and theorist Jean-Claude Milner furnishes me with yet another counter-objection to Pluth's ostensibly Lacanian criticisms of my materialism. Specifically, Milner's 2011 book *Clartés de tout: De Lacan à Marx, d'Aristote à Mao* opens with a 2009 interview in which he sketches an immanent critique of Lacan's wariness and reservations regarding the life sciences. Maintaining the Koyréian thesis having it that Galileo's privileging of formal language (as mathematics) establishes the definitive feature of modern scientificity – Lacan, like many of his contemporaries and successors in French theoretical circles, adheres to Alexandre Koyré's Galilean rationalism equating the scientific with the formalized (Koyré, 1958, pp. 99, 278) – Milner advances two premises: first, there are non-mathematical formalizations (what he calls "literalizations", with reference to the later Lacanian concept of the letter) sufficient to meet Galilean standards of scientificity; second, since Lacan's death, biology (with genetics as the paradigmatic instance in this context) has achieved precisely this degree of sufficiently scientific formalization *qua* literalization. Milner's conclusion from these two premises is that even the most orthodox, card-carrying Lacanians, as Lacan himself arguably would do if he were still alive to witness the recent progress of the life sciences, should shift to a more favorable, receptive stance with respect to various things biological (Milner, 2011, pp. 14–19, 22–24). I forward proposals similar to Milner's in the first volume of my *Prolegomena to Any Future Materialism* (2013b, pp. 39–58). The consequence with respect to Pluth is, once again, that Lacanianism itself undermines, rather than supports, treating psychoanalytic structures and dynamics as absolutely dissimilar with and different-in-kind from "the natural Real", whether that of physics or biology.

After formulating his just-disputed distinction between two Reals, Pluth (2013), two pages later in the same article ("On Adrian Johnston's Materialist Psychoanalysis"), brings up the tricky, controversial topic in philosophy of mind of "downward causation" (and, as he knows, psychical subjectivity is, for my transcendental materialism, something strongly emergent in relation to material beings that can and does react back upon these same beings). He elaborates:

> … must a theory of downward causation that wishes to be not only a dialectical but also a materialist orientation in some meaningful sense, not hold that there is a stopping point, a point at which some sort of natural 'object' is hit that is immune to at least *some* kinds of transformation? What I have in mind are changes that are not on the level of organization and configuring, transformations that the idea of downward causation certainly allows for, but on the level of the kind of 'stuff' itself. Whatever kind of downward causation there is between psychoanalytic objects and neurological ones, it would seem that no amount of downward causation would be able to transform the neurological stuff in question *qua* the stuff that it is; although it can of course organize it differently, affect its performance, and bring about different operational results from it. (p. 89)

Pluth's remarks in this passage seem to hinge upon an essentially Aristotelian distinction between matter ("the kind of 'stuff' itself", "the neurological stuff … *qua* the stuff that it is") and form ("the level of organization and configuring"). Thus, they provide me with an opening for an Aristotelian response: If any living or non-living substance (such as a human body, with its epigenetics, and brain, with its neuroplasticity) is what it is not only as the matter that it is (i.e., the "stuff … *qua* stuff that it is"), but as this matter 'organized' and 'configured' in a distinctive form, then the 'transformations' acknowledged by Pluth himself must count also as, so to speak, transubstantiations (with, for Aristotle, substance equaling matter plus form). That is to say, psychoanalytic objects 'downwardly cause' the transformation (i.e., change of form *qua* reorganization/reconfiguration) and, hence, transubstantiation of the matter/stuff of the neurological objects thereby taking on different forms. If "it [downward causation] can of course organize it [neurological stuff] differently, affect its performance, and bring about different operational results from it", then, coupled with the accompanying Aristotelian matter-form distinction, what is there for a convinced, confident materialist to be troubled by as regards what therefore would be the resulting not-very-reductionist 'reductionism'? Pluth's articulation of the worrying problem already is its own reassuring solution.

Just three pages after the above block quotation, Pluth (2013) mentally experiments with a 180-degree inversion of the "same matter, different form" model. According to this alternative hypothetical 'scenario':

> … what psychoanalysis is doing and finding may be legitimized by, supported by, endorsed by, not objects but *structures* that are outside of psychoanalytic theory and practice – and ones that are being found by the neurosciences. But, since it is only the *structures* that are identical, psychoanalysis need not be ontologically reducible to the neurosciences – for the objects it works on *are* very different from neurobiological objects. But in this scenario – which is maybe some kind of panlogicism? – in which the homologous *structure* between neurology and psychoanalysis is the red thread connecting the two, it is still not clear what kind of relationship there would be between the two disciplines, since the discovery of a structure at an ontological level cannot be said to confirm anything about another 'emergentist' structural level further down the chain (pertaining to psychoanalytic objects) without bringing back reductionism, I think. (p. 92)

At the end of the next paragraph, Pluth adds:

> Even if there is but one structure to rule them all – shared in common by neuroscience and psychoanalysis – this is no reason to think that the neurosciences offer us anything like an adequate *account* of the drives; for the two structures are operative in very different situations – one the natural-scientific real, and the other not just the real, the symbolic, or the imaginary, but let us say the practical-historical as well. (p. 92)

Starting with the second of these two passages, I previously both called into question the distinction Pluth here phrases as that between "the natural-scientific real" and "the practical-historical" one (if the proper name Darwin stands for anything, it is the profound problematization of such distinctions between nature and history) as well as stipulated my construal of Lacan's register theory generally and my register-theoretic parsing of drives particularly. Hence, I will not belabor these points further. I also already touched upon the topic of panlogicism in connection with Pluth's (mis)interpretation of Hegelianism.

Apropos panlogicism, my guess is that Pluth mentions it in the first of the two prior quotations ("maybe some kind of panlogicism"?) so as to summon up once more the revenant of Hegel (with his awareness of how Žižek and I each are committed to reactualizing multiple aspects of Hegel's philosophy). Assuming that this is so, I want to engage in a bit of argumentative judo by using Pluth's tacit pushing on my Hegelianism as an opportunity to shift into further clarifying my own orientation regarding the questions and difficulties raised by Pluth. Keeping in mind the difference between panlogicism and panpsychism I stressed earlier in the course of addressing Pluth on Hegel, I am inclined to own up to leaning in the direction of a Hegelian absolute idealism (again, as distinct from subjective idealism and, as such, compatible with materialism, [quasi-]naturalism and realism) with its dialectical-speculative identity of identity and difference (Hegel, 1977a, p. 156; Hegel, 2002, p. 154). To be more exact, and to appropriate Pluth's paraphrasing of J.R.R. Tolkien's *Lord of the Rings*: Although "there is but one structure to rule them all", this one structure, as itself a factical contingency (Pluth, 2012b, p. 110) existing only in and through the matter of physical nature (i.e., as never having been or being metaphysically real over and above this nature and its outgrowths), self-sunders by fragmenting itself into many irreducible-to-each-other structures, including the (relatively) autonomous structures essential to the mindedness and like-mindedness of full-fledged subjects.

Returning to Pluth's direct criticisms of me, he explicitly voices suspicions that I am both a reductionist and a verificationist (2012a, pp. 100–102, 111). In this vein, he (2013) has the following to say:

> In several places, along with his articulation of a nonreductionism, Johnston claims that the neurosciences reveal a 'basis' or a 'ground' for the objects of psychoanalysis … And he must do this if his view is going to be a materialism. Imagine that the neurosciences found nothing at all like psychoanalytic objects and structures in the natural real. Would this absence not discredit psychoanalytic theory and practice? Yet if one is inclined to answer that it would indeed discredit psychoanalysis, why is that? And how is one *not* for that reason a reductionist of at least some sort, however minimal? (p. 89)

Pluth continues:

> There may be different types and different degrees of reductionism. Which kind of reductionism does Johnston reject? No doubt, at a minimum, one according to which psychoanalytic objects just are neurobiological objects. (p. 89)

He soon adds:

> … I wonder if there are types of reductionism that are not avoided by Johnston's view, especially when he claims that the neurosciences offer a *ground* for the objects of psychoanalysis – a thesis with which I am inclined to agree, only I struggle with how to articulate it, and with its implications. (p. 89)

Pluth and I certainly share a common 'struggle'. Before addressing the anxieties about verificationism already raised in the first of these three quotations, I need to clarify in what sense I use such words as 'basis' and 'ground' apropos things neuro-biological in relation to the theory and practice of psychoanalysis. To begin with, I treat the brain (and body of which it is an inseparable part) as the always-necessary, but only rarely (if ever) on its own sufficient, ontological condition for the psychical subject front and center in analysis. Only if I were to insist on the central nervous system alone as the largely or completely sufficient condition for analytic subjectivity would I be the type of reductionist worrying Pluth. Hence, when I speak of 'basis' or 'ground', this should be construed usually as designating a necessary, but not sufficient, material condition – and, moreover, with the epigenetic, neuroplastic brain as solely one of a multitude of other ontological necessary conditions for the psyche/subject of analysis.

On the next page of the same article, Pluth (2013) elaborates further upon his hesitations around the topic of verificationism, itself closely bound up with the topic of reductionism. He muses aloud:

> If it were the case that the sciences ruled out the very possibility of psycho-analytic objects and phenomena, what would this mean? Clearly they do not, and Johnston shows how they do quite the opposite. But, when engaging with the sciences, it is difficult not to open the door to verificationism—by which I mean a view according to which if the sciences say there is no basis, no material correlate for X, then philosophers are obliged to say there is not really any such thing as X either. Now, Johnston is in the happy position of finding sciences that confirm the existence and possibility of psychoanalytic objects and phenomena … (p. 90)

A few lines later, he comments:

> If we were not to find any neurobiological correlates for psychoanalytic objects, I suspect that Johnston would find this to be a serious problem. But putting the neurosciences in the position of *confirming* psychoanalytic theory (or is it just in that they are in a position to confirm its objects?) almost certainly must degrade the status of psychoanalysis, for does it not make psychoanalysis dependent on another discipline for a large share of its validity? And even if the neurosciences do not *explain* anything that really goes on in psychoanalysis, it seems that on this view psychoanalysis is still *ontologically* dependent on what the neurosciences are finding. (p. 90)

At this point, I have a lot to say in response to all five preceding quotations taken together. First of all, and from what Pluth recognizes as my "happy position" (with my happiness itself having no bearing on the truth or falsity of the contents at stake), I am not entirely uncomfortable perhaps admitting that, for me as the materialist that I am, Pluth's counter-factual scenario in which psychoanalysis globally seems to be at odds with neurobiology (i.e., in which psychoanalytic structures and dynamics appear to be completely contradicted by neurobiological findings and facts) cannot arise to begin with. Put differently, I would wager that, in the counter-factual case of human neuroanatomy and neurophysiology being radically otherwise than as revealed thus far by neurobiology, the objects and processes delineated and handled in psychoanalysis as we know it would not surface in the first place. The consequence of this is that what Pluth himself concedes is the imagined, unreal scenario ("they do quite the opposite") of the "serious problem" of an apparently total incompatibility between the analytic and the biological he utilizes so as to motivate his critical questions regarding verificationism ("Imagine that the neurosciences found nothing at all like psychoanalytic objects and structures in the natural real", "If it were the case that the sciences ruled out the very possibility of psychoanalytic objects and phenomena", "If we were not to find any neurobiological correlates for psychoanalytic objects") actually never would occur, since no analytic appearances would be in evidence so as to generate the seeming incompatibility with biological grounds. In short, I feel no compulsion to angst much about the risks of verificationism insofar as they hinge upon such hypothetical, otherworldly eventualities. If this makes me minimally a verificationist, then so be it. It is a small price to pay for being a true materialist.

Additionally, there are a number of other components to my position, ones of which Pluth is well aware, that go a long way towards laying to rest Pluth's interrelated fears about reductionism and verificationism. For starters, and as I already argued at length above, neither neurobiology nor Lacanianism tolerates Pluth's non-dialectical distinction between natural and psychoanalytic Reals. Along similar lines, I am sympathetic to partisans of models of the extended mind/ brain in Analytic philosophy of mind, with epigenetics and neuroplasticity intra-biologically making it such that brains and bodies (i.e., biological first natures) are quite literally shaped and reshaped by extra-cerebral and extra-corporeal mediating forces and factors (i.e., more-than-biological second natures). Only complex, highly distributed nexuses of intertwined, entangled first and second natures, of entities and events both biological and more-than-biological, can and do constitute simultaneously both necessary and sufficient conditions for the effective existences of the subjects of philosophy and psychoanalysis, with these subjects' ineliminable uniqueness and autonomy. What is more, taking into account the immediately preceding in conjunction with my arguments (inspired by Kant and Hegel) against any and every epiphenomenalism as well as transcendental materialism's related "principle of no illusions" (all of this spelled out in detail by me on prior occasions [2008, pp. 269–287; 2013d; 2013f, pp. 91–99; 2014a, pp. 13–107; 2014c]), I grant downwardly causal powers to subjectivities both ontologically and epistemologically irreducible to the natural matter alone of the natural sciences (i.e., the explanatory jurisdictions excluding disciplines other than these sciences). Such stipulations put me drastically at odds with reductionism and verificationism, at least as these sorts of stances are understood by most people, including Pluth himself.

However, I must confess that I may indeed be guilty, as Pluth hints, of a more-restricted, less-global verificationism and a weakened, minimalist reductionism. As for the former, this perhaps is best elucidated with a non-hypothetical scenario, a factual (rather than counterfactual) instance. Within the past and present psychoanalytic world, specifically that of practicing clinical analysts, the topic of "therapeutic action" has been and continues to be a source of puzzlement, uncertainties, disagreement, controversies and so on, namely, an issue that is anything but settled and consensual. That is to say, questions about how and why analytic treatment effects changes in analysands (whether in individual analyses or in analysis overall) are far from being decisively and definitively answered within the community of analytic clinicians. What is therapeutically efficacious and why remains something of a mystery for theorists and practitioners of analysis.

Starting with Freud himself, transference (more precisely, the "transference neurosis" in which the figure of the analyst becomes the lightning rod for his/her analysand's symptoms and pathology) often is put forward as the real lynchpin of therapeutic action in the analytic process (*SE* 12, pp. 143, 153–155; *SE* 14, p. 196; *SE* 18, pp. 18–19; *SE* 23, pp. 174–177; Laplanche and Pontalis, 1973, pp. 462–464). In Freud's discourse and that of most analysts following him, this lynchpin typically is referred to as "the transference", with a definite article and in the singular, thereby implying the reality of a single, massive, block-like entity – specifically, a stable, enduring phenomenon over the course of the analysis in which an analysand consistently relates to his/her analyst as if the latter were one, and only one, other figure (for example, the analysand's father in "a paternal transference" or mother in "a maternal transference"). But, what if empirical investigations into brains provide evidence to the effect that there is not a/the transference as a uniform, homogeneous (mis-)identification of the sort traditionally spoken of by analysts? What if these investigations reveal instead that there are multiple neural networks operative in relationships like those between analyst and analysand, that a person's brain, when relating to someone else, shows simultaneous activation of a plethora of its synaptic webs corresponding to a plurality of significant figures other than the specific someone being related to in the *hic et nunc*? Would this not at least suggest that transference is really always transferences in the plural, that there is no such phenomenon in the analytic process as a one-and-only case of mistaken identity? If so, should clinical analysts not reconsider and maybe alter how they listen, intervene and interpret in their practices? Should they not revisit and perhaps revise some of their ideas about therapeutic action?

A number of Pluth's statements suggest that he is tempted to respond by asserting the right of analysts, taking refuge under the purported sovereignty of psychoanalysis as a non-scientific discipline, simply to ignore such possibilities blithely and serenely. Whether this would be to the benefit of the theory and practice of analysis, a good way for it to proceed and advance, is quite debatable. Who here is defending (as of continuing contemporary relevance and legitimacy), and who is burying (as an outdated and invalidated relic of ancient history) analysis? If anything resembling what I propose is neuro-psychoanalysis (transcendental materialist or otherwise) as reductionist and verificationist, why prefer anti-reductionism and anti-verificationism? Which of these two alternatives (i.e., analysis with or without neuroscience) really is worse or less desirable? Which is more irresponsible, reckless and dangerous?

Another example might help reinforce the same point. Mark Solms, the founder of neuro-psychoanalysis in the English-speaking world, draws upon the cross-species neuroscientific research of Jaak Panksepp (as well as that of Antonio Damasio and Joseph LeDoux, two other giants of affective neuroscience sympathetic towards psychoanalysis). Panksepp's empirical and experimental probings of the emotional and motivational (analysts would say 'affective' and 'libidinal') dimensions of the central nervous systems of human and non-human mammals have produced results leading Solms to challenge a fundamental tenet of classical Freudian metapsychology. Whereas Freud's post-1923 second topography (what Anglo-American analysts label the 'structural model') characterizes the agency of the id as unconscious (*SE* 19, pp. 23–24; *SE* 23, pp. 96–98, 101, 163–168, 170–171, 191), Solms's Panksepp-indebted counter-thesis is that the Freudian id is, in fact, primarily conscious, its affects/emotions and motivations/drives always being (mis)registered consciously, being felt and experienced in any number of ways one way or another (Solms, 2013, pp. 5–19) (incidentally, Solms's contention should be congenial to Lacanians, since Lacan, starting with his 1950s "return to Freud" as bound up with the proposition according to which "the unconscious is structured like a language", fiercely maintains a strict distinction between the Freudian unconscious proper and the id, tenaciously combatting pseudo-Freudian tendencies sloppily to conflate these notions). Per some of Pluth's cautionings, should Solms not do this? Why not? Should Solms and all other analytic thinkers preserve the disciplinary autonomy of psychoanalysis by stubbornly sticking to Freudian orthodoxy in the face of extra-analytic indications testifying against select elements of this orthodoxy? Why? Exactly what is to be lost here?

Incidentally, the mention of Panksepp's work provides the chance for me to respond to another of Pluth's reservations. Pluth (2013) asks, "Are we not able to induce psychoanalytic phenomena in animals that do not have the neurobiology Johnston highlights" (p. 91)? Obviously, this question is meant to cast doubt on there being neurobiological underpinnings of specifically analytic experiences and processes. Pluth probably is thinking here of Lacan's observations about human beings (partially) neuroticizing their canine and feline pets, with family dogs and cats sometimes manifesting their families' symptoms, domestication bringing with it domestic neuroses (Lacan, 1967–1968, 11/15/67; Lacan, 1973–1974, 6/11/74; Lacan, 1990b, p. 117; Lacan, 1994, p. 187; Lacan, 2006d, pp. 137–138) – "*homme*-sick animals, thereby called domestics [*d'hommestiques*] … for that reason are shaken, however briefly, by unconscious, seismic tremors" (Lacan, 1990a, p. 5). Yet, the comparative studies between mammalian species, human and non-human alike, conducted by Panksepp and like-minded biological researchers rest firmly and securely on the substantial, well-established continuities and likenesses of anatomy and physiology across the central nervous systems of various kinds of mammals. Although humans are distinctive primarily by virtue of their cognitive capacities supported by an evolutionarily recent neo-cortex unlike anything to be found even in humans' closest primate relatives, the neurobiology of emotion and motivation is basically more similar than dissimilar between human and non-human mammals. Despite not being entirely sure what "psychoanalytic phenomena in animals" Pluth has in mind, I would counter that it is more likely than not that (part of) what makes possible 'inducing' such phenomena is precisely the emotional and motivational neuroanatomy and neurophysiology non-human mammals have in common with humans.

To specify further what this philosophical and psychoanalytic relative autonomy involves – these specifications address Pluth's concerns about the reduction-related issue of verificationism – I should start by stating that it must be underspecified in advance of particular considerations of particular topics. Put differently, I see Lenin's historical materialist insistence on concrete analyses of concrete situations (Lenin, 1916) holding for dialectical/transcendental materialist analyses of potential or actual intersections between disciplines (such as between philosophy and/ or psychoanalysis, on the one hand, and the life sciences, on the other). To assuage partially (although not completely) Pluth's anxieties about verificationism – as with reductionism, I might at least be a weak verificationist – I think it safe to say that outright falsifications of the non-empirical (specifically as theoretical concepts in metaphysics or metapsychology) by the empirical (specifically as experimentally supported discoveries in physics, chemistry or biology) are rare, albeit not unheard of or unimaginable.

Nonetheless, I also think that, phrased in a Hegelian style, the distinction between the empirical and the non-empirical is a distinction internal to the empirical itself – in the sense that the initiative in drawing the dividing lines between empirical and non-empirical explanatory jurisdictions falls to the empirical side in this relationship (with the history of ideas bearing this out) (Johnston, 2013f, pp. 91–92). And, as I caution elsewhere (2013f):

> Acknowledging and accepting the preceding is not tantamount to a deplorable scientistic demotion of philosophy from the heights of extreme hubris, as the queen of the sciences, to the depths of equally extreme humility, as their handmaiden. A recognition of and reconciliation with the historically manifest unevenness in which the empirical has the initiative in shaping and reshaping the borders between itself and the non-empirical is not a surrendering of the rights of philosophy; this is not even a concession that such shaping and reshaping ever is, could, or should be wholly and completely decided exclusively from the side of the empirical, which itself never is

purely empirical anyway. Philosophy remains called to exercise its inalienable obligations to: critically posit and evaluate the more-than-empirical presuppositions behind the sciences; facilitate and partially structure discussions between the sciences; and, theoretically explore extrapolations from present states of interaction between philosophy and the sciences beyond the present to the benefit of all disciplines concerned. The multiple relations between the empirical and the non-empirical are not to be predetermined, but, rather, to be left open to ongoing negotiations informed by appropriate dialectical-speculative sensibilities (or, in Leninist terms, concrete analyses of concrete situations). (pp. 91–92)

Furthermore in the same vein, this theoretical Leninism of mine arguably is necessitated as the lone reasonable stance in response to the differing and unpredictable complexities taking shape within interfacings of empirical/scientific and non-empirical/extra-scientific materials. For instance, the intricacies of navigating always-specific cases of (non-)relationships between, on the one hand, philosophy and psychoanalysis and, on the other hand, neurobiology call for both a case-by-case approach as well as, correlatively, an abstention from hasty generalizations and premature predictions blanketing all past, present and/or future cases.

However, I may very well veer in a slightly verificationist direction insofar as I would insist that, in situations in which empirical/scientific information glaringly problematizes or seemingly contradicts non-empirical/extra-scientific concepts, pause for thought on the part of the practitioners of the non-empirical/extra-scientific disciplines in question is appropriate and, indeed, imperative. In addition to the neuro-psychoanalytic examples I provided earlier regarding the topics of transference and the id at the intersection of psychoanalysis and neurobiology, a perfect illustration of what I have in mind here is neuroscientist Benjamin Libet's deservedly famous discovery of the approximately 500-millisecond delay between the onset of a neural firing sequence and the surfacing of conscious awareness of this sequence as an intention to perform the action the sequence will lead to if not blocked from running its course (Libet, 2004, pp. 42, 56, 66–67, 80–81, 101–102, 107, 139, 208; Žižek, 2004, pp. 137–138; Žižek, 2006, pp. 240–241; Johnston, 2015e, pp. 121–152). Although this neuroscientific discovery by no means immediately and automatically entails that all philosophical talk of "free will" is now experimentally falsified garbage – the Libet delay, so to speak, admittedly is open to a number of philosophical/theoretical interpretations and appropriations – it still demands of intellectually honest philosophers that they seriously ponder in response whether to rethink their notions of agency, autonomy, self-determination and the like (explaining, if so, how to revise these notions and, if not, why revising is not requisite despite appearances to the contrary). Exercises in rethinking of this sort promise to generate lively, stimulating theoretical sparks – and to do so precisely through maintaining interdisciplinary friction rather than hermetically sealing off philosophy or metapsychology as frictionless spinning in an intra-disciplinary void (to appropriate wording from John McDowell).

By my lights, the key move to be made today is to repeat Hegel's gesture with respect to the natural-scientific *Weltanschauung* of the seventeenth and eighteenth centuries in the *Phenomenology of Spirit*'s discussion of "Observing Reason" (Johnston, 2012b, pp. 103–157; Johnston, 2013d; Johnston, 2014b, pp. 371–418; Johnston, 2014c; Johnston, 2014d, pp. 204–237; Johnston, 2016). For transcendental materialism in particular, this means harnessing through immanent critiques the life sciences' self-nullifying authority and auto-de/in-completing features (as exemplified by epigenetics and neuroplasticity). Although I am the furthest thing from an eliminative materialist, I indeed avow being a self-eliminative naturalist, namely, a materialist of phylogenetically and ontogenetically self-denaturalizing nature. This is of a piece with my confessed weak verificationism in that I believe it possible, mandatory and valid to verify scientifically the scientific unverifiability of a hybrid philosophical-psychoanalytic theory of subjectivity.

If, to re-quote an earlier-quoted Pluth, "the autonomy of psychoanalysis and its region of influence is" to be "preserved" in an uncompromisingly materialist manner (which, for me, also entails a certain carefully qualified empiricism and naturalism [Johnston, 2013f, pp. 91–99]), then, when all ultimately is said and done, it must be shown that the relevant matter *an sich* permits such an autonomy and its preservation (hence, this autonomy is relative as not being an absolute sovereignty unchecked by the empirical, experimental natural sciences). A non-reductive (or weakly reductive as not strongly reductive) materialism *qua* materialism proper is unavoidably obligated to explain how the material nature of the natural sciences allows for the intra-natural emergence and subsequent endurance of structures and dynamics irreducible, after their geneses, to their natural-material origins. This is precisely what my transcendental materialism, with its immanent-critical, dialectical-speculative engagements with the life sciences, attempts to accomplish: an explicit, non-dogmatic positing, passing through the explanatory jurisdictions of science, of the ontological and epistemological independence of the explanatory jurisdictions of such disciplines as psychoanalysis and philosophy (instead of an implicit, dogmatic presupposing of this independence simply bypassing these scientific regions) (Johnston, 2013c, pp. 204–205).

Pluth (2012a) is thoughtful enough to register, in his advocacy for Badiou against me, that, "It is not the case that Johnston is dismissive of philosophy at all, of course" (p. 100). However, he evidently believes that, despite my conscious aversion to anti-philosophical scientism, I still risk falling into such an intellectual and ideological bog. Pluth's essay (2012a) counter-critiquing my critique of Badiou's materialism concludes with a plea for philosophy's "independence" (pp. 111–112). Yet, Badiou certainly would join me in objecting to his self-appointed defender's plea. One of the things that Badiou and I concur about, *contra* Pluth, is philosophy's utter and thoroughgoing lack of sovereign self-sufficiency. In Badiou's parlance, philosophy is and should be "conditioned" by "events" in the four "generic procedures" of "truth production" (i.e., "art", "love", "politics" and "science") (Badiou, 1990, pp. 7–8, 11–12, 25–26; Badiou, 1999, pp. 35–39, 66, 79–80). Badiou and I disagree especially about exactly what the scientific conditioning of philosophy involves and contains. But, we nonetheless agree that the sciences, on one or the other of our conceptions of scientificity (his more Cartesian, mine more Baconian), are and ought to be key catalysts and spurs essential to the very vitality of philosophy (Johnston, 2013b, pp. 81–107, 175–178).

As I might put it paraphrasing Kant, without two-way friction between non-empirical theories and empirical sciences, the former end up empty and the latter blind. Winning a war of independence on behalf of philosophy or psychoanalysis would be, in fact, a Pyrrhic victory. It also would be a profound disservice to so many other areas of investigation (in the natural sciences, the social sciences and the humanities) standing to benefit, however much they would acknowledge this or not, from philosophical and psychoanalytic insights. Encasing metaphysics and metapsychology in an impregnable sovereign autonomy would be the surest way to ossify and kill them – and, in so doing, inflict untold collateral damage across a wide range of other disciplinary regions. There is nothing to gain and everything to lose, both intellectually and ideologically, in philosophers and psychoanalysts ceding vast swathes of terrain to others and beating a hasty retreat into the comfortable intradisciplinary confines of unconditioned and, hence, vacuous fortresses (which, in their free-standing vacuity, would not be worth defending anyway). For the sake of knowledge overall, including that uniquely nurtured and cultivated by philosophy and psychoanalysis, this defensive instinctual reaction must be steadfastly resisted and fiercely combatted. The direction of the general intellect hangs in the balance.

References

An Outline of Psycho-Analysis. SE 23: 139–207.

Badiou, A. (1990). "L'entretien de Bruxelles". *Les Temps modernes, 526*, 1–26.

Badiou, A. (1999). *Manifesto for Philosophy* (N. Madarasz, Trans.). Albany, NY: State University of New York Press.

Beyond the Pleasure Principle. SE 18: 1–64.

Eldredge, N., & Gould, S.J. (1972). Punctuated Equilibria: The Tempo and Mode of Evolution Reconsidered. In T.J.M. Schopf (Ed.), *Models in Paleobiology* (82–115). San Francisco, CA: Freeman Cooper and Company.

Freud, S. (1953–1974). *The Standard Edition of the Complete Psychological Works of Sigmund Freud, 24 Volumes* (J. Strachey, A. Freud, A. Strachey, and A. Tyson, Ed. and Trans.). London, UK: Hogarth Press and the Institute of Psycho-Analysis.

Hebb, D.O. (1949). *The Organization of Behavior: A Neuropsychological Theory*. New York, NY: John Wiley and Sons.

Hegel, G.W.F. (1969). *Science of Logic* (A.V. Miller, Trans.). London, UK: George Allen & Unwin.

Hegel, G.W.F. (1977a). *The Difference Between Fichte's and Schelling's System of Philosophy* (H.S. Harris and W. Cerf, Trans.). Albany, NY: State University of New York Press.

Hegel, G.W.F. (1977b). *Phenomenology of Spirit* (A.V. Miller, Trans.). Oxford, UK: Oxford University Press.

Hegel, G.W.F. (2002). Fragment of a System (R. Kroner, Trans.). In G.W.F. Hegel, *Miscellaneous Writings of G.W.F. Hegel* (J. Stewart, Ed.) (151–160). Evanston, IL: Northwestern University Press.

Hölderlin, F. (1972). *Über Urtheil und Seyn* (H.S. Harris, Trans.). In H.S. Harris. *Hegel's Development: Toward the Sunlight, 1770–1801* (515–516). Oxford, UK: Oxford University Press.

Inhibitions, Symptoms and Anxiety. SE 20: 75–175.

Johnston, A. (2008). *Žižek's Ontology: A Transcendental Materialist Theory of Subjectivity*. Evanston, IL: Northwestern University Press.

Johnston, A, (2009). *Badiou, Žižek, and Political Transformations: The Cadence of Change*. Evanston, IL: Northwestern University Press.

Johnston, A. (2011). "Repeating Engels: Renewing the Cause of the Materialist Wager for the Twenty-First Century". *Theory @ Buffalo, 15*, 141–182.

Johnston, A. (2012a). Reflections of a Rotten Nature: Hegel, Lacan, and Material Negativity. *Filozofski Vestnik, 33* (2), 23–52.

Johnston, A. (2012b). The Voiding of Weak Nature: The Transcendental Materialist Kernels of Hegel's *Naturphilosophie*. *Graduate Faculty Philosophy Journal, 33* (1), 103–157.

Johnston, A. (2013a). From Scientific Socialism to Socialist Science: *Naturdialektik* Then and Now. In S. Žižek (Ed.), *The Idea of Communism 2: The New York Conference* (103–136). London, UK: Verso.

Johnston, A. (2013b). *Prolegomena to Any Future Materialism, Volume One: The Outcome of Contemporary French Philosophy*. Evanston, IL: Northwestern University Press.

Johnston, A. (2013c). Misfelt Feelings: Unconscious Affect Between Psychoanalysis, Neuroscience, and Philosophy. In A. Johnston and C. Malabou, *Self and Emotional Life: Philosophy, Psychoanalysis, and Neuroscience* (73–210). New York, NY: Columbia University Press.

Johnston, A. (2013d). An Interview with Adrian Johnston on Transcendental Materialism (with Peter Gratton). *Society and Space.* http://societyandspace.com/2013/10/07/interview-with-adrian-johnston-on-transcendental-materialism/.

Johnston, A. (2013e). Drive Between Brain and Subject: An Immanent Critique of Lacanian Neuro-psychoanalysis. *Southern Journal of Philosophy, 51*, 48–84.

Johnston, A. (2013f). Points of Forced Freedom: Eleven (More) Theses on Materialism. *Speculations: A Journal of Speculative Realism, 4*, 91–99.

Johnston, A. (2014a). *Adventures in Transcendental Materialism: Dialogues with Contemporary Thinkers*. Edinburgh, UK: Edinburgh University Press.

Johnston, A. (2014b). Where to Start?: Robert Pippin, Slavoj Žižek, and the True Beginning(s) of Hegel's System. *Crisis and Critique, 1* (3), 371–418.

Johnston, A. (2014c). Interview About *Adventures in Transcendental Materialism: Dialogues with Contemporary Thinkers* with Graham Harman for Edinburgh University Press. http://www.euppublishing.com/userimages/ContentEditor/1397840563624/Adventures%20in%20Transcendental%20Realism%20-%20Author%20Q%26A.pdf.

Johnston, A. (2014d). Transcendentalism in Hegel's Wake: A Reply to Timothy M. Hackett and Benjamin Berger. *Pli: The Warwick Journal of Philosophy, 26*, 204–237.

Johnston, A. (2015a). This *is* orthodox Marxism: The Shared Materialist *Weltanschauung* of Marx and Engels. *Quaderni materialisti* (forthcoming).

Johnston, A. (2015b). 'Freedom or System? Yes, please!': How to Read Slavoj Žižek's *Less Than Nothing: Hegel and the Shadow of Dialectical Materialism*. In A. Hamza (Ed.), *Repeating Žižek* (7–42). Durham, NC: Duke University Press.

Johnston, A. (2015c). Marx's Bones: Breaking with Althusser. In N. Nesbitt (Ed.), *Reading Capital, 1965–2015* (forthcoming). Durham, NC: Duke University Press.

Johnston, A. (2015d). Materialism Without Materialism: Slavoj Žižek and the Disappearance of Matter. In A. Hamza and F. Ruda (Eds.), *Slavoj Žižek and Dialectical Materialism* (forthcoming). Basingstoke, UK: Palgrave MacMillan.

Johnston, A. (2015e). Bartleby by Nature: German Idealism, Biology, and the Žižekian Compatibilism of *Less Than Nothing: Hegel and the Shadow of Dialectical Materialism*. In L. de Sutter (Ed.), *Žižek and the Law* (121–152). New York, NY: Routledge.

Johnston, A. (2016). *Prolegomena to Any Future Materialism, Volume Two: A Weak Nature Alone*. Evanston, IL: Northwestern University Press (forthcoming).

Koyré, A. (1958). *From the Closed World to the Infinite Universe*. New York, NY: Harper Torchbooks.

Lacan, J. (1953). Some Reflections on the Ego. *International Journal of Psycho-Analysis, 34*, 11–17.

Lacan, J. (1967–1968). *Le Séminaire de Jacques Lacan, Livre XV: L'acte psychanalytique, 1967–1968* (unpublished typescript).

Lacan, J. (1973–1974). *Le Séminaire de Jacques Lacan, Livre XXI: Les non-dupes errent, 1973–1974* (unpublished typescript).

Lacan, J. (1977). *The Seminar of Jacques Lacan, Book XI: The Four Fundamental Concepts of Psychoanalysis, 1964* (J.-A. Miller, Ed. and A. Sheridan, Trans.). New York, NY: W.W. Norton and Company.

Lacan, J. (1990a). Television (D. Hollier, R. Krauss, and A. Michelson, Trans.). In J. Lacan, *Television/A Challenge to the Psychoanalytic Establishment* (J. Copjec, Ed.) (1–46). New York, NY: W.W. Norton and Company.

Lacan, J. (1990b). Impromptu at Vincennes (J. Mehlman, Trans.). In J. Lacan, *Television/A Challenge to the Psychoanalytic Establishment* (J. Copjec, Ed.) (117–128). New York, NY: W.W. Norton and Company.

Lacan, J. (1992). *The Seminar of Jacques Lacan, Book VII: The Ethics of Psychoanalysis, 1959–1960* (J.-A. Miller, Ed. and D. Porter, Trans.). New York, NY: W.W. Norton and Company.

Lacan, J. (1994). *Le Séminaire de Jacques Lacan, Livre IV: La relation d'objet, 1956–1957* (J.-A. Miller, Ed.). Paris, France: Éditions du Seuil.

Lacan, J. (2001a). *Les complexes familiaux dans la formation de l'individu: Essai d'analyse d'une fonction en psychologie*. In J. Lacan, *Autres écrits* (J.-A. Miller, Ed.) (23–84). Paris, France: Éditions du Seuil.

Lacan, J. (2001b). *Le Séminaire de Jacques Lacan, Livre VIII: Le transfert, 1960–1961* (J.-A. Miller, Ed.). Paris, France: Éditions du Seuil.

Lacan, J. (2006a). The Mirror Stage as Formative of the *I* Function as Revealed in Psychoanalytic Experience. In J. Lacan, *Écrits: The First Complete Edition in English* (B. Fink, Trans.) (75–81). New York, NY: W.W. Norton and Company.

Lacan, J. (2006b). Aggressiveness in Psychoanalysis, In J. Lacan, *Écrits: The First Complete dition in English* (B. Fink, Trans.) (82–101). New York, NY: W.W. Norton and Company.

Lacan, J. (2006c). *Le Séminaire de Jacques Lacan, Livre XVI: D'un Autre à l'autre, 1968–1969* (J.-A. Miller, Ed.). Paris, France: Éditions du Seuil.

Lacan, J. (2006d). *Le Séminaire de Jacques Lacan, Livre XVIII: D'un discours qui ne serait pas du semblant, 1971* (J.-A. Miller, Ed.). Paris, France: Éditions du Seuil.

Lacan, J. (2013). *Le Séminaire de Jacques Lacan, Livre VI: Le désir et son interprétation, 1958–1959* (J.-A. Miller, Ed.). Paris, France: Éditions de la Martinière.

170 Adrian Johnston

Laplanche, J., & Pontalis, J.-B. (1973). *The Language of Psycho-Analysis* (D. Nicholson-Smith, Trans.). New York, NY: W.W. Norton and Company.

Lenin, V.I. (1916). The Junius Pamphlet. https://www.marxists.org/archive/lenin/works/1916/jul/junius-pamphlet.htm.

Libet, B. (2004). *Mind Time: The Temporal Factor in Consciousness*. Cambridge, MA: Harvard University Press.

Milner, J.-C. (2011). *Rencontres avec Lacan, à l'horizon de la science*, In J.-C. Milner, *Clartés de tout: De Lacan à Marx, d'Aristote à Mao* (9–26). Paris, France: Éditions Verdier.

Moses and Monotheism: Three Essays. *SE* 23: 1–137.

"On Beginning the Treatment (Further Recommendations on the Technique of Psycho-Analysis I)". *SE* 12: 121–144.

Pluth, E. (2012a). The Black Sheep of Materialism: The Theory of the Subject. In S. Bowden and S. Duffy (Eds.), *Badiou and Philosophy* (99–112). Edinburgh, UK: Edinburgh University Press.

Pluth, E. (2012b). On Transcendental Materialism and the Natural Real. *Filozofski Vestnik, 33* (2), 95–113.

Pluth, E. (2013). On Adrian Johnston's Materialist Psychoanalysis: Some Questions. *Southern Journal of Philosophy, 51*, 85–93.

Project for a Scientific Psychology. *SE* 1: 281–397.

"Remembering, Repeating, and Working-Through (Further Recommendations on the Technique of Psycho-Analysis II)". *SE* 12: 145–156.

Solms, M. (2013). The Conscious Id. *Neuropsychoanalysis: An Interdisciplinary Journal for Psychoanalysis and the Neurosciences, 15* (1), 5–19.

"Some Points for a Comparative Study of Organic and Hysterical Motor Paralyses". *SE* 1: 155–172.

The Ego and the Id. *SE* 19: 1–66.

The Future of an Illusion. *SE* 21: 1–56.

"The Unconscious". *SE* 14: 159–215.

Žižek, S. (2004). *Organs without Bodies: On Deleuze and Consequences*. New York, NY: Routledge.

Žižek, S. (2006). *The Parallax View*. Cambridge, MA: MIT Press.

Žižek, S. (2012). *Less Than Nothing: Hegel and the Shadow of Dialectical Materialism*. London, UK: Verso, 2012.

Žižek, S. (2014). *Absolute Recoil: Towards a New Foundation of Dialectical Materialism*. London, UK: Verso.

PART III
Critical Praxes

9

THE ROLE OF BIOLOGY IN THE ADVENT OF PSYCHOLOGY

Neuropsychoanalysis and the Foundation of a Mental Level of Causality

Ariane Bazan

Psychology in Response to the Threatening Unveiling by Biology

While, since Ancient Greece, reflexion on the human condition took place under the term "philosophy", it was in the sixteenth century that the word *psychologia* appeared for the first time (Mengal, 2000). What made this word indispensable? It was a century of religious barbarism in what would become Europe, and corpses, often ripped apart, were strewn over the public scenery, overtaking effectively the informal Catholic ban on the dissection of human bodies. Progress in anatomy was major and, for the first time in the history of thought, the Brussels physician Andreas Vesalius, proposed, with his anatomical drawings, an image of internal human systems, and in particular, of muscular anatomy, as well as of the nerves innervating these muscles. These images were phenomenal, and we may suppose that their effect generated a turmoil comparable to the turmoil elicited by modern brain imagery. Indeed, they unveiled the fact that this bodily fabric is a logically articulated machinery whose movement can be understood mechanically by the mere beauty of how muscles and nerves intertwine.

Up until that time, *fysica*, the natural sciences of Aristotle, had been the principle source of medical knowledge in the Jewish, Christian and Muslim world for more than fifteen centuries. Aristotle proposed that the soul had a prerogative over the body: indeed, the body was merely a clay that must be moved to life by inspiration, i.e., by the breath of the soul – or *anima*. This medical doctrine underpinned the art of healing for so long a time that it seemed built to last forever (Mengal, 2000). But then, in the sixteenth century, anatomical drawings made the Aristotelian doctrine tremble: if it is no longer the *anima* which moves the body, then the world is in need of a new anthropology, one that redefines the soul. In 1540, the German religious reformer Philipp Melanchthon published a book which commented on the *De Anima* of Aristotle, and he added to the Aristotelian text a long treatise on anatomy (Mengal, 2000). On the basis of this new knowledge, Melanchthon attributed functions to the body which were previously reserved for the soul[1]. The brain became the principal organ of sensory functions and displaced the heart as the seat of emotional life and of thought. But the simple addition of an anatomical treatise was not enough. The images of the body fundamentally blurred the old maps: since the body seemed to be able to ensure a series of functions previously reserved to the soul, the soul must be redefined! To the Aristotelian position that all living beings, whether plant, animal or human, to varying degrees possess a soul which organizes the body, Melanchthon opposed a dualistic anthropology that divided the human into a moving body extended in space and a thinking soul. The two-dimensional *anthropologia* was articulated in *anatomia*, a doctrine of the body, and *psychologia*, a doctrine of the soul. This new anthropology was diffused into the world of the Reformation (Mengal, 2000). The use of the term *psychologia* by Melanchthon was its first intentional use and founded a new field of knowledge.

In its wake, the Dutch reformer Rudolph Snellius (1594, pp. 26–27) specified the essential properties that distinguish body from soul: "The rational soul of man is the thought that, coupled with the body, completes man. (…) The physical things closer to natural bodies that move naturally, have an extension and for that reason occupy a space. (…) The faculty of the rational soul is the mind or will. Thought is the faculty of the soul to discourse and think about things which are and which are not"[2] (Snellius, 1594, pp. 26–27). Wisely, thinking was defined as the ability to imagine things without them having to be actually present, that is to say, as imagination. The soul, threatened by the progress of anatomy, was therefore rescued by the attribution of new exclusive properties, especially thinking (imagination) and will. René Descartes (1648, p. 225) understood the rapid progresses of his time in terms of anatomy; he, himself, dissected animals and human cadavers and was familiar with research on blood circulation (Fuchs, 2001). He came to the conclusion that the body is a complex device capable of moving without the soul, thus contradicting the Aristotelian doctrine of the soul: "The soul can excite no movement in the body if not all bodily organs that are required for this movement are well prepared; but that, on the contrary, when the body has all the elements arranged for some movement, there is no need of the soul to produce them"[3]. The metaphysical order, which stated that the body exists by virtue of the soul, was broken. It was as a philosopher that Descartes proposed his dualistic view, which corresponded to Reformist views; he never used the new term *psychologia*. At the end of the seventeenth century, this way of presenting anthropology, the doctrine of man, in two parts, anatomy and psychology, was widespread, especially in medical literature (Mengal, 2000).

The word 'psychology' thus arose from 'the need to think the soul' in response to the threatened unveiling of man by biology. This paradox is repeated in the mid-nineteenth century, when psychology, which was still widely regarded as a branch of philosophy, emancipated itself as an autonomous domain of science. And, again, this was concomitant with a period of great advancement in biology. Indeed, in the nineteenth century some fundamental discoveries were made in physiology, including neurophysiology. Charles Bell and François Magendie, independently, discovered the distinction between sensory and motor nerves in the spinal column; Emil du Bois-Reymond mapped the electrical basis of muscle contraction; Pierre Paul Broca and Carl Wernicke identified brain areas responsible for different aspects of language, and Gustav Fritsch, Eduard Hitzig and David Ferrier localized the sensory and motor areas of the brain (e.g., see Brennan, 1998). One of the principal founders of experimental physiology, Hermann von Helmholtz, conducted studies on a wide range of topics including the natures of sound and colour, and of our perceptions of them (Warren & Warren, 1968). In the 1860s, while he held a position in Heidelberg, Helmholtz took on as an assistant a young M.D. named Wilhelm Wundt. Wundt used the equipment of the physiology laboratory to address more complicated psychological questions that had not, until then, been investigated experimentally. He experimentally studied the principles of sensory perception. He applied the method of reaction time measures, a measure proper to psychological research. In 1874, Wundt published his landmark textbook, *Grundzüge der physiologische Psychologie* (*Principles of Physiological Psychology*, 1874[4]) and in 1879, he founded a laboratory specifically dedicated to original research in experimental psychology, the first laboratory of its kind in the world. Psychology as an autonomous domain of science was born.

In other words, it was the confrontation with the amazing complexity of the body, respectively of the brain, in the sixteenth and nineteenth centuries that instigated the need to invoke, and then settle, the discipline of psychology. What seemed to happen in each of these moments was the recognition that what had previously been ascribed to the soul was in fact taken care of by the body. It is very paradoxical that it is precisely this recognition which, in turn, promotes psychology as an autonomous field. In the sixteenth century, the observation that anatomy in itself can explain how a body comes to move, for example, promoted the institution of a field, separate from anatomy, for the qualities of the soul which do not seem to have an extension and therefore do not occupy space, such as thought, discourse and will. In the nineteenth century, the observation that neurophysiology helps to explain perception and language definitively confirms psychology as a scientific discipline emancipated from philosophy.

Paradoxically, it also established psychology as a domain distinct from physiology itself, though firmly grounded in it: in fact, some philosophers and some of the first psychologists[5], proposed that psychology is characterized not by proper functions, but by proper laws. In 1867, Wundt, for example, rejected a naively materialistic approach and defended the idea of the autonomy of the mental: the laws that govern the mind are fundamentally different from those that govern material nature. The philosopher John Stuart Mill (1882 [1843], 590) also defended the autonomy of a psychological level of analysis and rejected the idea that mental phenomena were "generated through the intervention of material mechanisms". The study of mental phenomena must start from invariable laws which are distinct not only from metaphysics, but also from physicalist approaches to the mind or from a biologized psychology. Psychology was to describe "the uniformities of succession, the laws, whether ultimate or derivative, according to which one mental state succeeds another; is caused by, or at least, is caused to follow, another" (Mill, 1882 [1843], 490). The physiologist Helmholtz (1896 [1877], 187), also proposed that "memory, experience and custom" are "facts, whose laws are to be sought, and which are not to be explained away because they cannot be […] referred to the known laws of nervous excitation". In other words, at the end of the nineteenth century some of the major proponents of psychology sought to found psychology in laws and regularities proper to its domain.

On the Tragedy of Not Thinking the *Psyché* (Correctly)

In the twentieth century, then, it was Sigmund Freud, who, with psychoanalysis, offered a science of the soul, the organizing principles of which were radically distinct from those both of physiology and of philosophy. Freud, a neurologist, was trained at the physicalist physiology school of Berlin, and remained faithful to the teachings of his masters, Ernst Brücke and, especially, Hermann von Helmholtz. His feat was to propose a psychoanalytic metapsychology, which, along the lines of his other master, this one in philosophy, Mill, offers a real autonomous science of the soul, the laws of which are distinct from the biological while remaining faithful to the transcendental approach of the physiologists Fichte and von Helmholtz. That is, provided with an expertise in neurophysiology, Freud ended up assuming the physiological functioning of the mental apparatus if it was to be able to account for what he experienced in his clinical encounters. This, then, resulted in 1895 in his *Project for a Scientific Psychology* where he introduced, for example, the concepts of primary and secondary processes to describe the mind – with the primary process then seemingly directly inspired by the laws already proposed by Mill, namely the laws of association by contiguity and similarity.

However, the advent of psychotropic drugs in the 1950s, combined with the breathtaking advances in brain imaging of the last thirty years, have rearranged the field of psychology and have, in particular, blown new powerful life into the partializing resolutive-recompositive paradigm of its beginnings. Indeed, the founding model for *psychologia* is borrowed from anatomy: as science proceeds by analysis, by dissecting into the most simple to reconstructing to the most complex, in the same way, psychology is supposed to describe the faculties, the single components, from which to build up a mind. The empiricist philosopher David Hume (1938 [1740], 6; 1969 [1739 to 1740], 311), for example, described his project in terms of an anatomy of human nature: that is to say, he proposed to break down mental phenomena into more primitive elements (impressions and ideas) and to rebuild their formative history with a minimum number of mental laws. Wundt (1882: 399) also proposed that the purpose of scientific psychology is the "complete decomposition [*Zergliederung*] of conscious phenomena into their elements". Recent advances in neuroscience, then, allow for a totalitarian version of this ambition: in fact, nothing we might have wished to arrogate to the intimacy of the soul, neither passion, nor love, friendship, aspirations or even faith, morality, desire or orgasmic enjoyment … nothing escapes visualization. Is it any wonder, then, to infer that the mental would be merely some kind of phenomenology or direct expression of the brain? The paradoxical result of this progress seems to be then, on the one hand, the idea of the *psyché* as a phenomenology of the (neuro-)physiological realm, and, therefore, governed by biological and medical laws and, on the other, the inability to think the specificity of the mental.

What we now propose is that both the incorrect thinking and the 'non-thinking' of the mental are structurally doomed to failure and tragedy. Regarding the incorrect thinking: if the psyché is governed by biological laws, then it follows that the soul is to be treated according to the same principles as those applied to the body, that is to say, according to medical principles. We have proposed elsewhere (Bazan, 2013) how these medical principles, although they have led to valuable and spectacular advances in somatic medicine, are actually counterproductive when applied to mental health. We will here briefly critically assess three of these medical principles.

First, diagnosis by isolating (by dissecting) the problem from its logical chain through specialized clinical intervention renders the symptom meaningless. What the 'specialized' clinician is then left with is an essentialist approach, explaining the problem either in terms of an essence, a characteristic, a trait or in terms of nature or predisposition (Hyman, 2010). This essence is then crystallized in the name of a diagnosis. However, this diagnosis identifies the subject with his problem, without offering real indications for further intervention (see e.g., Casper, 2008)[6]. Moreover, this essentialist approach, in turn, instigates the identification of distinctive profiles of subjects with the 'same' problem and, as a result, new 'personality disorders' emerge. However, this then has its own effects (Hacking 1985, 102–103): indeed, subjects, worried about their distresses and disarrays, or those of their relatives, seek to understand their pains and are (temporarily) relieved by being able to stick a label onto them[7]. Formalizing a new diagnosis thereby increases the occurrence of this diagnosis and thus contributes to creating an epidemic (see e.g., Kutchins, 1997)[8]. Regarding the second medical principle, screening and prevention in the field of mental health, these have – along the same lines – an effect opposite to the desired one: indeed, active screening acts as an incentive for identifying with the publicized disorder and thus contributes to the creation of waves of psychopathological epidemics[9]. Thirdly and finally, then, the constitutive component of the medical approach in mental health is often the psychotropic drug. Even if it often remains to be shown that the treated problem refers to a particular physiological substrate or how most psychotropic drugs elicit their therapeutic effect, we are sure, however, that long-term use of these drugs induces changes in the physiological substrate[10]. After a certain period, it is even difficult to distinguish the supposed effects of the mental disorder from the effects induced by psychotropic medication. The discussion of these aspects requires a more substantiated contradictory debate, but we take the liberty, for the time being, of maintaining the idea that the application of medical principles to the field of mental health may be thought to induce psychopathology rather than to cure it (for further debate see e.g., Gonon, 2011).

Moreover, the choice of a medical approach is linked to a real inability to think the psyche both in scientific arenas[11] and, by backlash, in the 'general public'. Psychology does not really seem to have an answer to the question: if psychological functions and instances can be mapped to specific and determined structures in the brain, how is psychology different from neurophysiology? What does psychology mean beyond the brain? Far from being trivial, we propose that as subjects, we are 'doomed' by the inability to conceptualize the mental. Indeed, in this time of history, it appears most often impossible to explain suffering unless it is done within assumed biological or sociological parameters: if the explanation is not given in terms of genes, hormones or neurons, it must be in terms of education, family, context, society and so on. A subject can only be thought of as a bodily or as a social entity: that is, there is no subject who is not doomed to be a victim or an object. And, as a consequence, these 'victims' are claiming compensations and rights and are continuously on the lookout for possible culprits, which are invariably external and extraneous. Indeed, since there is no subject, there is no ethics of the subject, nor is there a subject who can be called upon to assume his or her proper role in the organization of the misfortune that has befallen him or her. It then follows that, like Sisyphus, unable to take measure of our proper involvement, we, subjects, are condemned to repeat indefinitely – and, worse even, that this not only befalls us as subjects of our singular history, but also as societies taken in the endless repetition of History.

A Third Momentum for Psychology

But we all have reason to rejoice: it is from 'the source of all evil' itself that salvation will arise! Indeed, the paradoxical consequences of the extreme sophistication of neuroimaging techniques lead to embarrassment in neuroscience. For, now that we see better and better, we can see 'everything', and that totality is staggering: in the brain everything is multiply connected to everything – and vice versa. In other words, it is only now that we can see it all, that we can finally take measure of the fact that in truth we cannot see anything: opening the body is not like opening a book, there are no captions or subtitles to its cells, the organs and tissues do not come with a manual attached. There is no truth about human nature that could be read from a neuron. But as long as we have not yet pushed our flashlights till the very end and turned the very last neuron inside out, the illusion that "someday, when we have better techniques, we will understand it all, and we'll be able to resolve the mysteries of the human mind" will continue to flourish. However, excess data will eventually wipe out all contrast – similar to how by seeing the pixels of a photo too well, one loses sight of the overall picture. And the need for an interpretative frame from another level will be felt more urgently and more precisely than ever before[12].

We therefore propose that the current neuroimaging revolution heralds a third moment for psychology and that, by virtue of its totalitarian unveiling, it pushes psychology into its last entrenchements, thereby provoking a new moment of truth (see Bazan, 2011): either psychology is exhaustively replaced by neuroscience and disappears as such, or the field is founded in a radically different way, and perhaps in a, for the first time, truly independent way. We propose that it is not so much the modules, the components, or the faculties that distinguish the psychological from the biological[13], but rather it is the organizational level from which to consider them. More specifically, psychology considers them from the level of the subject while neuroscience considers them from the level of the function[14]. At this stage we are thus summoned to give a definition of the subject, but the logic of the proposed reasoning does not require being restricted to a single definition, as long as this level provides a perspective on the body rather than a perspective coming from the body. We thus propose that it is this subject which founds the field of the psyché in its specificity and that, paradoxically, it is the brain imagery revolution which helps to create the need for that foundation.

Psychoanalysis and Neuroscience

Clinical listening is a methodology specific to psychology that can yield the materials for a conceptual framework that is coherent at the subject level. Among the clinical theories which share this epistemology of the subject, there is psychoanalysis. If psychoanalysis has proposed principles which are specific to mental functioning (e.g., primary and secondary processes, the signifier, jouissance), its history shows that this development has also implied, as concerns Freud, a journey through biology: it is by departing from the limits of biology that metapsychology was founded. It is through what reveals itself to be impossible to conceptualize within biology that a place is designated, opened up, in which the mental can be thought. In other words, and paradoxically, biology is vital for psychoanalysis.

Biology and psychoanalysis, neuroscience and psychoanalysis, especially intersect in this domain called neuropsychoanalysis. Both the name, and the thing itself, neuropsychoanalysis, are sometimes, and rightly so, considered to be a barbarism. The epistemological line most followed is that of Solms and Turnbull (2002), a dual aspect monism, that is to say, the idea that there is one single object, which can be approached either objectively or neuroscientifically – the brain – or subjectively or clinically – the mental apparatus. In the end, a more or less linear correspondence between the cerebral and the mental parameters is supposed: each phenomenon with consistency in the brain is thought to correspond to a phenomenon with consistency at the mental level. Research operates along the classical paradigm: neurophysiological observations are mapped to behavioral or personality characteristics, so that even within this psychoanalytic perspective the soul is thought to mirror the brain. This paradigm implies that knowledge of the brain can (directly) contribute to the psychoanalytic clinic. I reject this approach: I propose, instead, that an object cannot exist by itself, that is to say, as an (inert and already constituted) object regardless of its perception. I subscribe to a Kantian transcendental approach[15] which implies that the object, constituted by capturing part of Nature[16], is also determined by the procedure itself by which Nature is grasped, that is to say that the object is constituted in the negotiation between a grasping subject and a resisting Nature (Van de Vijver & Demarest, 2013). The idea is not that the subject can determine or exhaustively construct the object, but that the object is nevertheless marked by the question through which it appeared. In this approach, biology constitutes an object 'brain' on the one hand while the clinic constitutes a 'mental apparatus' object on the other. But there is not necessarily a linear correspondence between the two[17]. What is consistent in the brain cannot be mapped point by point to what is consistent in the mental apparatus; the soul is not the mirror of the neural substrate.

This epistemology is part of a more general approach to the organization of matter and life. The idea that although biology emerges from chemistry, biology and chemistry nevertheless constitute independent organization levels of matter, which are not in a reciprocal point-to-point correspondence and each of which has a conceptual apparatus of its own, as well as analysis and intervention techniques appropriate to each, is generally not subject to debate. Similarly, psychology does not relate differently to biology than biology does to chemistry: although it may be important in some respects to 'return' to the biological substrate, it would nevertheless be absurd to attempt to 'ultimately' replace mental phenomena by biological dynamics. Obviously this does not imply that the psyche materializes like a Genie coming out of a lamp. If we consider that material and living reality are respective organizational layers – consisting of the physical, the chemical, the biological and the social – then the mental is an organizational layer that emerges in between the biological and the social: the mental arises from the field of tension between the push from the biological substrate and the pull from the social level, that is to say, departing from a drive pressure and in response to a calling other. For example, the hungry child is moved by a drive pressure energizing all possible action pathways, making the child jiggle and cry. A caring Nebenmensch hears the cries and addresses the baby: "Oh, but you must be hungry. …" In the field of tension between the drive and the (linguistic) address a mental apparatus, a human subject, is called into being. From this ontology, it follows that the mental apparatus is marked both by biology and by the Other. The neuropsychoanalytic dimension in our approach tries to characterize the attachment or knotting points between the biological and the mental, that is to say, it tries to articulate how the same phenomenon at the heart of such a node can be spelled out in both biological and mental terms. These attachment points concern phenomena that account at the mental level for being in the human condition in a human body. At the level of these nodes the correspondence between the biological and the mental is direct[18]. There is nevertheless an essential difference between this and the monistic model: the biology involved in these nodes does not dictate in itself the organization of the mental. It does not have an organizing role for the mental, but it works as a constraint, limiting and at the same time making possible the mental constitution (Van de Vijver, 2010).

So it follows that our appraisal of neuroscience is subverted: its progresses will not contribute to a clinical understanding of the subject, but, inversely, this clinical understanding can lead to concepts which might prove precious for interpreting physiology, for seeing through an excess of physiological data in a meaningful way – in short, for "explaining the body". The aim is thus reversed: it is, in fact, those concepts concerning the subject[19], which will prove effective for interpreting physiology, which will gain consistency, and which will thereby give substance to a true mental apparatus with a proper architecture. Therefore, it is not the physiological substrate which demonstrates the clinical concept, but it is the clinical concept, which, since it is capable of bringing together a number of disparate physiological observations, acquires heuristic relevance.

We have previously proposed two possible nodes between the two levels, including the signifier (Bazan, 2007) and jouissance (Bazan & Detandt, 2013). These are at the same time two clinical dimensions of any transference relationship, including the irrational and the transgressive. Here are our proposals. The signifier is the phenomenon that reflects at the mental level what it means to be in the specifically human condition of language. Unlike any other form of animal language, the phonemes of human language are at the highest point dependent on their surrounding phonemes, that is to say on context, for their interpretation. The highly contextual dependence of interpretation imposes a huge constraint on the natural propensity of brain functioning, that is to say, it imposes an inhibition on the systematic and spontaneous tendency of direct interpretation dictated by the stimulus (the phonological stimulus especially). Signifier phenomena 'betray' the fact that we do not succeed in this inhibition all the time or in an exhaustive way: in psychotic decompensation, e.g., the subject is beset by the polysemia of language which explodes like a bomb in all-around associative effects; but outside of psychosis, symptoms structured by the signifier (phobias, rituals, preferences, dislikes, etc.) are also observed which betray the fact that language is not interpreted only contextually but can, in its quality as an emotionally charged object, shift meanings in a singular non-contextual way. At the biological level, the signifier is a phoneme fragment, at the mental level it is a mental tendency specific to the subject, and at the social level it is an irreducible dimension of human irrationality (and madness).

Jouissance is the phenomenon that reflects at the mental level the bodily condition of the drive. The first drive sources are located in the invertebrate body, the 'bag' of viscera, with the respiratory system, the circulatory system, the digestive system, the excretory system and the reproductive system. Needs or alarms of the internal body result in an excess of excitement that incites the external body, the vertebrate body - the skeleton and the skeletal muscles - to act. In many animal species, these two bodies are connected in a 'natural' way: a hungry newborn foal, for example, can stand on its feet and move toward the nipple of the mare. In other animal species, particularly in humans, there is a real gap between the internal body and the external body. When there is an alarm in the inner body, the human is prompted to act (with its external body), but this action is not naturally targeted toward a form that would be appropriate in relation to the alarm: the hungry newborn, for example, begins to cry and to jiggle, actions which in themselves do not alleviate the hunger and which simply reflect a non-directed tendency for discharge. When, by accident, or with the help of a Nebenmensch, an adequate action is found (for example, the mother puts the child at her breast), then this sequence of actions (e.g., suction) is rewarded biologically and encoded in the history of the body; this is thought to happen through the mesolimbic system (see Bazan & Detandt, 2013). This encoding has as a structural consequence, however, since, by disconnecting the action and its outcome, this encoding incites a repetition of the action as a motor sequence in and for itself, regardless of its outcome. In nature, it is seldom the case that one and the same action leads to results that are dramatically different from the inaugural result. In culture, however, context changes are frequent, and an action that was appropriate at the beginning (for example, the child who stands motionless in response to a stressed and irritable mother) can be at other times improper or even harmful (for example, an adult who withdraws in professional or social interactions). Jouissance 'betrays' the encoding of action sequences (or of body postures) regardless of their result. Biologically, jouissance is the mesolimbic registration of the 'adequate'[20] action, at the mental level it is a compulsion to repeat specific to the subject, and at the social level it is an irreducible dimension of transgression (since the subject is attached to the act in itself).

These two components with their heuristic potential would be able to found a mental architecture. Although a biological substrate can be proposed for both, the two nevertheless escape from the logic of the mirror: for both there is, beyond any tie to the biological, a particularly articulated theoretical deployment based on clinical observation, which is radically emancipated from the biological substrate. This theoretical deployment is then exclusively what gives conceptual weight to the idea of the mental apparatus, while the relevance of its biological articulation attests to the fact that the soul finds realization through man's bodily condition, and through the specific constraints that this body imposes.

A Plea for Mental Causality: Toward an Ethics of Subjective Accountability

The concept of an autonomous mental architecture is required as a foundation for any ethics of subjective accountability. Indeed, the brain paradigm offers only two extremes for the question of accountability: either there is an exhaustive flexibility through unlimited neural plasticity, or there is an inescapable determinism through identity profiles, personality structures and the demonstrable non-existence of free will. Likewise, the social paradigm imprisons the subject in the same two fates: either everything is solvable through education and training, or we are the inescapable victims of liberal capitalism, meritocracy, the rat race and increasing egoism. What gets lost in both these paradigms is the idea of subjective accountability. Indeed, if there is an autonomous level of the mental, then, that implies that whatever the body and brain are, and whatever family the subject was born in, he still has a margin of freedom when it comes to deciding his life. How, then, can we conceive of this autonomous mental level on the basis of which the subject can claim some accountability for his or her life? If we take seriously the idea of the two foundational nodes, the signifier and jouissance, then what they both amount to at the mental level is the dimension of the subject's history. For jouissance, this is very clear, since it is tied to actions that were once sanctioned for bringing (some) relief and thereby were encoded in bodily (neuro-)physiology inciting for their repetition. But of course, the whole historical dimension also runs through the highly particular grid of signifiers which are thought to organize a subject's singular action space (Bazan, 2007). Both the signifier and jouissance testify to the bodily inscription of a subject's history, but it is then solely at the mental level that a change or switch in the subject's position is possible. Indeed, if something is determined biologically, then it concerns motor action patterns (Libet et al. 1983; Libet, 1985; Haggard & Passingham, 2004; Brass & Haggard, 2007). Now there is something uniquely human which enables that condition to be at the same time determined in its movement, and yet also to possess freedom regarding its aspirations and fate: namely the extraordinary fact that (only) in the case of articulatory movements can one make point-by-point exactly the same movements but radically switch their meaning – as is the case for homonyms, polysemous words, ambiguous phrases etc. Therefore, it is through the switch from the determining signifier to a system of meaning that people can steer their lives within the margins for freedom that are given by linguistic ambiguity. And it is in so far as we have this margin of liberty, that we are bound to be accountable for what happens to us.

Notes

1. Not only movement, but also body heat through the production of blood and blood circulation with the discovery in 1628 by William Harvey of the distinction between small and large blood circulation (see the book: "The History of the Heart", which speaks of the nothingness of the spirits, the production of blood, the warmth of the

living bodies, etc.) At first an address to the readers, at the end a supplement on the bloodstream of Harveius (by) Dr. Jacob de Bak (our translation of de « Verhaal van 't Hart, waarin werd gesproken van de nietigheid der geesten, van de bloedmaking, van de warmte der levende lichamen, etc. In den aanvang een aanspreking tot de lezers, in 't einde een bijvoegsel voor de omloop des bloets van Harveius (door) Dr. Jacob de Bak », 1653, 't Amsterdam bij Lodewijk Spillebout).

2. Translated by the author from the French translation (in Mengal, 2000, p. 10) : « L'âme raisonnable de l'homme est la pensée qui, conjuguée au corps, parachève l'homme. (…) Les choses physiques plus proches des corps naturels qui se meuvent naturellement, possèdent une étendue et à cause de cela occupent un lieu.» Original text (Snellius, 1594, pp. 26–27) : « Animus hominis est mens quae corpori coniuncta hominem perficit. (…) Physica pressior in corporibus naturalibus, quae physice moventur, magnitudine sunt praedita, & propterea locum implent. (…) Rationalis animae facultas est mens aut voluntas. Mens est animae facultas de entibus & non entibus disserens & ratiocinans » Snellius, R. (1594). *Partitiones Physicae*. Hanoviae: apud Guilielmum Antoninum? 1594, pp. 26–27.

3. « L'âme ne peut exciter aucun mouvement dans le corps, si ce n'est que tous les organes corporels, qui sont requis à ce mouvement, soient bien disposés; mais que, tout au contraire, lorsque le corps a tous les organes disposés à quelque mouvement, il n'y a pas besoin de l'âme pour les produire. ».

4. *Grundzüge der Physiologische Psychologie*.

5. But not, for example, William James, who is an empiricist.

6. Moncrieff and others have shown that diagnostic labels are less useful than a description of a person's problems for predicting treatment response. *The British Journal of Psychiatry*. 167, 1995, pp. 569–573; Moncrieff, J., Kirsch, I., Efficacy of antidepressants in adults. *British Medical Journal*, 331, 2005, p. 155 doi: 10.1136; Moncrieff, J., Timimi, S., Is ADHD a valid diagnosis in adults? No. *British Medical Journal*, 2010, p. 340:c547 doi: 10.1136/bmj.c547.

7. Even the British Psychological Society states that "clients often, unfortunately, find that diagnosis offers only a spurious promise of such benefits [of recognition of their problems]" and that "diagnoses seem positively unhelpful compared to the alternatives". *The British Psychological Society Response to the American Psychiatric Association: DSM-5 Development*, June 2011.

8. For example, Ethan Watters (2010) reports that in Hong Kong, the first description of anorexia nervosa in the media in November 1994, precedes an explosive emergence of this disease which was previously virtually unknown (see also *The New York Times* of January 8, 2010, *The Americanization of Mental Illness*). Further, on February 6, 2012, *Der Spiegel* quoted this statement from Eisenberg, in an article that made the cover page: "ADHD [Attention Deficit and Hyperactivity Disorder] is a telling example of a fabricated illness". It is no small detail that this came from Leon Eisenberg, who in 1968 actually had ADHD added in the DSM-IV (Diagnostic and Statistical Manual of Mental Disorders). Leon Eisenberg also convinced the community that ADHD has a genetic origin without being able to prove it.

9. See also the journal *PLoS Medicine*, which devoted its April 2006 issue to the 'fabrication' of diseases.

10. For example, the studies of Waddington et al. (1993, 1998) and of Wade (1993) show the tardive dyskinesia side effects of neuroleptics intake (with, in particular, a number of cognitive and non-verbal deficits) and shows that the reason why schizophrenic patients have a lower life expectancy would be neuroleptics intake. Another study shows these same signs in patients younger than 40 (Pourcher, 1993). A more recent study (Harrow et al. 2014), which has followed patients over a period of twenty years, shows that after 20 years, the schizophrenic group that was not prescribed antipsychotic drugs had significantly less psychotic activity than the group, which took neuroleptics.

11. For example, in a BBC program commenting on his work the neuroscientist Jack Gallant at the University of California, Berkeley, who primed participants with video clips, put

them in a scanner and translated the electrical signals back into clips which looked very similar to what they had watched, denied that he would be able to do mind reading", as he doesn't really know what the mind is". (*The difficult task of reading the brain*, BBC program by Melissa Hogenboom of 5 May 2014). In another example, the neurologist Robert Burton (2013) says in his book *A Skeptic's Guide to the Mind*, that even after 2500 years of contemplation and research, we still have "no idea what a mind actually is".

12. See, e.g., the neurologist Robert Burton, in an interview of April 6, 2013 with journalist Jonathan Keats about the BRAIN initiative, an enormous investment of resources in neuroscience research: "Such a project is likely to produce abundant new data regarding electrical brain activity, but I don't sense any great underlying new idea or intuition. Data is informative, but what is really needed is some intellectual innovation that goes beyond technology – both present and future. (...) Improving our technologies without an accompanying breakthrough in thinking about the brain-mind connection is equivalent to upgrading a linotype machine to the world's greatest printer without having something to say". http://www.salon.com/2013/04/06/ neuroscience_needs_its_einstein/. See, also, the article by journalist Gary Marcus in *The New York Times* of July 12, 2014, about this same initiative: "But biological complexity is only part of the challenge in figuring out what kind of theory of the brain we're seeking. What we are really looking for is a *bridge*, some way of connecting two separate scientific languages—those of neuroscience and psychology. (...). But as anyone in a field richer in data than theory (like weather forecasting) can tell you, amassing data is only a start. The success of both the Human Brain Project and the Brain Initiative will ultimately rest not just on the data to be collected but also on what can be done with those data once they are collected. On that, too little has been said".

13. In line, therefore with Mill, Wundt and von Helmholtz.

14. Just as biology does not differ from chemistry by its components but considers them at another scale (see Bazan, 2011).

15. (Which is also in line with Fichte and von Helmholtz.)

16. Or of matter – or else even of the Real, in a Lacanian perspective.

17. This is therefore a form of dualism, even if it is not an ontological dualism. One could say that this is an epistemological dualism, that is to say, an approach that refuses to explain mental states in terms of bodily states. We subscribe to the non-reductionist psychological approach of von Helmholtz (as described in Hatfield, 1990, 182). See also the comments of neurobiologist Marc Jeannerod (2002): "The paradox is that personal identity, although it is clearly situated in the field of physics and biology, belongs to a category of facts that are beyond objective description and therefore appear as excluded from a scientific approach. It is not true that it is impossible to understand how meaning is rooted in the biological. But knowing that it has its roots there does not guarantee them to be accessible".

18. And even the idea is that these are direct nodes tying together the biological, the mental and the social.

19. Either concerning the mental, or concerning psychopathology.

20. But also of any action in case of trauma, since in that case any action is better than no action, regardless of its result – since in case of trauma any discharge, or any dischargeable form, of the excitation surplus is, in some ways, 'adequate'.

References

Bazan, A. (2007). *Des fantômes dans la voix. Une hypothèse neuropsychanalytique sur la structure de l'inconscient*. Montréal: Editions Liber.

Bazan, A. (2011). The grand challenge for psychoanalysis – and neuropsychoanalysis: taking on the game. *Frontiers in Psychology, 2011*, 2:220. doi: 10.3389/fpsyg.2011.00220.

Bazan, A. (2013). Een ziel laat zich niet als een lijf versnijden. Over de gevolgen van het medisch model voor de mentale gezondheidszorg. In Dans I. Devisch (ed.), *Ziek van gezondheid. Voor elk probleem een pil?* Anvers, Amsterdam: De Bezige Bij, 121–148.

Bazan, A., & Detandt, S. (2013). On the physiology of jouissance: interpreting the mesolimbic dopaminergic reward functions from a psychoanalytic perspective. *Frontiers in Human Neuroscience, 7*, 709. doi: 10.3389/fnhum.2013.00709.

Brass, M., & Haggard, P. (2007). To do or not to do: the neural signature of self-control. *Journal of Neuroscience, 27*, 9141–9145.

Brennan, J.F. (1998). *History and Systems of Psychology*. London: Prentice-Hall International.

Burton, R. (2013). *A Skeptic's Guide to the Mind: What Neuroscience Can and Cannot Tell Us About Ourselves*. New York, NY: St. Martin's Press.

Casper, M.-C. (2008). Le diagnostic comme effet de nomination. Un exemple la dyslexie. *L'Évolution Psychiatrique, 73*, 485–495.

Descartes, R. (1648). Description of the Human Body. In *The Philosophical Writings of Descartes, Volume 1*. Paperback - August 1998. Cambridge: Cambridge University Press.

Descartes, R. (1648). La description du corps humain. In Adam, C., Tannery, P. (eds.), *Dans Descartes, R. (1897–1913): Oeuvres de Descartes, Vol. XI*. Paris: L. Cerf.

Gonon F. (2011). La psychiatrie biologique: une bulle spéculative? *Esprit*, Novembre, 54–73.

Hacking, I. (1985). Making Up People. In T.C. Heller, M. Sosna, and D.E. Wellerby (eds.), *Reconstructing Individualism*. Stanford, CA: Stanford University Press, 222–236.

Haggard, P., & Passingham, R.E. (2004). Attention to intention. *Science, 303*, 1208–1210.

Harrow, M., Jobe, T., & Faiull, R. (2014). Does treatment of schizophrenia with antipsychotic medications eliminate or reduce psychosis? A 20-year multi-follow-up study. *Psychological Medicine*. March, 2014. doi:10.1017/ S0033291714000610.

Hatfield, G. (1990). *The Natural and the Normative. Theories of Spatial Perception from Kant to Helmholtz*. London: MIT Press.

Helmholtz, H. (1896 [1877]). *Das Denken in der Medicin*. In Helmholtz, *Vorträge und Reden* (Vol. II): 165–190. Braunschweig: Holzstiche.

Hobson, J.A., & McCarley, R.W. (1977). The brain as a dream state generator: an activation-synthesis hypothesis of the dream process. *American Journal of Psychiatry, 134*, 1335–1348.

Hume, D. (1938 [1740]). *An Abstract of a Treatise of Human Nature*. Cambridge: Cambridge University Press.

Hume, D. (1969 [1739/40]). *A Treatise of Human Nature*. London: Penguin Books.

Hyman, S.E. The diagnosis of mental disorders: the problem of reification. *Annual Review of Clinical Psychology*, 2010, *6*, 155–79.

Jeannerod, M. (1994). The representing brain: neural correlates of motor intention and imagery. *Behavioral and Brain Sciences, 17*, 187–245.

Jeannerod, M. (2002). *La Nature de l'Esprit*. Paris: Odile Jacob.

Kutchins, H., & Kirk, S. (1997). *Making Us Crazy: DSM the Psychiatric Bible and the Creation of Mental Disorders*. New York, NY: The Free Press.

Libet, B. (1985). Unconscious cerebral initiative and the role of conscious will in voluntary action. *The Behavioural and Brain Sciences, 8,* 529–566.

Libet, B., Gleason, C.A., Wright, E.W., & Pearl, D.K. (1983). Time of conscious intention to act in relation to onset of cerebral activity (readiness-potential). The unconscious initiation of a freely voluntary act. *Brain, 106*, 623–642.

Mengal, P. (2000/2001). La constitution de la psychologie comme domaine du savoir aux XVIème et XVIIème siècles. *Revue d'Histoire des Sciences Humaines, 2*, 5–27.

Mill, J.S. (1882 [1843]). *A System of Logic* (8th edition). New York, NY: Harper & Brothers.

Panksepp, J. (1998). *Affective neuroscience: The foundations of human and animal emotions*. Oxford: Oxford University Press.

Pourcher, E., (1993). Organic brain dysfunction and cognitive deficits in young schizophrenic patients with tardive dyskinesia. *Brain and Cognition, 23*, 81–87.

Snellius, R. (1594). *Partitiones Physicae, Hanoviae, apud Guilielmum Antoninum*.

Solms, M. (1997). *The neuropsychology of dreams: a clinico-anatomical study*. Hillsdale, NJ: Lawrence Erlbaum.

Solms, M., & Turnbull, O. (2002). *The brain and the inner world: an introduction to the neuroscience of subjective experience*. New York, NY: Other Press.

Stremler, E., & Castel, P-H. (2009). Pour une histoire des débuts de la neuropsychanalyse: premiers éléments de réflexion à partir de sources inédites. In L. Ouss, B. Golse (eds.), *Vers une Neuropsychanalyse?* Paris: Odile Jacob.

Van de Vijver, G. (2010). Het spoor van de psychoanalyse - Een schuinse pas ten aanzien van alle mogelijke aanpassing. *Tijdschrift voor Psychoanalyse, 16, 4*, 229–239.

Van de Vijver, G., & Demarest, B. (2013). Objectivity: its meaning, its limitations, its fateful objections. In *Objectivity after Kant. Its meaning, Its limitations, its fateful objections*. Hildesheim: Georg Olms Verlag, vii-xxviii.

Waddington, J. et al. (1998). Mortality in schizophrenia: Antipsychotic polypharmacy and absence of adjunctive anticholinergics over the course of a 10-year prospective study. *British Journal of Psychologie, 173*, 325–329.

Waddington, J. (1993). Cognitive dysfunction in schizophrenia: organic vulnerability factor or state marker for tardive dyskinesia? *Brain and Cognition, 23*, 56–70.

Wade, J. (1993). Factors related to the severity of tardive dyskinesia. *Brain and Cognition, 23*, 71–80.

Warren, M., & Warren, P. (1968). *Helmholtz on Perception: Its Physiology and Development*. New York, NY: John Wiley & Sons.

Watters, E. (2010). *Crazy Like Us: The Globalization of the American Psyche*. New York, NY: Free Press, 306.

Wundt, W. (1867). Über die Physik der Zelle in ihrer Beziehung zu den allgemeinen Prinzipien der Naturforschung. *Handbuch der medicinischen Physik*. Erlangen: Enke.

Wundt, W. (1874). *Grundzüge der physiologischen Psychologie*. Leipzig: Engelmann.

Wundt, W. (1882). Die Aufgaben der experimentellen Psychologie. *Unsere Zeit, 3*, 389–406.

10
EMBODIED SIMULATION AS SECOND-PERSON PERSPECTIVE ON INTERSUBJECTIVITY[1]

Vittorio Gallese

"What we commonly mean by 'understand' coincides with 'simplify' [...]: with this purpose in view we have built for ourselves admirable tools in the course of evolution, tools which are the specific property of the human species – language and conceptual thought".[2]

Introduction

One of the core objectives of cognitive neuroscience is to understand the relationship between the functional mechanisms of our brain-body system and our social cognitive skills, shedding new light on the notion of intersubjectivity. However, the notion of intersubjectivity is intrinsically related to the notion of the self. Thus, the neuroscientific study of intersubjectivity cannot elude the issue of subjectivity and of the experiences constituting it. In this chapter I discuss the relation between intersubjectivity and a minimal notion of the self, the bodily self.

The second half of the twentieth century witnessed the enormous progress of cognitive neuroscience, also fostered by the development of new technologies like brain imaging, enabling for the first time a thorough non-invasive study of the human brain. Since then, cognitive neuroscience started addressing topics related to social cognition like intersubjectivity, the self, empathy, free will, decision-making, ethics and aesthetics, many of which were traditionally the object of investigation of different disciplines like psychology, philosophy, economy and politics. These recent developments are stirring an ever growing debate on the heuristic value of cognitive neuroscience when applied to these topics.

At this point a crucial question is perhaps worth asking what is cognitive neuroscience after all? Cognitive neuroscience is first and foremost a methodological approach whose empirical results are strongly influenced by the assumptions posed by the theoretical framework inspiring its very same approach. The scientific investigation of single neurons and/or of brain areas doesn't necessarily prefigure either the questions cognitive neuroscience addresses to the brain nor their answers.

Some quarters of cognitive neuroscience are still today strongly influenced, on the one hand, by classic cognitivism and, on the other, by evolutionary psychology. Broadly speaking, classic cognitive science endorses a methodologically solipsistic view of the mind according to which focusing on the individual's mind is all one needs to define what the mind is and how it works. Indeed, according to classic cognitive science the mind basically is a functional system whose processes can be described in terms of symbolic information processing, according to a series of formal syntactical rules. Understanding others would square with representing in propositional format in one's mind the propositional contents of others' minds.

According to evolutionary psychology the human mind can be conceived of as a conglomerate of cognitive modules, selected in the course of evolution because of their adaptive value. Prominent figures in evolutionary psychology like Leda Cosmides and John Tooby went as far as arguing that the brain is a physical system working like a computer (Cosmides & Tooby, 1997), while according to Steven Pinker (Pinker, 1994, 1997) our cognitive life can be reduced to the functioning of a series of modules, like the language module, the Theory of Mind (ToM) module and so on.

On the basis of this composite theoretical framework, it is no surprise that many cognitive neuroscientists during the last twenty years, when investigating social cognition, mainly aimed at localizing in the human brain the above mentioned cognitive modules, thus implicitly – when not even explicitly – relying on the views heralded by classic cognitive science and evolutionary psychology. This approach can be characterized as a form of ontological reductionism, which treats the individual – the self – as a mass of information-processing neural networks. Such a reduction also suffers of an excessive reliance on brain imaging as the sole method of investigation. The point is that fMRI by itself falls short of enabling a thorough picture of how the brain works, unless its correlational data are benchmarked with the more finely grained invasive sub-personal level of investigation, consisting in the recording of single neurons in non-human primates or – more rarely – in humans. Furthermore, if brain imaging is not complemented with a detailed phenomenological analysis of the perceptual, motor and cognitive processes it aims at investigating and, most importantly, if brain imaging results are not interpreted on the basis of our knowledge of clinical neuropsychological cases, this approach loses much of its potential heuristic value (for similar views, see Cacioppo & Decety, 2011).

Here I propose an alternative – or, at the very least, complementary – approach to the study of social cognition, which focuses on the pivotal role played by the lived body in the constitution of the way we understand the world of others. Such a bottom-up approach can shed new light on the genesis of the self and intersubjectivity by relying on a methodological reductionism that does not sacrifice the rich experience we make use of in our daily transactions with the world. To solve the problem of what it means to be a human subject, a self-reflective self, we should not consider the brain in isolation, but focus on its tight interrelated connections with the body. We should also abandon the solipsistic stance and address the issue from a social point of view.

The hypothesis developed in the present article rests on four premises:

1. The minimal notion of the self, the bodily self, tacitly presupposes ownership of an action-capable agentive entity. Hence, this primitive sense of the self primarily rests on the workings of the motor system. As will be shown, empirical evidence supports the neural realization of this implicit aspect of selfhood in the brain's motor cortex.
2. Since minimal bodily selfhood rests neurally and psychologically on the motor system, it logically follows that characteristics of the latter are defining for the former. That is, minimal bodily selfhood could be attributed to known features of the motor system, including its capacities and limitations.
3. One of the relevant features of a prominent component of the motor system, the mirror neurons mechanism, is that it is active both during performance and perception of goal-directed action. This mechanism underpins one way – likely the most basic and direct one – of understanding the goals of others' motor behavior.
4. The motor aspects of the bodily self provide the means to integrate self-related multimodal sensory information about the body and the world it interacts with.

Resting on these four premises, it could be inferred that minimal bodily selfhood has a dual function. On the one hand, it constitutes the basic sense of the self. On the other, it shapes our perception and pre-reflective conception of others as other selves incarnated in a motorly capable physical body with capacities and experiences similar to ours. Through the bodily self's resonance, others become second selves, or second persons,[3] and this is a more vivid experience of intersubjectivity, relative to the detached, propositional deliberation on the experiences of others.

I challenge the standard solipsistic theoretical account of intersubjectivity offered by classic cognitive science, capitalizing upon a new take on intersubjectivity, as defined by the second-person perspective. The second-person perspective offers a different and deflationary epistemic approach to the problem of other minds, by reducing the mental gap that supposedly separates them. Some wide-ranging implications of this model are briefly discussed.

In the following sections I introduce motor cognition, mirror neurons and the mirror mechanism in humans. I discuss the role in intersubjectivity of a minimal notion of the self, the bodily self and propose a second-person perspective on intersubjectivity.

Motor Cognition

For many years the cortical motor system was conceived of as the neural controller of elementary physical features of movement such as force, direction and amplitude. On a theoretical level, however, many scholars in the past emphasized the strict connection between movement and cognition. The German psychiatrist and philosopher Erwin Straus, for example, pointed out that even the apparently simplest form of human behavior enabled by the motor system, like keeping an upright position, can be directly connected to its metaphorical extensions (e.g., 'an upright member of the community') (Straus, 1960). Such connection is made possible by humans' structural project (*Bauplan*), that is, by human bodily nature. According to Straus, bipedalism and the conquest of the upright position not only redefined the function of human sensory organs, like the eyes and the ears, and surrendered the hand from its role of supporting the body, enabling its fullest expressive power, but also deeply changed humans' stance toward the physical world, which could be finally viewed from a distance, henceforth objectified.

In spite of such theoretical anticipations, it took quite a while for neuroscience to even conceive of the possibility of assigning a cognitive role to the motor system. The classic picture of the motor system radically changed since the discovery that many cortical motor neurons do not discharge during the execution of elementary movements, but are active before and during motor acts such as grasping, tearing, holding or manipulating objects (see Rizzolatti et al., 1988; Rizzolatti & Gallese, 1997; Rizzolatti, Fogassi, & Gallese, 2000). The motor goal-relatedness of cortical premotor neurons is independent from the hand movements required to accomplish the goal (Umiltà et al., 2008; Rochat et al., 2010). Teleology made its way into the cortical motor system.

A further element of novelty about the functional properties of the cortical motor system concerns its role in perception, since we now know that it is indeed endowed with sensory properties. Several studies consistently showed that premotor and parietal areas contain neurons that perceptually respond to visual, auditory and somatosensory inputs (see Rizzolatti et al., 1988; Rizzolatti & Gallese, 1997; Fogassi et al., 1992; Fogassi et al., 1996; Gentilucci, Scandolara, Pigarev, & Rizzolatti, 1983; Gentilucci et al., 1988; Graziano, Yap & Gross, 1994; Graziano, Hu, & Gross, 1997a; Graziano, Hu, & Gross, 1997b; Graziano, Reiss, & Gross, 1999). Altogether, these findings led to the formulation of the Motor Cognition hypothesis as a leading element for the emergence of social cognition (see Gallese, Rochat, Cossu, & Sinigaglia, 2009; Gallese & Rochat, 2009). According to this hypothesis, cognitive abilities like the hierarchical representation of action with respect to a distal goal, the detection of motor goals and action anticipation are possible because of the peculiar functional architecture of the motor system, organized in terms of goal-directed motor acts. The proper development of such functional architecture likely scaffolds more cognitively sophisticated social cognitive abilities.

Empirical evidence (Matelli, Luppino, Rizzolatti, 1985; Rizzolatti & Luppino, 2001; Rizzolatti, Fadiga, Fogassi, & Gallese, 1997; Gallese, 2005; Bremmer et al., 2001; Serino, Canzoneri, & Avenanti, 2011) shows that the cortical motor system both in non-human primates and humans maps the body's motor potentialities and that such mapping enables the multisensory intergration of self bodily-related stimuli affecting the body and its surrounding space.

Let's now address some of the neural mechanisms enabling intersubjectivity and mutual understanding by introducing mirror neurons in macaques, mirror mechanisms in humans and embodied simulation.

Mirror Neurons, Mirror Mechanisms in Humans and Embodied Simulation

Mirror neurons are another class of multimodal motor neurons. They were originally discovered in ventral premotor area F5 of macaque monkeys (di Pellegrino, Fadiga, Fogassi, Gallese, & Rizzolatti, 1992; Gallese, Fadiga, Fogassi, & Rizzolatti, 1996; Rizzolatti, Fadiga, Gallese, & Fogassi, 1996). Mirror neurons are activated not only when the monkey performs a particular object-related action, but also when observing someone else performing the same action. Also for macaques' mirror neurons, what really matter are not specific movements, but the motor goal that movements are supposed to accomplish (Gallese et al., 1996). Neurons with similar properties were also found in regions of the inferior parietal lobe (Gallese, Fogassi, Fadiga, & Rizzolatti, 2002; Fogassi et al., 2005), reciprocally connected with area F5 (Rizzolatti & Luppino, 2001). The intensity of mirror neurons' discharge is significantly stronger during action execution than during action observation (Rochat et al., 2010). Thus, the mirror mechanism is not opaque to the issue of agency, that is, it implicitly discriminates between *who* is the agent and *who* is the observer.

Since their very discovery, mirror neurons were interpreted as enabling a direct form of understanding others' motor behavior (di Pellegrino et al., 1992; Gallese et al., 1996; Rizzolatti et al., 1996), while arguments were made that the mere visual description of others' motor behavior cannot account for its goal-relatedness (see Cattaneo, Sandrini, & Schwarzbach, 2010). According to the same proposal, the relational character of behavior as mapped by the cortical motor system would enable the appreciation of purpose without relying on explicit inference.

Many studies employing different methodologies revealed also in humans a mirror mechanism (MM) mapping the perception of others' motor behavior onto motor representations of the observers' brain (Rizzolatti, Fogassi & Gallese, 2001; Rizzolatti & Sinigaglia, 2010; Gallese, Keysers & Rizzolatti, 2004; Gallese & Sinigaglia, 2011b). A distinctive feature of the MM for movement in humans consists in its much wider scope. Motor resonance in humans can be evoked not only by the execution/observation of goal-directed motor acts, but also by simple movements, like raising one's arm, jumping, or flexing one's finger. This wider 'motor palette' likely played a role in fostering the distinctive mimetic nature of the human species.

Very early on it was hypothesized that the MM for movement might have been just the tip of a much bigger iceberg (Goldman & Gallese, 2000; Gallese, 2003). Indeed, numerous neurophysiological, neuroimaging and behavioral studies confirmed the initial hypothesis that a similar MM could underpin the social perception of others' bodily experiences and mental states, (see Goldman & Gallese, 2000). Indeed, the same cortical regions underlying the experience of emotions and sensations are also activated when witnessing others' emotions (Carr, Iacoboni, Dubeau, Mazziotta, & Lenzi, 2003; Wicker et al., (2003); Leslie, Johnson-Frey, & Grafton, 2004; Pfeifer, Iacoboni, Mazziotta, & Dapretto, 2008) and sensations, like touch (Keysers et al., 2004; Blakemore, Bristow, Bird, Frith, & Ward, 2005; Ebisch et al., 2008; Ebisch et al., 2011; Ebisch et al., 2012), pain (Hutchison et al., 1999; Morrison, Lloyd, di Pellegrino, & Roberts, 2004; Singer et al., 2004; Botvinick et al., 2005; Jackson, Meltzoff, & Decety, 2005) and pleasant touch (McCabe, Rolls, Bilderbeck, & McGlone, 2009). Furthermore, it has been recently shown that action and emotion are not segregated domains, as the emotion dynamically expressed by the face of an observed agent modulates the cortical motor circuits activated during the perception of her/his grasping action (Ferri, Frassinetti, Ardizzi, Costantini, & Gallese, 2012b). These results show that the MM is modulated by the affective state of others: the emotional context is combined with the motor representation of the observed action at the level of the cortical motor system. The observed dynamic facial expression of others thus modulates the embodied simulation of the observed action.

The theory of embodied simulation (ES, Gallese, 2005; Gallese & Sinigaglia, 2001b; Gallese, 2003) provides a unified theoretical framework for all of these phenomena. It proposes that our social interactions become meaningful by reusing our own mental states or processes in functionally attributing them to others. In this context, simulation is conceived of as a non-conscious, pre-reflective functional mechanism of the brain-body system, whose function is to model objects, agents and events. This mechanism can be triggered during our interactions with others, but is also plastically modulated by contextual, cognitive and personal identity-related factors. ES theory challenges the notion that the sole account of intersubjectivity consists in explicitly attributing to others propositional attitudes like beliefs and desires, mapped as symbolic representations. As previously argued before and below mind reading is *intercorporeality* as the main source of knowledge we directly gather about others (Gallese, 2007).

As pointed out by De Preester, following the French philosopher Merleau-Ponty, the body of intercorporeality is primarily perceived as a systematic means to go towards objects. This is the reason why, De Preester argues, "the other is seen as a behavior and the 'I' is primarily a 'motor I'" [56, p. 137]. This perspective on simulation holds that the same neural structures involved in our own bodily self-experiences are also reused when facing others, enabling the pre-reflective understanding of their behaviors and of some of their mental states, thus introducing a novel conceptualization of simulation with respect to its standard account in philosophy of mind (see Goldman, 2006).

What and who are the selves relating to one another in the course of human interpersonal relationships? To address these questions, we should focus upon the multilevel notion of the self.

From the Bodily Self to Intersubjectivity

The Danish psychiatrist Josef Parnas, building upon a phenomenological perspective, identified three levels specifying the self (Parnas, 2000; Parnas, 2003). The first level consists in the implicit awareness that any of our experiences are 'ours', defined as 'ipseity'. The second level consists of the more explicit awareness of being the invariant subject of experience and action. Finally, the third level pertains to the social or narrative self. The first level has been variously identified with the notions of 'core self' or 'minimal self'. A bottom-up approach to intersubjectivity could thus benefit from the empirical investigation of the elements allowing the emergence of implicit and pre-reflective self-knowledge.

Most research on the self employs the notions of body ownership, sense of agency and first person perspective. Body ownership refers to the perceptual status of one's own body, which makes bodily sensations seem unique to oneself (Tsakiris, Hesse, Boy, Haggard, & Fink, 2007). Empirical evidence shows that the experience of our body as our own mainly relies on multisensory integration, which, however, is conditioned by the possibility – or not – to perform actions with a given body part (Tsakiris & Haggard, 2005; Tsakiris, Prabhu, & Haggard, 2006). Sense of agency refers to the sense of being the one who generates the action. We recognize ourselves as agents when we experience congruence between self-generated movements and their expected consequences. However, as argued by Marc Jeannerod (2007), the sense of agency also arises in situations where action representation is formed, but no movement is executed. Since frequently actions in our daily life remain covert, the existence of overt behaviour should not be a prerequisite for self-identification. This form of motor simulation occurs, for example, in the case of mental motor imagery (Jeannerod, 1995), when perceiving perceptual events within our peri-personal space with the activation of F4 neurons or of their human homologue, or during the observation of others' actions with the activation of the MM as its neural counterpart. First-person perspective, finally, refers to the fact that the world appears to be constrained by a mobile bodily self, that is, by the situated point of view, the orientation and the attitudes proper of the self's sensorimotor background capacities (Cermolacce, Naudin, & Parnas, 2007). Thus, many notions adopted to answer the question of how we distinguish ourselves as bodily selves from other human bodies refer to the crucial role of the motor system.

Indeed it was proposed that there is a sense of body, enactive in nature, which enables one to capture the most primitive sense of self as bodily self (Gallese & Sinigaglia, 2010; Gallese & Sinigaglia, 2011a). Our body is primarily given to us as source or power for action. Our body is experienced as specifying the variety of motor potentialities defining the horizon of the world we interact with. Such a primitive sense of self as bodily self is conceived of as being antecedent to the distinction between sense of agency and sense of ownership.

The relationship between this minimal sense of self and the cortical motor system was recently revealed. The motor experience of one's own body, even at a covert level, allows an implicit and pre-reflective bodily self-knowledge to emerge, leading to a self/other distinction, as measured by participants' faster responses during a mental rotation task to pictures of their dominant hand, with respect to others' hands (Ferri, Frassinetti, Costantini, & Gallese, 2011). The same study also showed that when participants were requested to explicitly discriminate between their hands and the hands of others, the self-advantage disappeared. Implicit and explicit recognition of the bodily self dissociate: only implicit recognition of the bodily self, mapped in motor terms, facilitates implicit bodily self processing. A subsequent fMRI study (Ferri, Frassinetti, Ardizzi, Costantini, & Gallese, 2012a) based on a similar hand mental rotation task showed that a bilateral cortical network formed by the supplementary and pre-supplementary motor areas, the anterior insula and the occipital cortex activated during processing of participants' own hands. Furthermore, the contralateral ventral premotor cortex was uniquely and specifically activated during mental rotation of participants' own dominant hand. These authors concluded that the ventral premotor cortex might represent one of the essential anatomical and functional bases for the motor aspect of bodily selfhood, also in light of its role in integrating self-related multisensory information. This hypothesis is corroborated by clinical and functional evidence showing its systematic involvement with body awareness (Ehrsson, Spence, & Passingham, 2004; Berti et al., 2005; Arzy, Overney, Landis, & Blanke, 2006). Thus, there seems to be a tight relationship between the bodily self-related multimodal integration carried out by the cortical motor areas specifying the motor potentialities of one's body and guiding its motor behavior and the implicit awareness one entertains of one's body as one's own body and of one's behavior as one's own behavior.

After having clarified some basic aspects of a minimal notion of the self as bodily self, I turn now to a second-person perspective on intersubjectivity.

I and You: A Second-Person Perspective on Intersubjectivity

When meeting others, we can relate to them in the detached way, typical of an external observer. We can 'objectively' explain others, reflect and formulate judgments, categorize their actions, emotions and sensations by adopting a third-person perspective, aimed at objectifying the content of our perceptions and predictions. The purpose of such cognitive operations is the deliberate categorization of an external state of affairs, that is, the mental representations of others.

However, when relating to others we also experience them as bodily selves, similarly to how we experience ourselves as the owners of our body and the authors of our actions. When exposed to others' expressive behaviors, reactions and inclinations, we simultaneously experience their goal-directedness and intentional character as we experience ourselves as the agents of our actions, the subjects of our affects, feelings and emotions, the owners of our thoughts, fantasies, imaginations and dreams.

All of these peculiar qualities of our social transactions qualify as ingredients of the so-called second-person perspective on intersubjectivity[4]. This approach differs from the third-person approach because it specifies a radically different and deflationary epistemic approach to the problem of other minds, since it greatly reduces the mental gap supposedly separating us from others.

The three minimal requirements any epistemic approach should meet in order to be qualified as second-person were recently outlined by the German philosopher Michael Pauen (2012, pp. 38–39). I posit that all these requirements are compatible with the neuroscientific account of the basic aspects of intersubjectivity outlined here. As briefly reviewed in the previous sections, ES and its underpinning MMs provide, one the one hand, a sub-personal characterization of what enables an empathic sharing of others' states based on vicarious brain activity in the sensory-motor and viscero-motor systems while, on the other, they are sensitive to self-other discrimination (see also below).

All of our social relationships can be lived and experienced in different ways. What changes is our attitude towards others. The German philosopher and theologian Martin Buber (1878–1965), a precursor to the second-person perspective on intersubjectivity, in his seminal book *I and Thou* (*Ich und Du*, Buber, 1923/1970), posited that human interpersonal relations can be second-person relations, i.e., *I-you,* or third-person relations, i.e., *I-it* (and *I-she, I-he*). The other can in fact be conceived of as an instrument, thus one can relate to another human being in a manner similar to how one relates to inanimate objects. Hence, the choice is not between a second- and a third-person perspective, since as human beings we clearly entertain both. We are beginning to understand what the sub-personal neural mechanisms enabling the former are, while we still know very little about those enabling the latter.

According to Buber (1923/1970), the full-blown I only emerges once one perceives oneself as a 'you', when interpersonal dialogue turns into a self-centered inner dialogue. Indeed, as infant research clearly demonstrated, the rhythm, synchronicity and asynchronous engagements humans systematically experience from the very beginning in every inter-human relationship mark the birth of intersubjectivity (Stern, 1985; Trevarthen, 1979; Trevarthen, 1993; Tronick, 1989), see also (Castiello et al., 2010). It should be added that Buber's account of intersubjectivity prefigures Stein Bråten's notion of alter-centric participation, that is, the innate capacity of experiencing what the other is experiencing, as being centered in the other (Bråten, 1988, 1992, 2007).

Since the longing for relation is primary, as infant research has copiously shown, the you of the interpersonal dyad could be initially viewed as the outcome of the Appetitive Motivational (or Seeking) system[5], conceptualized as the functional network evoking appetitive eagerness (see Panksepp, 1998; Solms & Panksepp, 2012), coupled with a relationally programmed motor system (Rizzolatti & Gallese, 1997;

Gallese, 2000). This basic 'package' would enable the parallel genesis of the I and of his/her objects. In sum, currently available neuroscientific evidence seems to allow for a sub-personal description – albeit a still sketchy one – of some of the neural mechanisms enabling and underpinning basic forms of intersubjectivity, based on partly shared brain circuits. These circuits can both allow for vicarious experience of the other as another self, while at the same time preserving the self/other distinction.

Conclusions

The solution to the hotly debated issue of intersubjectivity can't be a forced choice between a third-person and a second-person perspective, because we constantly switch between these two modes of interpersonal relation. If this holds to be true, we should oppose the idea that a theoretical meta-representational approach to the other is the sole or main key to intersubjectivity. It appears more fruitful to explore the possibility that the phrase 'mind reading'[6] might qualify a variety of epistemic approaches to the other. My proposal is to consider mind reading, conceived of in a broad sense, as a non-metarepresentational way of understanding others, basically sharing a common crucial feature: the mapping of the other onto the self, reciprocated by the mapping of the self on the other. Mind reading conceived of in a narrow sense should instead qualify the type of explicit third-person form of understanding we refer to when others' behaviors or mental states are opaque and ambiguous, thus requiring explanations. Unfortunately, the classic approach to mind reading is to date unable to convincingly explain why a series of brain areas like medial frontal areas and the temporo-parietal junction (TPJ) systematically activate during explicit mentalizing tasks, besides making the tautological claim that mind reading happens to be located there (for a detailed discussion of this point, see Ammaniti & Gallese, 2014, pp. 3–6). As argued by Erwin Straus (1960), Cartesian solipsism – and, one could add, its contemporary heir, classic cognitive science – not only divides the mind from the body, but also divides the self from the world, perception from action and the I from the Thou.

Understanding others is a complex enterprise. At the very least it requires us to represent which proximal and distal goals others' behavior is directed to, others' emotional state, the identification of the beliefs, desires and intentions specifying the reasons explaining why a given behavior occurred and the understanding of how those reasons are linked to agents and to their behavior. I posit that ES and the underpinning MMs by means of neural reuse can constitutively account for the representation of the motor goals of others' actions by reusing one's own bodily formatted motor representations, as well as of others' emotions and sensations by reusing one's own visceromotor and sensorimotor representations. ES can provide a unified explanatory framework for mind reading as conceived of in the broad sense specified above. Our bodily acting and sensing nature appears to constitute the real transcendental basis upon which our experience of the social world is built.

In conclusion, I think it's fair to say that the discovery of mirror neurons and the huge empirical research such discovery generated in the following two decades has allowed us to start explaining basic aspects of intersubjectivity, like mind reading in the broad sense as delineated here, on the basis of well documented neurophysiological mechanisms. The discovery of mirror neurons, within the broader context of a new account of the motor system demonstrating its cognitive role, allowed for the possibility to conceive intersubjectivity and social cognition from a novel neuroscientifc perspective that emphasizes the crucial role of the acting body. This new perspective, in turn, greatly contributed to a revitalization of the notion of empathy and the philosophical tradition that originally identified empathy as a key element of human social intelligence, long forgotten in the debate on human cognition. I am afraid much work has still to be done to shed new light on the neural mechanisms enabling cognitively more sophisticated ways of understanding others. Perhaps a bottom-up approach could be fruitfully pursued also in this domain.

Acknowledgments

This work was supported by the EU Grant TESIS to Vittorio Gallese.

Notes

1. A lengthier version of this article appeared as: Gallese, V. (2014) Bodily Selves in Relation: Embodied simulation as second-person perspective on intersubjectivity. *Philos Trans R Soc Lond B Biol Sci.* 2014 Apr 28; 369(1644):20130177. doi: 10.1098/rstb.2013.0177.
2. Primo Levi, *The Drowned and the Saved*, 1989, London: Abacus, p. 36.
3. The notion of second person is used here compositionally and not in the linguistic sense of being the addressee of our linguistic output.
4. For a thorough discussion of this topic, see Schilbach, L., Timmermans, B., Reddy, V., Costall, A., Bente, G., Schlicht, T., & Vogeley, K. (2013). *Toward a second-person neuroscience.* Behavioural and Brain Sciences, 36(4), 393e414.
5. The transhypothalamic "reward" system that is facilitated by dopaminergic circuits arising from the brainstem ventral tegmental area (VTA).
6. I use the phrase 'mind reading' here because it is almost universally employed to refer to the human ability to understand others' expressive behavior and the causes and reasons producing it. However, I don't commit myself to the notion that understanding others just consists of literally 'reading their minds'.

References

Ammaniti, M., & Gallese, V. (2014). *The Birth of Intersubjectivity. Psychodynamics, Neurobiology and the Self.* New York, NY: W. W. Norton & Company, 236.

Arzy, S., Overney, L.S., Landis, T., & Blanke, O. (2006). Neural mechanisms of embodiment: Asomatognosia due to premotor cortex damage. *Archive of Neurology, 63*, 1022–1025.

Berti, A., Bottini, G., Gandola, M., Pia, L., Smania, N., Stracciari, A., Castiglioni, I., Vallar, G., & Paulesu, E. (2005). Shared cortical anatomy for motor awareness and motor control. *Science, 309*, 488–491.

Blakemore, S-J., Bristow, D., Bird, G., Frith, C., & Ward, J. (2005). Somatosensory activations during the observation of touch and a case of vision–touch synaesthesia. *Brain, 128*, 1571–1583.

Botvinick, M., Jha, A. P., Bylsma, L. M., Fabian, S. A., Solomon, P. E., & Prkachin, K. M. (2005). Viewing Facial Expressions of Pain Engages Cortical Areas Involved in the Direct Experience of Pain. *Neuroimage, 25*, 315–319.

Bråten, S. (1988). Dialogic Mind: The infant and the adult in protoconversation. In M. Carvallo (Ed.), *Nature, Cognition and System*. Vol. I. (187–205). Dordrecht: Kluwer Academic Publishers.

Bråten, S. (1992). The virtual other in infants' minds and social feelings. In H. Wold (Ed.) *The Dialogical Alternative* (77–97). Oslo: Scandinavian University Press.

Bråten, S. (2007). *On Being Moved: From Mirror Neurons to Empathy* (333). John Benjamins Publishing Company.

Bremmer, F., Schlack, A., Shah, N.J., et al. (2001). Polymodal motion processing in posterior parietal and premotor cortex: a human fMRI study strongly implies equivalencies between humans and monkeys. *Neuron, 29*, 287–96.

Buber, M. (1923/1970). *I and Thou*. English Translation by W. Kaufman. New York, NY: Touchstone.

Cacioppo, J.T., & Decety, J. (2011). Social neuroscience: challenges and opportunities in the study of human behavior. *Annals of the New York Academy of Science, 1224*, 162–173.

Carr L., Iacoboni M., Dubeau M.-C., Mazziotta J.C., & Lenzi G.L. (2003). Neural mechanisms of empathy in humans: A relay from neural systems for imitation to limbic areas. *Proceedings of the National Academy of Sciences, 100*, 5497–5502.

Castiello, U., Becchio, C., Zoia, S., Nelini, C., Sartori, L., Blason, L., D'Ottavio, G., Bulgheroni, M., & Gallese, V. (2010). Wired to be social: The ontogeny of human interaction, *PLoS ONE*, 5 (10), e13399.

Cattaneo, L., Sandrini, M., & Schwarzbach, J. (2010). State-Dependent TMS Reveals a Hierarchical Representation of Observed Acts in the Temporal, Parietal, and Premotor Cortices. *Cerebral Cortex, 20*(9), 2252–8.

Cermolacce, M., Naudin, J., & Parnas, J. (2007). The "minimal self" in psychopathology: Re-examining the self-disorders in the schizophrenia spectrum. *Consciousness and Cognition, 16*, 703–714.

Cosmides, L., and J. Tooby, J. (1997). The Multimodular Nature of Human Intelligence. In A. Schiebel & J.W. Schopf (Eds.), *Origin and Evolution of Intelligence*. Center for the Study of the Evolution and Origin of Life, UCLA, CA. (71–101).

De Preester, H. (2008). From *ego* to *alter ego*: Husserl, Merlau-Ponty and a layered approach to intersubjectivity. *Phenomenology and the Cognitive Sciences, 7*, 133–142.

di Pellegrino, G., Fadiga, L., Fogassi, L., Gallese, V., & Rizzolatti, G. (1992). Understanding motor events: a neurophysiological study. *Experimental Brain Research, 91*(1), 176–180.

Ebisch, S.J.H., Perrucci, M.G., Ferretti, A., Del Gratta, C., Romani, G.L., & Gallese, V. (2008). The sense of touch: embodied simulation in a visuo-tactile mirroring mechanism for the sight of any touch. *Journal of Cognitive Neuroscience, 20*, 1611–1623.

Ebisch S.J.H., Ferri F., Salone A., d'Amico L., Perrucci M.G., Ferro F.M., Romani G.L., & Gallese V. (2011). Differential involvement of somatosensory and interoceptive cortices during the observation of affective touch. *Journal of Cognitive Neuroscience, 23*(7), 1808–22.

Ebisch S.J.H., Salone A., Ferri F., De Berardis, D., Mantini, D., Ferro F.M., Romani G.L., & Gallese V. (2012). Out of touch with reality? Social perception in first episode schizophrenia. *Soc Cogn Affect Neurosci*. 2012 Jan 24. [Epub ahead of print].

Ehrsson, H.H., Spence, C., & Passingham, R.E. (2004). That's my hand! Activity in premotor cortex reflects feeling of ownership of a limb. *Science, 305*, 875–877.

Ferri, F., Frassinetti, F., Ardizzi, M., Costantini, M., & Gallese, V. (2012a). A sensorimotor network for the bodily self. *Journal of Cognitive Neuroscience, 24*, 1584–1595.

Ferri, F., Frassinetti, F., Ardizzi, M., Costantini, M., & Gallese, V. (2012b). A sensorimotor network for the bodily self. *Journal of Cognitive Neuroscience, 24*, 1584–1595.

Ferri, F., Frassinetti, F., Costantini, M., & Gallese, V. (2011). Motor simulation and the bodily self. *PLoS One, 6*, e17927.

Fogassi, L., Ferrari, P.F., Gesierich, B., Rozzi, S., Chersi, F., & Rizzolatti, G. (2005). Parietal lobe: from action organization to intention understanding. *Science, 308(5722)*, 662–7.

Fogassi, L., Gallese, V., di Pellegrino, G., Fadiga, L., Gentilucci, M., Luppino, G., Matelli, M., Pedotti, A., & Rizzolatti, G. (1992). Space coding by premotor cortex, *Experimental Brain Research, 89*(3), 686–90.

Fogassi, L., Gallese, V., Fadiga, L., Luppino, G., Matelli, M., & Rizzolatti, G. (1996). Coding of peripersonal space in inferior premotor cortex (area F4). *Journal of Neurophysiology, 76*(1), 141–157.

Gallese, V. (2000). The inner sense of action: agency and motor representations. *Journal of Consciousness Studies, 7*, 23–40.

Gallese, V. (2003). The manifold nature of interpersonal relations: The quest for a common mechanism. *Proceedings of the Royal Society of London, B., 358*, 517–528.

Gallese, V. (2005). "Being like me": self-other identity, mirror neurons and empathy. In S. Hurley & N. Chater (Eds.), *Perspectives on Imitation: From Cognitive Neuroscience to Social Science* (Vol. 1, 101–118). Cambridge, MA: MIT Press.

Gallese, V. (2007). Before and below Theory of mind: Embodied simulation and the neural correlates of social cognition. *Proceedings of the Philosophical Transactions of the Royal Society of London B. Biological Science, 362*, 659–669.

Gallese, V., Fadiga, L., Fogassi, L., & Rizzolatti, G. (1996). Action recognition in the premotor cortex. *Brain, 119*, 593–609.

Gallese, V., Fogassi, L., Fadiga, L., & Rizzolatti, G. (2002). Action Representation and the inferior parietal lobule. In Prinz, W., and Hommel, B. (Eds.), *Attention and Performance* XIX, (247–266). Oxford, UK: Oxford University Press.

Gallese, V., Keysers, C., & Rizzolatti, G. (2004). A unifying view of the basis of social cognition. *Trends in Cognitive Science, 8*, 396–403.

Gallese, V., Rochat, M., Cossu, G., & Sinigaglia, C. (2009). Motor cognition and its role in the phylogeny and ontogeny of action understanding. *Developmental Psychology, 45*, 103–13.

Gallese, V., & Rochat, M. (2009). Motor cognition: The role of the motor system in the phylogeny and ontogeny of social cognition and its relevance for the understanding of autism. In Zelazo, P.D., Chandler, M., and Crone, E., (Eds.), *Developmental Social Cognitive Neuroscience*. Psychology Press.

Gallese, V., & Sinigaglia, C. (2010). The bodily self as power for action. *Neuropsychologia, 48*, 746–755.

Gallese, V., & Sinigaglia, C. (2011a). How the body in action shapes the self. *Journal of Consciousness Studies, 18(7–8)*, 117–143.

Gallese V., & Sinigaglia, C. (2011b). What is so special with Embodied Simulation. *Trends in Cognitive Sciences, 15*, 512–519.

Gentilucci, M., Fogassi, L., Luppino, G., Matelli, M., Camarda, R., & Rizzolatti, G. (1988). Functional organization of inferior area 6 in the macaque monkey. I. Somatotopy and the control of proximal movements. *Experimental Brain Research, 71(3)*, 475–490.

Gentilucci, M., Scandolara, C., Pigarev, I.N., & Rizzolatti, G. (1983). Visual responses in the postarcuate cortex (area 6) of the monkey that are independent of eye position. *Experimental Brain Research, 50(2–3)*, 464–468.

Goldman, A. (2006). *Simulating Minds: The Philosophy, Psychology and Neuroscience of Mindreading*. Oxford: Oxford University Press.

Goldman, A., & Gallese, V. (2000). Reply to Schulkin. *Trends in Cognitive Sciences, 4*, 255–256.

Graziano, M.S., Hu, X.T., & Gross, C.G. (1997a). Coding the locations of objects in the dark. *Science, 277*(5323), 239–241.

Graziano, M.S., Hu, X.T., & Gross, C.G. (1997b). Visuospatial properties of ventral premotor cortex, *Journal of Neurophysiology*, 77(5), 2268–2292.

Graziano, M.S., & Reiss, L.A., Gross, C.G. (1999). A neuronal representation of the location of nearby sounds. *Nature, 397*(6718), 428–430.

Graziano, M.S., Yap, G.S., & Gross, C.G. (1994). Coding of visual space by premotor neurons. *Science, 266*(5187), 1054–1057.

Hutchison, W.D. et al. (1999). Pain Related Neurons in the Human Cingulate Cortex. *Nature Neuroscience 2*, 403–405.

Jackson, P. L., Meltzoff, A. N., & Decety, J. (2005). How Do We Perceive the Pain of Others: A Window into the Neural Processes Involved in Empathy. *NeuroImage, 24*, 771–779.

Jeannerod, M. (1995). Mental imagery in the motor context. *Neuropsychologia, 33*, 1419–1432.

Jeannerod, M. (2007). Being oneself. *Journal of Physiology (Paris), 101*, 161–168.

Keysers, C., Wicker, B., Gazzola, V., Anton, J.-L., Fogassi, L., & Gallese, V. (2004). A touching sight: SII/PV activation during the observation and experience of touch. *Neuron, 42*, 335–346.

Leslie, K.R., Johnson-Frey, S.H., & Grafton, S.T. (2004). Functional imaging of face and hand imitation: towards a motor theory of empathy. *Neuroimage, 21*(2), 601–607.

Matelli M., Luppino G., & Rizzolatti G. (1985). Patterns of cytochrome oxidase activity in the frontal agranular cortex of the macaque monkey. *Behavioral Brain Research, 18*, 125–137.

McCabe, C., Rolls, E.T., Bilderbeck, A., & McGlone, F. (2009). Cognitive influences on the affective representation of touch and the sight of touch in the human brain. *Social, Cognitive and Affective Neuroscience, 3*(2), 97–108.

Morrison, I., Lloyd, D., di Pellegrino, G., & Roberts, N. (2004). Vicarious responses to pain in anterior cingulate cortex: is empathy a multisensory issue? *Cognitive, Affective and Behavioral Neuroscience, 4*(2), 270–278.

Panksepp, J. (1998). *Affective neuroscience: The Foundation of Human and Animal Emotions*. Oxford, UK: Oxford University Press.

Parnas J. (2000). The self and intentionality in the pre-psychotic stages of schizophrenia: A phenomenological study. In Zahavi D. (Ed.), *Exploring the Self: Philosophical and Psychopatological Perspectives On Self-experience*. Amsterdam: John Benjamins, 115–148.

Parnas J. (2003). Self and schizophrenia: A phenomenological perspective. In Kircher T., David A., (Eds.), *The Self in Neuroscience and Psychiatry*. Cambridge: Cambridge University Press, 127–141.

Pauen, M. (2012). The second-person perspective. *Inquiry, 55*(1), 33–49.

Pfeifer, J.H., Iacoboni, M., Mazziotta, J.C., & Dapretto, M. (2008). Mirroring others' emotions relates to empathy and interpersonal competence in children. *Neuroimage, 39*(4), 2076–2085.

Pinker, S. (1994). *The Language Instinct*. New York, NY: Harper Collins.

Pinker, S. (1997). *How the Mind Works*. New York, NY: Norton.

Rizzolatti, G., & Gallese, V. (1997). From action to meaning. In: *Les Neurosciences et la Philosophie de l'Action* (217–229). J.-L. Petit (Ed.). Paris: Librairie Philosophique J. Vrin.

Rochat, M.J., Caruana, F., Jezzini, A., Escola, L., Intskirveli, I., Grammont, F., Gallese, V., Rizzolatti, G., & Umiltà, M.A. (2010). Responses of mirror neurons in area F5 to hand and tool grasping observation. *Experimental Brain Research, 204*(4), 605–16.

Rizzolatti, G., Camarda, R., Fogassi M., Gentilucci M., Luppino G., & Matelli M. (1988). Functional organization of inferior area 6 in the macaque monkey: II. Area F5 and the control of distal movements. *Experimental Brain Research, 71*, 491–507.

Rizzolatti, G., Fadiga, L., Gallese,V., & Fogassi, L. (1996). Premotor cortex and the recognition of motor actions. *Cognitive Brain Research, 3*, 131–41.

Rizzolatti, G., Fadiga, L., Fogassi, L., & Gallese, V. (1997). The space around us. *Science, 277*(5323), 190–191.

Rizzolatti, G., Fogassi, L., & Gallese,V. (2000). Cortical mechanisms subserving object grasping and action recognition: a new view on the cortical motor functions. In Gazzaniga, M.S. (Ed.), *The New Cognitive Neurosciences, 2nd Edition* (539–552). Cambridge, MA: A Bradford Book, MIT Press.

Rizzolatti, G., Fogassi, L., & Gallese,V. (2001). Neurophysiological mechanisms underlying the understanding and imitation of action. *Nature Review of Neuroscience, 6*, 889–901.

Rizzolatti, G., & Luppino, G. (2001). The cortical motor system. *Neuron, 31,* 889–901.

Rizzolatti, G., & Sinigaglia, C. (2010). The functional role of the parieto-frontal mirror circuit: interpretations and misinterpretations. *Nature Review Neuroscience, 11*, 264–74.

Serino, A., Canzoneri, E., & Avenanti, A. (2011). Fronto-parietal areas necessary for a multisensory representation of peripersonal space in humans: an rTMS study. *Journal Cognitive Neuroscience, 23*(10), 2956–2967.

Singer,T., Seymour, B., O'Doherty,J., Kaube, H., Dolan, R.J., & Frith, C.D. (2004). Empathy for pain involves the affective but not sensory components of pain. *Science, 303*(5661), 1157–1162.

Solms, M., & Panksepp,J. (2012). The Id Knows More than the Ego Admits: Neuropsychoanalytic and Primal Consciousness Perspectives on the Interface Between Affective and Cognitive Neuroscience. *Brain Sciences, 2*, 147–175.

Stern, D.N. (1985). *The Interpersonal World of the Infant.* London: Karnac Books.

Straus, E. (1960). *Psychologie der menschlichen Welt.* Berlin; Göttingen; Heidelberg: Springer, 224–235.

Trevarthen, C. (1979). Communication and cooperation in early infancy: a description of primary intersubjectivity. In M. Bullowa (Ed.), *Before Speech: The Beginning of Interpersonal Communication* (321–347). NewYork, NY: Cambridge University Press.

Trevarthen, C. (1993). The self born in intersubjectivity: An infant communicating. In U. Neisser (Ed.) *The Perceived Self* (121–173). NewYork, NY: Cambridge University Press.

Tronick, E. (1989). Emotion and emotional communication in infants. *American Psychologist, 44*, 112–119.

Tsakiris, M., & Haggard, P. (2005). Experimenting with the acting self. *Cognitive Neuropsychology, 22,* 387–407.

Tsakiris, M., Hesse, M.D., Boy, C., Haggard, P., & Fink, G.R. (2007). Neural signatures of body ownership: A sensory network for bodily self-consciousness. *Cerebral Cortex, 17,* 2235–2244.

Tsakiris, M., Prabhu, G., & Haggard, P. (2006). Having a body versus moving your body: How agency structures body-ownership. *Consciousness and Cognition, 15,* 423–432.

Umiltà, M.A., Escola, L., Intskirveli, I., Grammont, F., Rochat, M., Caruana, F., Jezzini, A., Gallese,V., & Rizzolatti, G. (2008). How pliers become fingers in the monkey motor system. *Proceedings of the National Academy of Science, 10,* 2209–2213.

Wicker, B., Keysers, C., Plailly,J., Royet, J-P., Gallese,V., & Rizzolatti, G. (2003). Both of us disgusted in my insula: The common neural basis of seeing and feeling disgust. *Neuron, 40,* 655–664.

11
EMPATHY AS DEVELOPMENTAL ACHIEVEMENT

Beyond Embodied Simulation[1]

Mark Solms

Introduction

There can be few better examples of the limits that hard-won knowledge in the humanities places on contemporary neuroscience than the problem of 'other minds'. This philosophical problem reminds cognitive neuroscientists that they can never make external observations upon their object of study: the mind. The mind is not an object. You can only know your own. But science demands objectivity. So this problem – the radically subjective nature of the mind – apparently makes it impossible to have a science of the mind. It makes 'scientific psychology' an oxymoron.

There was until recently, therefore, only one way for mental scientists to proceed. Loathe as they may have been to admit it, they observed the relationship between their own (subjective) mental states and their own (objective) bodily states, and then inferred or hypothesised that equivalent mental states probably accompany the equivalent bodily states they observed in others. In other words, to the extent that they aspired to do mental science at all, they projected their own mental states into the bodies (and ultimately the brains and neural processes) of others. This projective process is traditionally called 'empathy'. And empathy is not a respectable empirical method.

Some 'mental' scientists chose instead to exclude the mind from nature, as the behaviourists did, but that is another story. (Many neuropsychologists are in fact neurobehavioursts, still today, in my experience.) There are also non-scientists – mystics and psychotics and the like – who claim direct, supernatural knowledge of other minds. But here I am concerned only with the mainstream of contemporary mental science, which believes that the mind does indeed exist, accepts that it is indeed part of nature, notwithstanding the fact that we demand objective evidence for all scientific claims.

I count myself among these believers. Although few mental scientists seem willing to admit it, this is what we are: believers. Due to the problem of other minds, the attribution of mental states to other creatures that look and behave like ourselves (whether they be human or animal) remains a matter of 'faith' (see Bion 1970). It cannot be a matter of observation.

Against this philosophical background, the discovery of mirror neurons was a major step forward (Di Pellegrino et al. 1992; Gallese et al. 1996). Mirror neurons seemed to provide a mechanism by means of which the subject can perceive directly the mental states of others, in a manner not fundamentally different from how we perceive any old object (Fogassi et al. 2005). We are told that the pattern of premotor neuronal activity producing the voluntary movements of the other is mirrored in our own premotor neurons, and their intentionality is thereby reproduced in us (i.e., in our own brains). Please note: this implies that mirror neurons perceive other minds in much the same way that sensory neurons perceive other objects, by mapping the surface features of the objects.

(Here I am leaving aside the 'hard problem' of how mapped activity in the sensory cortex generates the experience of an object. This problem applies equally to all perception, including the supposed perception of other minds via mirror neurons; see Solms, 2014. The fact that I am leaving this problem aside – because it is not specific to the matter at hand – does not make it a small problem. It is in fact a huge problem for cognitive neuroscience, which for the most part simply ignores such philosophical conundrums.)

The mirroring mechanism just described, now called 'embodied simulation' (see previous chapter), seems to circumvent the ancient philosophical problem of other minds, and therefore the epistemological problems of empathy. It seems to make it possible to observe other minds empirically.

There is no reason to doubt that embodied simulation does indeed exist. But I want to argue that the problem of empathy remains. The mechanism of empathy is a lot more complicated than embodied simulation theory would have us believe. I believe that embodied simulation is a simple, reflexive mechanism which may well have an indirect relationship with empathy, but it is not the mechanism of empathy. In this paper I want to discuss the mechanism of empathy proper.

Embodied simulation via mirror neurons is an innate capacity of primate brains, and it functions automatically: monkey see, monkey do (Carey, 1996). Empathy, by contrast, is very difficult to achieve. Empathy is an acquired capacity. It is better thought of as a developmental achievement.

What is Empathy?

It is well known that the conception of 'empathy' has shifted over time, between languages and across disciplines. The mechanism in aesthetics by means of which the viewing subject projects its intentional states into inanimate objects ('*Einfühlung*') became a mechanism in psychology through which the subject apperceives the intentional states of others ('empathy'). The distinction between 'empathy' (feeling into) and 'sympathy' (feeling with) was blurred in this disciplinary transition, mainly due to the fact that psychological objects possess subjective intentionality whereas aesthetic objects, despite appearances, do not. Artworks are actually as dead as doornails.

I raise this historical point, despite the fact that it is extraneous to my main argument, for the reason that the transition from projective *Einfühlung* to apperceptive empathy raises the possibility of empathic error in psychology – a problem that does not arise in aesthetics. It is possible to misperceive the state of another mind in ways that do not arise with, say, the appreciation of a landscape. Who is to say whether or not a willow is weeping?[2]

The change in the directionality of empathy (from aesthetic projection to psychological apperception) was, however, only apparent. The illusion of a change in direction is reducible to the problem of error. I claim that in both the aesthetic and the psychological cases, the subject attributes its own intentional states to objects; the empathizing subject 'feels its way into' objects, not the other way around. When the objects in question are other minds, the subject may get the intentional feelings of the object wrong. This is misperception of feeling. But when the objects in question are inanimate artworks, the subject always gets the feelings wrong (artworks do not really possess intentional feelings).

So the mechanism of empathy remains the same; it is always projective, albeit projection constrained – and hopefully corrected – by error.

This rule applies even in the case of embodied simulation – which is not empathy proper. Embodied simulation is said to involve direct perception of the intentional states of others. But when the pattern of premotor activity in the perceiving subject directly mirrors that of the other, how does the subject know whether the intended movement is its own or not? A recent study by Gallese's group answers this question: something must be added to the premotor neuronal activity before the subject can perform 'me' versus 'not me' attributions, namely activity in cortical areas higher in the processing stream than mirror neurons (Ebisch et al. 2012). When this 'something extra' is missing (as occurs in schizophrenia, for example) the subject misattributes intentionality – the subject cannot determine who willed the movements. The locus of the attributed intention, then, no matter what the subject thinks, is always inside the subject.

But let me return to my main argument. I have said that empathy involves a unitary mechanism: the empathic subject always projects itself (always 'feels its way') into the object. The structure and etymology of the word reflect this:

ἐμ/πάθεια
em/pathy
Ein/fühlung
into/feeling

So empathy involves two things – 'feeling' and 'into' – one of them being affective and the other being spatial. The 'feeling', as I have said, by definition, belongs to the subject. The 'into' (the attribution) is where the difficulty lies. This is the source of empathic error. The crux of the problem of empathy, therefore, is the accurate spatial attribution of affect.

In the Beginning was the Affect …

I want to lay stress on the affect. I believe feelings come first, then we ask where they came from. Answering such questions (about the sources of feelings) is difficult. Two properties of affect explain why.

First, affect is devoid of spatial qualities. We might experience a feeling of fear (say) as coming from an object, but really the fear is a subjective response *to* the object. Our subjective responses do not actually arise from things outside of ourselves. Affect can only ever arise from within us.

We must also remember that subjective space is metaphorical. When we say that affect arises 'within' us, we position our subjectivity with reference to the objects around us, and in doing so we objectify it. Subjectivity itself (as Descartes [1641] pointed out) lacks spatial extension; it lacks substance. This applies especially to what I claim is the core feature of subjectivity, namely affect. You can never see, touch, taste and so on, an affect. To objectify affect you must bring it into conjunction with other things. And this is what we typically do.

Second, affect has peremptory motivational qualities. In this respect, too, it is different from space. Space is neutral. We may feel compelled to approach or withdraw from places (or from objects in space) but this is due to the feelings they evoke, it is not due to the objective features of the places or things themselves. Things that are attractive to one person may be repulsive to another.

These two qualities of affect – immateriality and peremptory motivation – make affect more difficult to think about than it is to think about objects. Affect is typically discharged, it is acted upon (or reacted to) rather than thought about. To think about an affect we have to 'tame' it first. Objectifying affect (turning it into external, visualisable, localizable stuff that we can think with) is the standard way of taming it. (See Solms in press.)

This is what cognition does to affect. But the taming of affect takes time, and the outcome is usually unstable.

The Structure of Consciousness

Consciousness has two major components: first we are aware of ourselves and then of a world around us. This distinction (between ourselves and the world) coincides with the distinction between subject and objects. (See Solms, 2013, 2014.)

Objects are registered in the classical sensory modalities: we see, hear, smell and so on, things. Space is computed from an integration of these modalities; it maps the location of things in relation to the external surface of the own body. The subjective equivalent of the objective perceptual modalities is affect. Affect registers the internal state of the subject – the interior of the body, if you will (see Solms, 1997, 2013). But it does not do so by means of somatotopic maps. In its most elemental form, it does so by monitoring the state of vital functions and then converting these physiological parameters into feeling states in the pleasure-unpleasure series (see Damasio, 2010).

In this way, affect tells us how we are doing within a biological scale of values – how we feel, including how we feel about objects. Affect in this rudimentary form broadcasts the state of the subject to itself, in relation to its vital needs (survival and reproductive success). Viewed anatomically, elemental affect derives from primitive 'need detector' mechanisms located in the medial hypothalamus and other structures of the visceral brain (e.g., solitary nucleus, area postrema, parabrachial nucleus, circumventricular organs) which project to the periaqueductal grey (PAG) and the rest of the extended reticulothalamic activating system.[3]

By contrast, space and its objects derive from thalamocortical mechanisms and the sensory receptor organs associated with them. Via these mechanisms we construct, through our lifetimes, a model of the outside world – a predictive representation of it (see Friston, 2010). The purpose of doing so is to learn how best to meet our needs there – that is, how best to marry affect with objects.

Affective consciousness (which arises mainly from brainstem structures) is then extended upwards into thalamocortical structures so that we may know what our feelings are about (aboutness = intentionality; cf. Brentano, 1874). The structure of all perceptual consciousness therefore coincides with the structure of empathy; it projects feelings into space.

It is important to recognise that the re-representation of the affective self as an object (as a body in space) relies heavily on a particular cortical region: the perisylvian cortex of the right cerebral hemisphere. Speaking anatomically, this is where the spatial learning process described above unfolds – the process whereby a subject progressively comes to know the minds of others. When this part of the brain is damaged, as we shall see later, empathy collapses.

It is true that not all affect/object relationships need to be learned. Some emotional responses are 'unconditioned' (to use a technical psychological term). These instinctual affect/object complexes are called 'basic emotions' (see Panksepp, 1998). Basic emotions are built-in predictions – predictions that are so vital for survival and reproductive success that you cannot afford to learn them via your own experience (Friston calls them 'priors'). For example: approaching a cliff triggers a degree of fear, always. And the fear tells you what to do, what action is appropriate, namely, in this case: freeze or retreat. If you had to learn what might happen if you continued over the cliff, that would be the last thing you learned; and such genes would (appropriately) not be propagated.

I suspect that embodied simulation relies on just such inbuilt mechanisms. When another mind is gripped by fear (and its body moves accordingly) the state of fear is mirrored in the perceiving subject. But such exceptions only prove the rule: most emotional states are far more complicated than the elemental instinctual emotions. The affective state of others is an ever-changing landscape. You have to feel your way into them in order to read them. This type of mind reading – the everyday type – must be performed *in vivo*; there are no genetic stereotypes for it. And predicting what others are going to do, divining their intentional states, is a very important activity.

This is the type of mind reading that is a developmental achievement. When a child says that a glass lying on its side is 'tired', that is not good empathy. The child is wrong; the glass is not tired (just as the willow is not weeping). This is presumably why we value empathy. Not everybody is good at it.

What is more, we value empathic capacity morally. Feeling your way into the affective state of others (accurately) is a good thing. It is not only good for you, it is also good *of* you. Likewise, failing to feel someone's pain (say) is bad. This moral dimension of empathy requires explanation, too.

But why is empathy so difficult? As I have said: the difficulty resides in the non-topological quality of affect. It is not difficult to feel a feeling; what is difficult is to discern where it comes from, which in turn reveals what it is about: What events in the world might have caused me to feel this? And what actions might be required to change it?

Now I come to the crux of my argument, namely that the second quality of affect mentioned above, the peremptory quality, is what makes it so difficult to localise.

The Theory of Narcissism

In the beginning was the affect (see Fig. 11.1). This seems to be a reasonable assumption. Everything we know about the phylogeny and ontogeny of consciousness-producing structures points to this conclusion (Merker, 2007; Solms & Panksepp, 2012). The most rudimentary form of affect, generated at the level of the PAG (and associated with its ventral and dorsal columns, respectively) is pleasure versus unpleasure. Higher (limbic) varieties of affect/object complexes, too, can be classified in this way; they are special kinds of pleasure and unpleasure. (Orgasm, attachment, safety and so on are varieties of pleasure; pain, loss, fear and so on are varieties of unpleasure.) Affect, nevertheless, comes in two fundamental forms: pleasurable and unpleasurable feelings.

FIGURE 11.1 First Developmental Stage: Undifferentiated Feelings (The figure depicts the fluctuating affective state of the primal subject, where + is pleasure and – is unpleasure.)

Feelings in themselves, as I have said already, do not possess spatial attributes. However, all animals approach pleasure inducing stimuli and avoid unpleasure inducing ones. The same applies to us; we want to be (and to remain) in pleasurable states, and to avoid unpleasurable ones. This is the 'pleasure principle', which forms the basis of the theory of narcissism (see Freud, 1925).

The theory of narcissism applies the pleasure principle to the formation of the human subject – to the first spatial differentiation. The subject (the 'within') is a place set apart from objects. Since we aspire to be in pleasurable states as opposed to unpleasurable ones, the first conception of 'me' (of the place where my subjectivity intends to exist) is where the pleasure is; conversely, the place my subjectivity intends to avoid (the 'not me') is where the unpleasure is. In the beginning, therefore, 'me' coincides with pleasure and 'not me' with unpleasure (see Fig. 11.2). It seems reasonable to assume that our first intentional states take roughly this form. This is the default mode of subjectivity. Observations of immature minds (e.g., very young children) and of severe psychopathologies (e.g., schizophrenia) point to the same conclusion.

In this state, called narcissism, the subject maintains a rigid split between pleasurable and unpleasurable feelings, by 'introjecting' the sources of the former

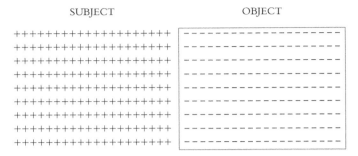

FIGURE 11.2 Second Developmental Stage: Split Feelings (The figure depicts the state of narcissism, where positive and negative feelings are split and allocated to subject and object respectively, via mechanisms of introjection and projection.)

and 'projecting' the sources of the latter. Thus feelings acquire their first spatial attribution: pleasurable feelings belong inside (they are me) and unpleasurable feelings belong outside (they are not me). In short, the nascent subject rids itself of bad feelings by relegating them to nascent objects. This leads to the not very nice but unavoidable conclusion that 'hate, as a relation to objects, is older than love' (Freud, 1915a, p. 136).

Now consider the implications for our topic, empathy. When something feels good, we try to locate it within our beloved selves; when something feels bad, we compulsively locate it in objects. We accordingly want to distance ourselves from things imbued with feelings other than our own. This is not a good basis for empathy. Yet this would seem to be our default mode of response. That is why I do not think empathy relies on automatic mechanisms.

I am not arguing this from first principles. I am arguing it from my experience as a psychoanalyst. The principles derive from the experience. It turns out that people in primitive states of mind are not very empathic; they typically grossly misread (misattribute or mislocate) the feelings of others.

Fortunately, the exigencies of life militate strongly against the viability of narcissism. We living creatures need objects if we are to survive and reproduce. We, therefore, have to allow some bad feelings to be relocated inside us (e.g., 'I feel hungry') and some good ones outside (e.g., 'she provides relief'). On this basis, we have to accept that we are not fundamentally different from other objects, in that we possess 'objective' (unwanted) attributes of a kind that we would rather attribute only to others. This mature state, the basis for what Freud called 'object love', is the opposite of narcissism. The transition from narcissism (self love) to object love is necessitated by the reality principle.

Having made this transition – against strong emotional resistances – the subject is in a position to attribute feelings more realistically (see Fig. 11.3). Now it can begin to properly answer the question: Where does this feeling come from? Such questions, if they are going to be answered accurately, require the subject to tolerate objects. It requires a receptive attitude towards them. But remember: real objects by their very nature are apt to produce unwelcome feelings in us, such as lack and

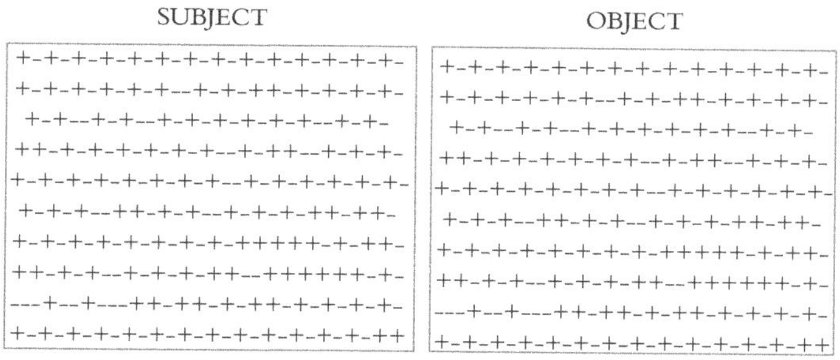

SUBJECT   OBJECT

```
+-+-+-+-+-+-+-+-+-+-+-+-+-     +-+-+-+-+-+-+-+-+-+-+-+-+-
+-+-+-+-+-+--+-+-++-+-+-+-     +-+-+-+-+--+-+-++-+-+-+-
 +-+--+-+--+-+-+-+-+-+--+-+-    +-+--+-+--+-+-+-+-+--+-+-
++-+-+-+-+-+--+-++--+-+-+-     ++-+-+-+-+-+--+-++--+-+-+-
+-+-+-+-+-+-+-+--+-+-+-+-+-    +-+-+-+-+-+-+--+-+-+-+-+-+-
 +-+-+--++-+-+--+-+-+-++-++-    +-+-+--++-+-+--+-+-+-++-+-
+-+-+-+-+-+-+-+-+++++-+-++-    +-+-+-+-+-+-+-+-+++++-+-++-
++-+-+--+-+-+-++--++++++-+-    ++-+-+--+-+-+-++--++++++-+-
---+--+---++-++-+-++-+-+-+-    ---+--+---++-++-+-++-+-+-+-
+-+-+-+-+-+-+-+-+-+-+-+-++     +-+-+-+-+-+-+-+-+-+-+-+-++
```

FIGURE 11.3 Third Developmental Stage: Integrated Feelings (The figure depicts realistic self/object relations.)

need. In these circumstances, allowing oneself to feel the intentional state of the object as it actually is opens us to unwelcome truths. For example, it may be that the object has no intention of rectifying our lack, meeting our need, requiting our desire. Since 'hate, as a relation to objects, is older than love', locating pleasure in the other is apt to arouse envy, just as finding pain there may arouse guilt. To tolerate such things is to overcome narcissism. It is therefore only after narcissism is overcome (or to the extent that it is overcome) that empathy is possible.

With these simple facts, I believe we have explained why empathy is considered good, both practically and morally.

The Theory of Repression

Having stated my main argument, I would like to consider some more subtle issues.

Freud made an interesting observation about how we deal with the vulnerabilities introduced by object love. Since the exigencies of life require us to tolerate separateness – the 'otherness' of the things we need and want – and therefore to tolerate unwelcome feelings within ourselves, we try to avoid thinking about things that evoke such feelings. We relegate such things to a part of our minds that we pay no attention to. That is, we render them unconscious, we 'repress' them (see Fig. 11.4).

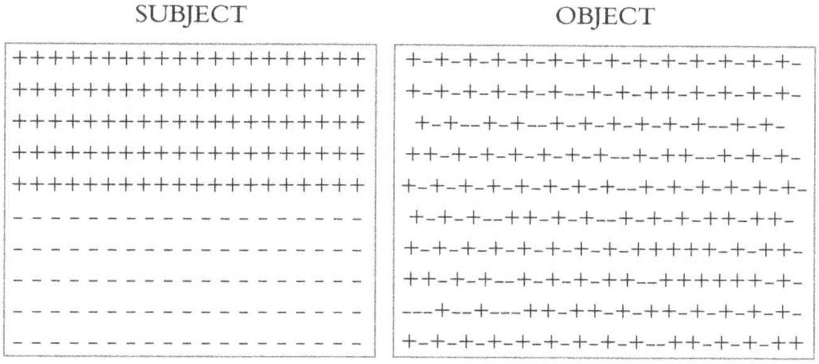

SUBJECT   OBJECT

```
++++++++++++++++++++++     +-+-+-+-+-+-+-+-+-+-+-+-+-
++++++++++++++++++++++     +-+-+-+-+-+--+-+-++-+-+-+-
++++++++++++++++++++++      +-+--+-+--+-+-+-+-+--+-+-
++++++++++++++++++++++     ++-+-+-+-+-+--+-++--+-+-+-
++++++++++++++++++++++     +-+-+-+-+-+-+-+--+-+-+-+-+-
- - - - - - - - - - - - - - - - - - - -     +-+-+--++-+-+--+-+-+-++-++-
- - - - - - - - - - - - - - - - - - - -     +-+-+-+-+-+-+-+-+++++-+-++-
- - - - - - - - - - - - - - - - - - - -     ++-+-+--+-+-+-++--++++++-+-
- - - - - - - - - - - - - - - - - - - -     ---+--+---++-++-+-++-+-+-+-
- - - - - - - - - - - - - - - - - - - -     +-+-+-+-+-+-+-+-+-++-+-+-++
```

FIGURE 11.4 Fourth Developmental Stage: Suppressed Feelings
(The figure depicts repression.)

In his famous essay on 'The Unconscious', Freud elaborated:

> The assumption of an unconscious is … a perfectly *legitimate* one, inasmuch as in postulating it we are not departing a single step from our customary and generally accepted mode of thinking. Consciousness makes each of us aware only of his own states of mind; that other people, too, possess a consciousness is an inference which we draw by analogy from their observable utterances and actions, in order to make this behaviour of theirs intelligible to us. (It would no doubt be psychologically more correct to put it this way: that without any special reflection we attribute to everyone else our own constitution and therefore our consciousness as well, and that this identification is a *sine qua non* of our understanding [of others – please note: this is empathy – MS]) … Psychoanalysis demands nothing more than that we should apply this process of inference to ourselves too – a proceeding to which, it is true, we are not constitutionally inclined. If we do this, we must say: all the acts and manifestations which I notice in myself and do not know how to link up with the rest of my mental life must be judged as if they belonged to someone else: they are to be explained by a mental life ascribed to this other person.
>
> *(Freud, 1915b, p. 169)*

This so-called other person, Freud explained, is the unconscious part of our own intentionality. It is the other within us: the repressed. The 'fundamental rule' of clinical psychoanalysis asks the patient to adopt the same tolerant and receptive attitude toward this unconscious part of its self that it (hopefully) learned to adopt towards other people. It asks us to 'empathise' with unwanted parts of ourselves.

I quoted this passage from Freud to remind readers how difficult it is to empathise and to clarify the nature of the attitude it entails.

Every psychoanalyst knows how much mental work is required to (accurately) know the mind of another person. The mechanism of embodied simulation does not begin to do justice to this task.

It is also noteworthy in this respect that analysts seek to know the patient by looking inward, by allowing themselves to notice what they feel, and then working out what belongs to the analyst and what to the patient. This also involves talking to patients, putting hypotheses to them, and taking in their responses (correcting our errors). Only then can we begin to know what the patient's feelings are really about.

A Clinical Vignette

To put flesh to these theoretical bones, I will conclude with a brief vignette. The patient is a middle-aged woman who suffered a stroke (a few days before the interview reported below) which destroyed a large part of the perisylvian region of her right cerebral hemisphere (see Fig. 11.5). As I said earlier: this is the part of the brain where spatial learning unfolds – the process whereby a subject progressively comes to know the minds of others. When this part of the brain is damaged, as we shall now see, empathy collapses.

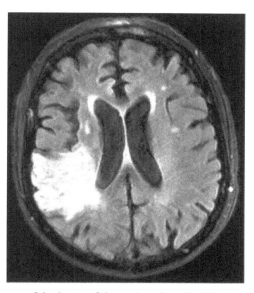

FIGURE 11.5 MRI scan of the brain of the patient described in the text, showing infarction in the territory of the right middle cerebral artery.

This stroke left the patient bedridden, due to dense paralysis of the left side of her body (arm and leg). However, she flatly denied that she was paralysed, and she asked incessantly to be sent home. This symptom is called 'anosognosia'. Anosognosia is quite common after right hemisphere stroke, that is, after damage to the part of the brain that internalises the rules of space. Patients with right persylvian damage unlearn those rules. Then they regress to narcissism (see Kaplan-Solms & Solms, 2001). They represent space as they would like it to be, rather than as it *is* (they regress from the reality principle to the pleasure principle). They forget the most difficult of all spatial rules, namely that one's self is no different from other objects. Although I love myself so much more, I am bound by the same indifferent rules. From the point of view of others, it is me who is the object and they who are the subject.[4] Thus these patients lose the capacity to know the intentional state of others, particularly when it requires them to face such unwelcome objective facts.

In the vignette that follows, I have explained to the patient that I am interviewing her in front of a camera so that I can demonstrate her case to other doctors. You (the reader) are therefore explicitly included in the conversation.

ME: Can you tell me why you're in hospital?

PATIENT: [Silent.]

ME: Can you tell me why you're here?

PATIENT: Apparently I had a stroke; that's why I'm here.

ME: That's right. But why did you say 'apparently'; do you agree that you've had a stroke?

PATIENT: Yes, but I don't feel any symptoms. What do you feel? How are you supposed to feel?

ME: Well, one of the most common consequences of a stroke is paralysis; you get loss of movement in an arm or a leg. Are you having those symptoms?

PATIENT: [Lifts up her paralysed left arm with her intact right arm.] Here, they [the other doctors] can see; I'm lifting my arm up.

ME: You're lifting it up so that the doctors can see?

PATIENT: Yes.

ME: So are you showing them that you *can* move that arm or that you *can't* move that arm?

PATIENT: I *can* move it.

ME: But you're lifting it by lifting it with this [right] hand. Can you lift it by itself?

PATIENT: I lift it with my mind.

ME: With your mind?

PATIENT: [Nods.]

ME: And when you lift it with your mind, do you actually see it and feel it moving?

PATIENT: Yes.

ME: So if I had to ask you the question – 'Is this arm working normally or not?' – what would your answer be?

PATIENT: No.

ME: No, it's not working normally?

PATIENT: [Shakes her head.]

ME: Okay; what's the matter with that arm?

PATIENT: Nothing. There's nothing wrong with it.

ME: There's nothing wrong with it?

PATIENT: Because I can move it.

ME: There's nothing wrong with it because …?

PATIENT: Because I can touch it.

ME: There's nothing wrong with it because you can touch it?

PATIENT: [Nods]

ME: And when you touch it, it feels normal?

PATIENT: [Nods.]

ME: And when you try to move it by itself does it feel normal?

PATIENT: [Nods.]

ME: So, as far as you are concerned, there's absolutely nothing wrong with you now?

PATIENT: [Nods.]

ME: Even though apparently you had a stroke?

PATIENT: [No response.]

ME: The normal effect of a stroke, which is paralysis, that hasn't happened to you?

PATIENT: [Shakes her head.]

ME: Okay, can you lift up this hand? [Points to her right hand.]

PATIENT: [Lifts the hand.]

ME: That's it. Okay, put it down. Can you lift up this hand? [Points to her left hand.]

PATIENT: [No response.]

ME: Do you see, Mrs—, when you lift up this hand [right], it actually goes up, you see, but when you lift up this hand [left], it stays there. You see, that's what we call paralysis. Do you see?

PATIENT: [No response.]

ME: That's because of the stroke. That's what has happened as a result of the stroke. So when you say you don't have any symptoms, it's not quite right, because this is a symptom you *do* have as a result of the stroke. Do you see? [Points to the left arm.]

PATIENT: [No response.]

ME: So now, while you are here in hospital, the physiotherapists are going to work with you and they are going to see what they can do to help you, to regain the movement in that arm. Okay?

PATIENT: [No response.]

ME: Just so that the doctors [via the camera] understand, can you tell me again now, after we have discussed this: is there anything wrong with you as a result of this stroke?

PATIENT: [Shakes her head.]

ME: No?

PATIENT: [Shakes her head.]

ME: Nothing? Are you sure? But what have we just discussed now; what did I just tell you?

PATIENT: [Points to her left hand.] This side has a symptom.

ME: I said that that side has a symptom; that's right. And did I say what the symptom was?

PATIENT: Not lifting up this hand. [Lifts up her left arm with her right arm.]

ME: I beg your pardon?

PATIENT: Because I'm not lifting up this hand by itself.

ME: I said that you can't lift that hand by itself. That's right. Isn't that true?

PATIENT: [Yawns. Nods.]

ME: So do you agree with me, you can't lift this [left] hand by itself?

PATIENT: [Nods.]

ME: So do you agree: that is the effect of the stroke?

PATIENT: [Nods.]

ME: That's very important. That's very good. So may I just ask you again – because the doctors are going to be watching this from the camera, so I just want to be sure that you and I agree, and that they understand that you and I agree – can you tell me again: this stroke, has it caused you any problems, has it caused any harm to any part of your body?

PATIENT: [Nods.]

ME: It has. And what has that harm been, what has that effect been?

PATIENT: [No response.]

ME: What symptoms has it caused you, that stroke?

PATIENT: At home, when I know its bedtime, I get into a bath. But here they don't have that.

ME: At bedtime you can't get into a bath?

PATIENT: [Nods.]

ME: But why are you telling me that?

PATIENT: Because I can only sleep when I've had a nice bath.

ME: Oh, so it's affecting your sleep …

PATIENT: Yes.

Me: … so you would rather not be here. I understand that; you would rather be at home.

PATIENT: Yes.

ME: I know you would rather be at home. But remember what I told you: the reason that you're here is because of this paralysis [pointing to her left hand] because of the stroke. That's why you can't be at home right now. But you will be able to get back home; it won't be very long.

PATIENT: You see, at home you're comfortable.

ME: That's right.

PATIENT: Everybody knows at a hospital that you are sick.

ME: Yes.

PATIENT: And they come and talk crap to you every time.

ME: I see. So am I busy talking crap to you?

PATIENT: No.

ME: But it makes you feel bad for everybody to be coming and talking to you about being sick.

PATIENT: [Nods.]

ME: You don't want to feel sick.

PATIENT: Yes.

ME: You don't want to be treated as a sick person.

PATIENT: [Nods.]

ME: Nobody does. Well, most people don't like to be treated as a sick person.

PATIENT: [No response.]

ME: The important thing is that, at the moment, even though you don't *feel* sick – that's why you don't feel like a sick person – this arm [left] isn't working at the moment, because of that stroke. And remember, that's the thing we have agreed about; because I think it is very important for us to be able to help with that. Okay?

PATIENT: [No response.]

ME: So can we discuss it one last time? Can you tell me again: this arm [left] is it working or not working? At the moment; is it working or not working? At the moment; right now. Is this arm working properly or not?

PATIENT: [Nods.]

ME: Are you saying it is working properly? Are you saying that it's not paralysed?

PATIENT: [Nods.]

ME: But just a few minutes ago you agreed with me that it is.

PATIENT: No I didn't.

ME: Is that just because I forced you to?

PATIENT: No, you didn't force me; how did you force me?

ME: No, I am trying to understand. Why did you agree with me a few minutes ago and now you're not agreeing?

PATIENT: [Points to her head.] Because you can't read my mind. In my mind's eye you can see that you are lifting your hand. But *you* can't see that.

ME: I understand. That's very important. So in your mind's eye you can see that you're lifting the hand?

PATIENT: [Nods.]

ME: But what about with your physical eyes? Even though in your mind's eye you *believe* you are lifting it, because you've made the decision that you're going to lift it, and you feel yourself putting that decision into effect – in your mind's eye, therefore, you feel that you are lifting it – but if you look at your hand with your physical eyes, with your actual eyes, can't you see it is actually not lifting?

PATIENT: [Nods.]

ME: So, as you say, I'm outside of you, I'm not inside of your mind, I'm outside; I look at it with my eyes and I don't see it moving, and that's why I think it is paralysed.

PATIENT: Yes.

ME: So now which one do you think is right: what our actual eyes see or what our mind's eye sees?

PATIENT: What your mind's eye sees.

ME: Does your mind's eye see something that is more real than what your actual eyes see?

PATIENT: [Nods.]

ME: So that's why you believe you're not paralysed?

PATIENT: [Nods.]

ME: Okay. Alright Mrs—, I don't want to keep pestering you. Okay, I'll come back and talk to you again another time.

PATIENT: [Nods.]

Discussion

The patient described above illustrates the general principle that right perisylvian damage causes people to perceive things from a narcissistic perspective – to see things as they want them to be rather than as they really are. This is because the right perisylvian region is the part of the brain that computes space accurately, and, therefore, locates feelings correctly. The patient in our clinical vignette reversed the actual spatial state of affairs when she claimed that her disorder was caused by my inability to see things from her point of view. Like an immature child (or petulant adolescent) who construes the world according to their subjective wants, it was the patient who could not see her disability from my point of view. The problem with anosognosic patients, in a word, is that they are unable to empathise. They cannot tolerate the viewpoint of the other, so they are highly prone to empathic errors.

The process of learning how space works in relation to our feelings (i.e., learning how it works in contradiction of the pleasure principle) is all too easily reversed. Our minds' (subjective) eye readily sees things that our physical (objective) eyes do not, even without the devastation of a right hemisphere stroke.

I have just illustrated this truism with reference to an extreme example, to render the mechanisms at work as clear as possible. But we recognise the same mechanisms in our selves, albeit in subtler forms. Who among us finds it easy to know the minds of others when they contain unwelcome truths about us, and thereby require us to see ourselves objectively? Narrowing the gap between the subjective and objective perspectives in the face of peremptory feelings is a developmental achievement of capital importance. But a gap always remains.

That is why empathy is difficult. I hope I have conveyed my main point clearly. The current approach of most cognitive neuroscientists to the problem of empathy is hopelessly reductionistic. It does not even nearly do justice to the facts.

There can be few better examples of the limits that the hard-won knowledge of the Humanities places on cognitive neuroscience than the radically subjective nature of the mind. This makes it impossible to have a physical science of psychology.

But 'scientific psychology' is only an oxymoron if 'scientific' is considered synonymous with 'physical'. That is to say, we cannot have a scientific psychology if we limit ourselves to spatial concepts (to the *res extensa* of Descartes) and if we disregard the peremptory power of affect, because we thereby disregard the motivational forces that so easily distort the supposed neutrality of 'objective' spatial cognition.

Considering the problem of other minds; to the extent that we aspire to do mental science we simply must project our own subjective states into others. This projective process is empathy. But empathy is not a respectable empirical method … precisely because it is so unreliable, so difficult to achieve and to maintain. In psychoanalysis – a science of the mind that does not consider 'scientific' to be synonymous with 'physical' – we rely very heavily on empathy as a method of investigation. But we can only do so because we have proper respect for feelings.

Notes

1. This chapter is a substantially revised version of my paper 'Empathy and other minds: A neuropsychoanalytic perspective' presented at the Zentrum für Literatur - und Kulturforschung, Berlin, 2013.

2. Misperception of the intentionality of the artist (as opposed to the artwork) is another matter entirely. It is a psychological matter.
3. When we view affect anatomically it is important to remember that we are re-representing it in a visual/spatial format. We are not reducing affect to anatomy but rather correlating it with anatomy (see Solms, 2014).
4. One is reminded of the Christian empathic moral: 'Love thy neighbour as thyself'.

References

Bion, W. (1970). *Attention and Interpretation*. London: Tavistock.

Brentano, F. (1874). *Psychologie vom empirischen Standpunkte*. Leipzig: Dunker & Humbolt.

Carey, D.P. (1996). "Monkey see, monkey do" cells. *Current Biology, 16*, 1087–8.

Damasio, A. (2010). *Self Comes to Mind*. London: Pantheon.

Descartes, R. (1641). *Meditations on First Philosophy*. [Trans. from the Latin by J. Cottingham.] Cambridge: Cambridge University Press.

Di Pellegrino, G., Fadiga, L., Fogassi, L., Gallese, V., & Rizzolatti, G. (1992). Understanding motor events: a neurophysiological study. *Experimental Brain Research, 91*, 176–180.

Ebisch, S., Salone, A., Ferri, F., et al. (2012). Out of touch with reality? Social perception in first-episode schizophrenia. *Social Cognitive & Affective Neuroscience, 8*, 394–403.

Fogassi, L., Ferrari, P.F. Gesierich, B., Rozzi, S., Chersi, F., & Rizzolatti, G. (2005). Parietal lobe: from action organization to intention understanding. *Science, 308*, 662–667.

Freud, S. (1915a). Instincts and their vicissitudes. *Standard Edition, 14*, 117–140.

Freud, S. (1915b). The unconscious. *Standard Edition, 14,* 159–204.

Freud, S. (1925). On negation. *Standard Edition, 19*, 235–239.

Friston, K. (2010). The free-energy principle: A unified brain theory? *Nature Reviews Neuroscience, 11*, 127–138.

Gallese, V., Fadiga, L., Fogassi, L., & Rizzolatti, G. (1996). Action recognition in the premotor cortex. *Brain, 119*, 593–609.

Kaplan-Solms, K., & Solms, M. (2001). *Clinical Studies in Neuropsychoanalysis: Introduction to a Depth Neuropsychology*. London: Karnac.

Merker, B. (2007). Consciousness without cerebral cortex: A challenge for neuroscience and medicine. *Behavioral & Brain Sciences, 30*, 63–134.

Panksepp, J. (1998). *Affective Neuroscience: The Foundations of Animal and Humans Emotions*. Oxford: Oxford University Press.

Solms, M. (1997). What is consciousness? *Journal of the American Psychoanalytic Association, 45*, 681–778.

Solms, M. (2013). The conscious id. *Neuropsychoanalysis, 15*, 5–19.

Solms, M. (2014). A neuropsychoanalytical approach to the hard problem of consciousness. *Journal of Integrative Neuroscience, 13*, 173–85.

Solms, M. (in press). Affect theory today. *Psychoanalytic Psychology*.

Solms, M., & Panksepp, J. (2012). The id knows more than the ego admits. *Brain Sciences, 2*, 147–175.

AFTERWORD

12

THE FRAGILE UNITY OF NEUROSCIENCE

Joseph Dumit

This book begins by questioning the conditions of possibility and impossibility of the neurosciences and the humanities: "How far does the legitimacy of the neurosciences extend? How is the relation of the neurosciences to the humanities to be thought"? Yet, as I have been delving into the contributors' ideas, the power of the claims of neuroscience has never seemed more weak and fragile. For all of the increasing repetition of 'brain talk' in policy, business, medicine, education and everyday speech, the connection between this brain talk and power seems less and less persuasive. Foucault once said, "critique is the movement by which the subject gives himself the right to question truth on its effects of power and question power on its discourses of truth" (Foucault, ([1978]1997, p. 47). The first step in a critique of neuroscience, then, might be to question the apparently ubiquitous claims about the legitimacy of neuroscience (the Decade of the Brain, the Human Brain Project, and the BRAIN Initiative) and equally to interrogate the power that so easily speaks in the name of neuroscience. In other words, what if the operative nexus of power-knowledge is not the brain (in the hands of neuroscience), but neuroscience in the hands of other discourses? Then perhaps these papers point to neuroscience coming to occupy a position similar to psychiatry at the beginning the twentieth century: "the weaker it is epistemologically, the better it functions" (Foucault, 1999, p. 33).

As a provocative thought experiment, I will start from this counter-hypothesis: how weak is neuroscience? The first suggestion these chapters provide is that it is historically in continual crisis, because its object cannot be delimited: at times it is 'the brain' as the squishy three-pound organ in the head, or the entire central nervous system, or the subject of psychiatry, or the human subject of psychology, or the human subject that exceeds psychology, or the ideal simulation of rationality. The historical attention in many of these papers suggests that whichever object is chosen, it varies greatly, and what is really behind this variation cannot be handled within neuroscience. The result is that along both of these dimensions – object and history – it is not clear that these papers talk to each other any more than neuroscience papers talk to each other across different journals, methods, objects or visions of the future.

While the frame of neuroscience versus the humanities sets the stage, the real fights are revealed to be within neuroscience, and between neuro- and other sciences, including computer science, behavioral economics, economics, psychology, psychiatry, sociology, education, marketing and so on. There is a recursive issue here: each of these disciplines is undergoing its own neuro-crisis, struggling over the acceptance of neuroscience findings, and how they are used within disciplinary debates. On one hand, as discussed by Pykett and drawing on Schüll and Zaloom (2011), neuroscience is deployed to amplify existing debates over behavioral economics, with each side selectively filtering neuroscientific results. On the other hand, as they all point out, there seems to be only evidence that neuroscience is not changing anyone's mind, but rather it is reinforcing the very prejudices and assumptions about human nature and social good that the researchers started with.

Nonetheless, in many cases, a regular occurrence on campuses is whether someone who tries to hinge an argument on a neuroscience finding (e.g., mirror neurons) should actually know what the actual studies did, should have some familiarity with the methods used, should be able to do neuroscience, or whether the findings actually change the long-standing debates to which they are deployed. My current assessment is that they should, but that they do not. Neuroscience is most often imported as a means not to think any further, rather than as an actual provocation to put at risk the theories one started with. Similarly, as I have documented in my work on brain imaging in courtrooms (Dumit, 2004, 2014a), neuroscientific studies have almost no power to control the meaning they are given by lawyers and judges, often to the great dismay of the practicing researchers. Bassiri in this volume details the long history in which neurology and nascent neuroscience has always been co-produced with legal regimes, precisely because the notions of persons it depends upon are already wrapped up in legal definitions.

I will suggest that the deployment of neuroscience findings in other disciplines, and in policy and law, is not the same as legitimacy. I would like to raise the stakes and ask for cases where the neuro findings produced something surprising and did not serve as an intriguing, but not decisive, type of scientific ornamentation – a case where an academic argument or a policy would have been changed had the neuroscience results been different. This may be a high bar for the claim of 'legitimacy', but the joke that one can always find justification for one's argument somewhere in neuroscience is difficult to shake (Kraus makes this point regarding the contradictory claims on behalf of plasticity). Would anything change about arguments for altruism (or performance studies), if mirror neurons were found to not exist, or to function differently from how they are currently conceived? (See Solms.) The insights of many of the papers here (particularly those offered by Reynaert) are that the explanatory gap between persons and neuroscience, experience and mechanisms or circuits, remains as vexing as the uses of neuroscience despite the gap.

The most profound example of neuroscience crossing this gap I have found in Carol Dweck's research into 'mindsets'. She researched how different views of intelligence held by children affected their school performance. Kids with a 'fixed mindset' notion that intelligence is innate gave up when they encountered really hard problems, apparently because they imagined they had hit their plateau; if they were really talented, then the problems would have been easy. Those who had a 'growth mindset' approached intelligence as something improved through hard work, and therefore treated difficult problems as opportunities, rather than as confirmations of their limitations. Dweck conducted an experiment in which one group of children received an anatomical lecture about the brain, while the other heard about how neurons continue to grow throughout life and are encouraged to grow through effort. The latter kids tended to adopt a growth mindset and did better in school than the other kids, even years later (see Dweck, 2006). The strange thing about this finding is that it is not about whether neuroscience can decide which theory of the brain is more correct, rather it is that the neuroscience theory you read affects your mindset (and in practice, your intelligence). In other words, 'neuroscience' can change people, even if neuroscience does not.

With Dweck in mind, we might reconsider the position of philosopher Catherine Malabou as described by de Kesel in this volume, that the true theory of the brain is the one that we make our freedom with. "A revolutionary brain research should enable 'resistance'" (Malabou, 2008 cited in de Kesel). In a manner of speaking, what we do with our lives can have something to do with what we do with our brains, and that has something to do (in our era) with what we do with our neuroscience. I hear in this a turn toward a version of 'ideokinesis', a term coined by Mabel Todd in the 1930s at the Columbia University Posture Lab, wherein she showed how the ideas we have about how our anatomy works shape our ability to move our bodies (Todd, 1937). Gallese traces some of the neuroscience research on cognitive motor systems that bear upon this issue, but perhaps Bazan is most powerful in suggesting that the issue is not what the brain does per se, but what the brain-body does and what we (persons) do with what the brain-body does. Where to draw the line between the brain that any particular neuroscientist studies and the body that it is engaged with and presumably directs it is one that divides neuroscience over and over, and recalls Elizabeth Wilson's amazing critique *Neural Geographies,* in which the (active)mind vs. (passive)body split is only duplicated by the (active)brain vs. (passive)body (see Wilson, 1998).

Gallese, Bazan, Reynaert and De Vos all traffic in what I have playfully called 'plastic neuroscience', wherein neuroscience is simultaneously put at risk by liberal arts critique and by the brains it studies (Dumit, 2014b). De Vos' powerful point that "what is put under the scanner is not a body, it is even not the psychological features one wants to find the neural underpinning for, it is, I argue, psychological theory".

By scanning a theory, neuroscience wards against challenging its own assumptions about personhood, human nature and the society it is defending. Intriguingly, many neuroscientists I talk to fully agree with this critique. They are not that interested in the results of their studies, which they feel must take the form of a scanned theory. Those results are what pay the bills so that they can explore what brains do, and a number of them have insisted that it is the weirdness of brains, and not persons, that interest them. If we who want to critique neuroscience want to also change it, then following Kraus we may very well want to exacerbate tensions within it, as well as between it and other disciplines. The contributions in this book provide a fascinating set of maps to these tensions and help identify the points of leverage within them. Maps of fragility can be very useful!

The second suggestion of the weakness of neuroscience is that it participates in the general weakness of science in the contemporary world. Kraus and De Vos point to the core issue of asymmetries of funding between social and neurosciences, and the issue here is the zero-sum game in which less funding for social sciences means that certain arenas of inquiry are being starved of evidence (the defunding of political science at the NSF being one of the most recent example; Mole, 2013). Yet there could be no better demonstration of the strangeness of the crisis in the humanities than the notion that neuroscience brings it on, when the current target is precisely the lack of jobs (Zakaria, 2015).

On a larger scale, it is unclear how we should appraise the almost geometric growth that neuroscience research has received since its naming the 1960s. While we have funding events like the Decade of the Brain, it is quite clear that there do not need to be events to declare the decade of banking, of oil, fracking, drones or GMOs. Neuroscience is big, but not that big. Furthermore, it is subject to the very type of disciplinary capture that the humanities have claimed for it. As most profoundly revealed by Haueis and Slaby regarding the large-science Human Brain Project in the European Union (EU), it appears as if brain research has been torqued into virtual brain research, in which a new research infrastructure is going to be built around computing rather than what had previously been called neuroscience. This could be the most visible signal that data science, simulation and machine learning are supplanting neuroscience as the priority prefix of the next few decades.

But we should also step back and consider the wider economic context in which the 2013 EU Human Brain Project as well as the 2014 Obama BRAIN Initiative have been launched. Between 2009 and 2012, almost all of the major multinational drug companies (GlaxoSmithKline, AstraZeneca, Pfizer, Merck, Sanofi and Novartis) "[abandoned their] traditional drug-discovery programmes and treatments for brain disorders" (Abbott, 2011: 161). Central nervous system and neuroscience research labs were shuttered, leaving hundreds of researchers out of jobs.

Steve Hyman, former director of the National Institute for Mental Health, explained that despite there being a growing prevalence of mental illness in the first-world markets and globally, and the lack of effective treatments, there has been basically no truly new treatments discovered since the initial big molecules of the 1950s and '60s (imipramine, clozapine, etc.). He cataloged what medical anthropologists and other critics of the pharmaceutical industry have been saying for decades: (1) research has concentrated on me-too drugs and known mechanisms, (2) even though those mechanisms (such as serotonin transporter, or lithium) have not been verified, (3) animal models have been used to justify research even though the animal models are poor, or worse, irrelevant, and (4) the brain-mental-illness connection is almost a complete mystery.

Merck's former vice president for neuroscience William Potter explained the past 35 or so years of pharmaceutical brain research in terms of relative profitability:

> In the 1980s and '90s, drug companies realized that they could make billions of dollars a year off drugs that were slightly modified versions of already-approved medications, particularly the SSRI antidepressants like Prozac, Potter says: "The investment in truly innovative projects was not as deep as it might have been because you could make so much money from 'me, too,' drugs."
>
> *(Miller, 2010, p. 503)*

Neuroscience had consciously been held back from fundamental research in order to preserve the growth that was available by standing still. There would be no point in researching truly new antidepressants if you were making enough money from me-too ones, as they would only cannibalize your own markets. Across the research field, the consensus was that relative to the new specialty drugs in cancer and diabetes, "neuroscience [became] an expensive and risky prospect for industry" (Cressey, 2011). And this was despite the continuing growth in antidepressant and other central nervous system (CNS) prescriptions. In terms of generic drugs, the market size in dollars was shrinking.

Neuroscience as a research field was therefore instrumentalized and hamstrung by industry, a cautionary tale for every research field to be sure. The value of science to a company is precisely the capital growth it is seen to provide compared to that of a different investment. The stunning statement by the Human Brain Project that "previous neuroscientific research has already generated most of the data necessary for understanding the human brain from genes to cognition" (see Haueis and Slaby) might unintentionally mirror the stasis imposed on it by industry, reading the flat line in fundamental questions as definitive, and therefore justifying the expenditure of money in terms of computationally simulating all future results on the basis of the existing data.

For those of us who support the Whitehead–Stengers' definition of science as the directed application of the everyday insight that there is more to see in nature with due attention (see Stengers, 2002), the fragility of science as a domain is bad enough. Even scarier is the current situation in Canada, in which the conservative government who had bet on oil and gas industry projects systematically shut down a large swath of environmental and other federal science programs and muzzled the ability of all government scientists to openly describe their results. Resistance to this overall program include the Idle No More movement by First Nations tribes, researchers picketing with "Death of Science" placards and the Write2Know campaign (see Callison).[1]

I hope these examples, though they stray from neuroscience, demonstrate the new era of critique in which "the right to question truth on its effects of power and question power on its discourses of truth" (Foucault, [1978]1997, p. 47), takes on dimensions that are only tenuously grasped in the language of the legitimacy of neuroscience. Our critique must engage with a world (and each society specifically) where multiple overlapping legitimacies compete and where science is helpful and often used, but unfortunately neither necessary nor sufficient in even environmental and health struggles. Similarly, neuroscience is ubiquitous in the changing landscape of learning disabilities, autism accommodations, mental illness treatments, many mass-tort cases and insanity defenses, but its explanatory power is but one stream of discourse among other, often louder ones (see Callison, 2014; Oreskes and Conway, 2010; Brandt, 2007; Proctor, 2011; Orr, 2006).

So where do I stand in my critique of neuroscience? As powerful as neuroscience can appear to be, I think it is fragile and almost defenseless against larger social regimes and I want to help defend its right to explore brains against its instrumentalization by industries. But I also want to put it more at risk by insisting that it take its own inquiry into brains-bodies-persons-subjects seriously, as requiring a much stranger view of people and biology than the one it has currently built into its experimental systems. And, wearing my critical science and technology studies (STS) hat, I want to insist that the ornamental use of neuroscience findings, ones that pretend to buttress a disciplinary claim with brain facts, should be called out. In those instances, I do suspect that the tables could be turned and the disciplinary claim and its counter-claim could be returned to the neuroscientific researcher in order to show how weakly thought-through the experiment's humanistic premises were. In this way, we might create a stronger epistemological basis for neuroscience, social science and the humanities, than they seem to think they need. Less writing, more thinking.

Note

1. See their website: http://write2know.ca.

References

Abbott, A. (2011). Novartis to shut brain research facility. Drug giant redirects psychiatric efforts to genetics. *Nature, 480*(7376), 161–162.

Brandt, A.M. (2007). *The cigarette century: The rise, fall, and deadly persistence of the product that defined America.* New York, NY: Basic Books.

Callison, C. (2014). *How climate change comes to matter: The communal life of facts.* Durham and London: Duke University Press.

Callison, C., & Hermida, A. (forthcoming). Dissent and resonance: #Idlenomore as an emergent middle ground, *Canadian Journal of Communication.*

Cressey, D. (2011). Psychopharmacology in crisis. *Nature online,* June 14. Available at: http://www.nature.com/news/2011/110614/full/news.2011.367.html.

Dumit, J. (2004). *Picturing personhood. Brain scans and biomedical identity.* In-Formation Series. Princeton, NJ and Oxford: Princeton University Press.

Dumit, J. (2014a). How (not) to do things with brain images. In C. Coopmans, J. Vertesi, M. Lynch and S. Woolgar (eds.), *Representation in scientific practice revisited,* 291–313. Cambridge, MA and London: The MIT Press.

Dumit, J. (2014b). Plastic neuroscience: Studying what the brain cares about. *Frontiers in Human Neuroscience, 8*(176), 1–4.

Dweck, C. (2006). *The new psychology of success.* New York, NY: Random House.

Foucault, M. ([1978]1997). What is critique? In *The politics of truth,* 41–82. Los Angeles, CA: Semiotext(e).

Foucault, M. (1999). *Abnormal. Lectures at the Collège de France, 1974–1975.* New York, NY: Picador.

Human Brain Project (2012). *The Human Brain Project. A report to the European Commission.* Lausanne: The HBP-PS Consortium.

Malabou, C. (2008). *What should we do with our brain?* Bronx, NY: Fordham University Press.

Miller, G. (2010). Is pharma running out of brainy ideas? *Science, 329(5991),* 502–504.

Mole, B. (2013). NSF cancels political-science grant cycle: US funding agency said to be dodging restrictions set by Congress. *Nature.* doi:10.1038/nature.2013.13501.

Oreskes, N., & Conway, E.M. (2010). *Merchants of doubt: How a handful of scientists obscured the truth on issues from tobacco smoke to global warming.* New York, NY: Bloomsbury Publishing.

Orr, J. (2006). *Panic diaries. A genealogy of panic disorder.* Durham, NC and London: Duke University Press.

Proctor, R. (2011). *Golden holocaust: Origins of the cigarette catastrophe and the case for abolition.* Berkeley and Los Angeles: University of California Press.

Schüll, N.D., & Zaloom, C. (2011). The shortsighted brain: Neuroeconomics and the governance of choice in time. *Social Studies of Science, 41*(4), 515–538.

Stengers, I. (2002). *Penser avec Whitehead. Une libre et sauvage creation de concepts.* Paris: Éditions du Seuil.

Todd, M.E. (1937). *The thinking body: A study of the balancing forces of dynamic man.* Princeton: Princeton Book Company.

Wilson, E.A. (1998). *Neural geographies: Feminism and the microstructure of cognition.* New York, NY: Routledge.

Zakaria, F. (2015). *In defense of a liberal education.* New York, NY: W. W. Norton & Company.

INDEX